Roots of the Present:
Napa Valley 1900-1950

by
Lin Weber

Wine Ventures Publishing
St. Helena, CA 94574

Library of Congress Control
Number 2001 135150

ISBN 0-9667014-3-7

Cover photo by Priscilla Upton.
Cover design by Matthew Shelley.

Table of Contents

To Chris, with love

Foreword

By Dr. Kevin Starr
California State Librarian

History happens – and thus history can be written – in sweeping terms and grand cycles. Think of Edward Gibbon on the fall of the Roman Empire, or William Hickling Prescott on the conquest of Mexico, or Francis Parkman on the epic of the exploration and settlement of Canada by France. When history is thus perceived and presented on an heroic scale, entire decades, entire centuries even, can be marshaled to telling effect.

And yet history is also a matter of specifics, of day-by-day experience, of the minutes and hours and minutiae of daily experience as encountered by ordinary people in their daily lives. History on a grand scale – which is to say, history as social philosophy and/or social science – searches for patterns and paradigms that explain entire epochs. History up close and personal, however, is also not exempt from seeking larger patterns of interpretation, although such patterns can be difficult to ascertain and to present when the historian is caught in the labyrinthine web of the daily and the particular.

The beauty of *Roots of the Present: Napa Valley 1900-1950* by Lin Weber is that it is history that is simultaneously wedded to the particular yet possessed of larger social patterns of importance to American history in California and to universal human experience. First of all, *Roots of the Present* is solidly based in an exhaustive survey of newspaper and grand jury records from the Napa Valley in the 1900-1950 era, augmented by extensive personal interviews with survivors from these decades and further amplified by an array of secondary sources. Journalism has been called history in a hurry. This is another way of saying that good journalism sweeps up like a cyclone or tornado the multiple facts attached to significant events. Having exhaustively reviewed the

i

newspaper records of the Napa Valley from the first five decades of the twentieth century, Lin Weber has encountered the feel, the texture, the specific detail, the particular and poignant moments of past experience. Grand jury reports are also known for their detail and for their candor, and Lin Weber has made good use of these sources as well. The result is a pointillist-realist narrative of the Napa Valley replete with telling – indeed, existential – detail. *Roots of the Present* challenges us to re-live these decades in all their vivid immediacy, day by day, sometimes, in fact – as in the case of the influenza epidemic of 1918 – hour by hour; for that plague could, as Lin Weber depicts, carry off people who were seemingly healthy just hours earlier.

The specificity of *Roots of the Present* gives it the density and the narrative satisfaction of a good novel. Here is American life in the Napa Valley in these years as only exhaustive research can reveal. Here also is the humor, tragedy, and pathos of daily experience. The earlier chapters of *Roots of the Present* are especially poignant in their evocations of just how fragile human life was in the early twentieth century: how routine diseases (much less the dreaded influenza epidemic of 1918), broken bones, household or work accidents, could result in sudden fatalities. So too were the Napa Valley residents of this era up against demanding economic challenges in an uncertain farming environment compounded by high railroad shipping rates. And yet life could be good in these early years as well, as testified to by Lin Weber's highly detailed accounts of church gatherings, Sunday baseball games, barn dances, harvest festivals, and other rural and/or small town celebrations.

So satisfying is *Roots of the Present*, in fact, as pointillist-realist narrative based on primary sources, so scrupulous is Lin Weber in earning the power of her narrative through vivid detail, readers of this fine history might initially miss an equally vivid play of pattern and paradigm also at work. The Napa Valley of these years was its own special place; indeed, the conclusion of Lin Weber's narrative in the organization of the Napa Valley wine industry in 1949 establishes a pattern for the next fifty years, in that the 1949 organization involved an upgrading of self-conscious ambition among winemakers that would over the next five decades transform the Napa Valley into an Euro-American landscape known to the world for its vines and wines, its restaurants and cuisine, its continuing testimony to the pleasures of the good life. And yet this very same Napa Valley in the years between 1900 and 1950 was also a representative Californian and American place experiencing its own dynamics along with the larger dynamics of the state, the nation, and the world.

Thus through Lin Weber's eyes we experience how the Napa Valley made the transition to irrigation and engineered urbanism along with the rest of California. We experience the horrific outbreak of anti-German-American sentiment in World War I. We go through Prohibition in a specially intense manner, for the Volstead Act struck at the very heart of the Napa Valley economy. We experience the Depression in an especially keen and sympathetic context, thanks to Lin Weber's vivid mini-portraits of how the economic collapse of the nation affected individual lives in the Valley. Portraits of Napa Valley residents serving abroad in harm's way during the Second World War are especially vivid, as is the telling of the story of the great explosion at Port Chicago. And then, in the postwar years, the Napa Valley began, ever so tentatively, its transition into national, then international, importance.

The Napa Valley of *Roots of the Present*, then, is at once its own special place – and part of American history in California. If we were to judge by this history alone, we could reconstruct the larger history of California as being, among other things, shaped by the immigration experience (the story, in fact, seems at times almost dominated by immigrants from Europe), shaped by agriculture (still the lead element in the California economy), shaped by the desire of ordinary men and women to find a better way of life. At this point, *Roots of the Present* – so overwhelmingly detailed and contextual – edges into the universal patterns of human experience. The more detailed the protagonists of this history are, the more human they become; and the more human they become, the more universal becomes the importance of who they were, what they hoped and struggled for, how they succeeded and how they failed. The Napa Valley, in this context, while part of California and the United States, reaches out to

iii

something more: the immemorial quest of human beings to live on the land and in smaller communities and to find there, hour by hour, day by day, detail by detail, event by event, the consolations and challenges of human life.

Thanks...

For their very helpful contributions of memories and memorabilia I am indebted to Mary Avist, George Blaufuss, Dick and Carol Cavagnaro, Rita Franceschi, Edna Gibbello, Herb Gunn, Marilouise Kornell, Georgene Larsen, the late Ray and Gen Lawler, Sheriff Richard Lonergan, Kathleen Patterson, Stella Raymond, Walt and Geri Raymond, Rosemary Wehr and John York.

Photographer Priscilla Upton braved a cold March morning to shoot a roll of vineyard film for me, from which came the cover photo of a gnarled old vine. My son-in-law, graphic artist Matthew Shelley, designed the cover.

Curator Randy Murphy at the Napa Valley Museum, Dennis Gonsolin at the Napa Firefighters' Museum, Diane Ballard at the Napa County Historical Society, Mary Jean McLaughlin at the Napa County Superior Court, surveyor Bruce Alfonso, Bismarck Bruck's grandson Kergan Bruck, Carol Dibelle at the Yountville Veterans' Home and the friendly staff at the Sharpsteen Museum provided me with much useful material. Thanks, too, to Meg Scantlebury at Charles Krug, Lorna Ippel at Beaulieu and Jessica Keefe at Louis Martini Winery; and to Brenda Brown and Eric Nolff at Malloy Lithographers for their technical support.

I've spent a great portion of the last three years peering into the monitors of microfilm machines at the St. Helena, Napa and Calistoga libraries, a task that was facilitated by the wonderfully helpful librarians there, all of whom run satisfyingly tight ships.

Finally, I want to express heartfelt thanks to my editorial readers, Peg and Bob Beardsley, Nancy Haynes, Margaret Johansen, Marilouise Kornell, Carol Lawler, Eric Nelson, and Virginia Snowden; and especially to Dr. Kevin Starr, Chief Librarian for the State of California, for writing his eloquent preface.

Most of all, however, I want to thank my husband Chris for his unfailing support and encouragement.

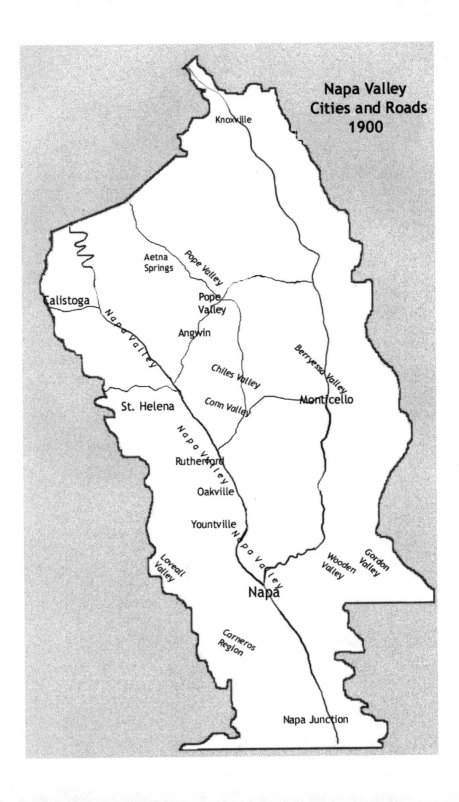

Napa Valley
Cities and Roads
1900

Chapter One

The New Era

The year 1900 arrived in the Napa Valley with high winds and an inch of rain. Washouts on the main line forced the Southern Pacific railroad to reroute its Sacramento passengers through the little south county train town of Napa Junction, which had once been called "Adelante." The storm took out part of the quay in Vallejo, and rough seas on the San Pablo Bay shattered all the windows on one side of the commuter steamship *Berkeley*, terrifying the passengers.

A professional hunter was returning to Vallejo with the hold of his sloop full of ducks that he had just shot at Napa Creek. The boat capsized that night, and because he was still wearing his heavy rubber waders, he drowned. Another sloop nearly suffered the same fate. The *Napa Daily Journal* told the story with a spin that minimized an ethnic group that may have seemed marginal to the editor, but which would play a leading role in the city of Napa very soon:

> The local Italian colony is having considerable sport over the misfortunes of a quartette of young men who, according to the story furnished us by one of the jokesters, went duck hunting Monday night on the sloop *Little Maine*. The crew of the boat is said to have consisted of Tony Fracht, captain; Dave Cavagnaro, stevedore; Henry Cavagnaro, supercargo, and T. Navone, chief cook. They are credited with losing their bearing

several miles below town and tying up their boat and walking home.[1]

The bad weather affected attendance at the Alert Hose Company's annual masquerade ball at Crowey's Napa Opera House, although the place looked festive and patriotic enough in its red, white and blue bunting with evergreens. Miss Maurie Hillis (dressed as a cake-walk dancer) and S.H. Hortmann ("Lord Fauntleroy") won $8.00 each as the "best sustained characters." M.M. Haas cross-dressed as "Old Sarah," and Robert Even came as "The Back Yard and the Front Yard." Haas and Even won $6.00 each as the "most original" contestants.

The door prize, a "valuable porcelain seat,"[2] went to young Peter Feliz, who came to the party with his wife. Peter worked for the County's biggest employer, the State Insane Asylum, a few miles down Soscol Avenue, the main road south of town. County Coroner Dave Kyser donated the prize. Once a professional plasterer, Kyser now had a combination furniture store and mortuary,[3] a macabre confluence of trades that was common at the time. Dave himself was was among the revelers, but he was not entirely happy. Someone had shot a pistol through the front window of his store on Main Street, and the bullet had damaged some of his merchandise. Dave Kyser's experience of the 1900's would reach satisfying heights, but another County Coroner would be dealing with him sooner than anyone expected, while the Peter Felizes would live on to enjoy many more New Years.

Most St. Helenans ushered in New Year's alone or in quiet groups. The owner/editor of the *St. Helena Star*, Frank B. Mackinder, reported on the happenings at the Presbyterian Church,

---

[1] *Napa Daily Journal (NDJ)* 1-3-1900.

[2] probably a commode

[3] Thomas Jefferson Gregory, *History of Solano and Napa Counties*, Historic Record Company, Los Angeles, 1912, p. 184. The fact that Kyser was both the coroner and a funeral director was not considered a conflict of interest then.

of which he was a member. The congregation observed the New Year by presenting their beloved pastor, the Reverend James Mitchell, with a gift of $40.[4] At a time when a 10-pound sack of flour went for 25¢, this was serious money.

The honored recipient spent part of the weekend officiating at a quiet wedding. Miss Meda Grigsby, daughter of Robert F. Grigsby,[5] was given in marriage to Fred Kellett at the home of Fred's mother in Calistoga.[6] The Grigsby family was one of the Napa Valley's very oldest. Miss Meda's branch had left to mine for silver in Mexico, but many other Grigsbys remained. Great Uncle John had been co-leader of the Grigsby-Ide party, one of the first wagon trains ever to cross the Sierras. He figured prominently in the Bear Flag Revolt, a short-lived but extraordinarily well-timed uprising of US pioneers in the Napa and Sonoma Valleys against the Mexican government back in 1846.[7] Like so many of the Napa Valley's earliest American pioneers, John Grigsby was a southerner through and through. During the Civil War this son of the Confederacy slipped away, leaving behind a spate of nephews to keep the Grigsby name alive. Most Grigsbys were "Up-Valley" people, the term used for the region north of Rutherford.

From the start the Up-Valley had tended to collect people with ties to the old South. There had once been tension between the Confederate-leaning Up-Valley and the folks in Napa City, who were mainly Yankees; but memories of the Civil War were fading. These days a new war was on peoples' minds. Several men from the Napa Valley were still stationed in the Philippines, site of the Pacific theater of the Spanish American War. Young Willis Grigsby, a St. Helenan, had gotten into deep trouble there. He was caught impersonating a fellow officer, and during the pursuant

---

[4] *St. Helena Star (SHS)*, 1-5-1900.

[5] and granddaughter of Terrell Grigsby, a vintner who died in 1892. See "A Brief History of the Grigsby Family of Lake and Napa Counties," Harriet Reinmiller, undated, unpublished manuscript, p. 7.

[6] *Weekly Calistogian (WC)* 1-5-1900.

[7] See Lin Weber, *Old Napa Valley*, Wine Ventures Publishing, St. Helena, 1998.

investigation it came out he had not one, but three wives in California. Just a week before Meda Grigsby's wedding, Willis was sentenced to prison for fraud. All the local papers carried word of the scandal.

The papers also reported on a sorrow that struck the Bales, the very first family of European stock to make the Up-Valley their home. Fred Bale, grandson of Edward Turner Bale,[8] had volunteered in the Spanish American War as a soldier, and after America's victory he re-enlisted. He encountered disease in the tropics, and just as the new year turned he succumbed.[9]

John and Lucinda York had found the Napa Valley very much to their liking. These transplanted southerners had made it their home longer than any other couple. They had raised 10 children in their big home on York Creek in St. Helena, and they now had so many grandchildren and great-grandchildren that they had trouble remembering all the little ones' names. John walked with a cane, the result of an accident breaking a horse when he was in his 50's, but on the whole they still had their health. On September 6, 1901, most of the members of the "Native Sons of St. Helena Parlor No. 53" surprised the old–timers by dropping in on them to help celebrate their 60th wedding anniversary. Most nights, though, John and Lucy just sat together in the kitchen, quietly smoking their pipes.[10]

The Joseph Mecklenburgs would soon be observing their 50th anniversary, too. Joe Mecklenburg had managed both the old Bale mill in Calistoga and Yount gristmill in Yountville. Some old-timers called the Bale place the "Kellogg" mill, after its principal builder, Florentine Kellogg. Newer folks referred to it as the "Lyman mill," because since 1872 it had been in the hands of the W.W. Lyman family: erudite, well-connected people whose main

---

[8] Edward Turner Bale received a land grant from the Mexican government in 1841 that gave him title to much of the Napa Valley.

[9] *SHS*, 1-5-1900.

[10]Rodney McCormick, "Recollections of Rodney McCormick of Grandfather York, Vol. 2," unpublished, St. Helena, 1938, p.13.

interest was the wine industry. The mill was in its senescence and would cease to function altogether in 1905.[11]

Many wealthy families like the Lymans had country homes or were frequent guests in the Up-Valley, especially in St. Helena. While most St. Helenans were folks of modest means, a significant number were *ante bellum* bluebloods, social lions who dominated San Francisco's upper crust. The *Star* mentioned, from time to time, the "capitalists" who visited with the W.W. Lymans and other persons of note.[12]

Cracks were beginning to appear, however, on the fine veneer of the Up-Valley's social luster. Economic crises had plagued the state in the 1890's, and quite a few people who had invested in vineyard land suffered heavy losses. They sold out, often to recent immigrants whose intent was simply to farm the land.

On the whole only the extravagant or politically ambitious held lavish weddings in the Napa Valley in the year 1900. The world's great monarchies were still thriving, or anyway appearing to. It would have seemed presumptuous for anyone but titled nobility, the fabulously rich or someone running for office to create fantasies involving hand-maidens (bride's maids) and retainers (groom's men). Napa lawyer Raymond Benjamin had a big wedding in 1901, but he wanted to run for District Attorney. Glitzy displays of wealth were certainly not unheard of, however, especially in the Valley's tourist resorts, but most Americans held fast to a world view that honored hard work, frugality and personal privacy.

The President, William McKinley, a reserved, cordial, rather stoic Republican from Ohio, was perceived by most Americans to personify this ideal.[13] Large, slow-moving and impeccably dressed, McKinley looked, sounded and thought like the embodiment of The Establishment. Like the Alaskan mountain that was named for

---

[11] Denzil and Jennie Verardo, *The Bale Grist Mill*, California State Parks Foundation, Oakland, 1984, p.13.

[12] W.W. Lyman's father, Theodore, left the Valley after the Civil War to become the Episcopal Bishop of North Carolina.

[13] See Henry F. Pringle, *Theodore Roosevelt*, Harcourt & Brace Company, Orlando, FL, 1931 and 1984.

him, he gave the impression of being a motionless solid. He was, above all things, a man who resisted change: the premier guardian of the *status quo*. His political career was the personal project of a Midwest industrialist named Mark Hanna. In the eyes of many, this wasn't necessarily a bad thing; it was just how it was.

St. Helena Star editor Frank B. Mackinder was as proud and stalwart a McKinley Republican as one could find. He rhapsodized in his 1900 New Year's editorial that an "era of good feeling" was about to begin. Supply and demand, he wrote, had finally found harmony. Prices were fair, and both buyer and seller were satisfied, especially in St. Helena's all-important wine industry. "Granaries and barns are full, the fertile fields are well-tilled and productive,...the whir of factory wheels and the hum of industry can be heard on every side."[14] Mackinder was ecstatic when McKinley was re-elected.

John E. Walden of the *Napa Daily Journal* and the *Weekly Journal* grieved over the fact that his party's candidates—William Jennings Bryan and Adlai E. Stevenson—not only lost, but lost big in Napa County. "Everything seems to be Republican," he lamented, "even Carneros Creek."[15] The outspoken editor tried to comfort his fellow Democrats with a dollop of Victorian solace: "One thing that can make this new year happier," he wrote, "is to have that one feeling, that one thought, that one faith always with us: that 'whatever is, is right,' and for the best...[N]othing ever comes into our lives except what is for our good."[16] Walden's passive acceptance of the *status quo's* bitter pills would change before the decade had passed.

Most who had known success in the 1890's were carrying their good fortune into the new era. Luther Turton, only 38 years old, had already designed many of the important buildings in Napa and St. Helena. He continued to win contracts for important, highly visible projects. One of his most delightful was a Napa City landmark: a fanciful tower on the Semorile Building, home to

---

[14] *SHS*, 1-5-1900.

[15] *NDJ*, 11-7-1900

[16] *NDJ*, 12-29-1899.

Johnny Walden's two newspapers. "Architect Turton," as Walden liked to call him, was an agile, athletic man who liked to make round-trip bicycle rides from Napa to St. Helena.

Ervine W. Doughty, known to most folks as "E.W.," erected many of the structures that Turton designed.[17] He would continue to be Napa City's leading building contractor for the next four decades. His success eventually enabled him to build for himself a lovely estate near the bridge on Trancas Street.

An English-born stonemason, James B. Newman, often worked with Turton and Doughty. He had just bought out his partner, the second-generation Napan, H. Wing. Using Turton's architectural plans, Newman and Doughty would soon fit the stones of the Goodman Library and the expanded Migliavacca Building. Newman also erected many of the important stone bridges in Napa City.

A Scottish colleague, R.H. Pithie, was at the height of his career, too. Pithie began by building stone bridges and now was erecting elegant structures for wealthy patrons in many Northern California locations. Pithie's experience of the new era would prove to be brief. He would die of pneumonia at his St. Helena home in February, 1901.

"Home" was of paramount importance to families. Babies were born there, couples got married there and when it was time, most people, like Pithie, entered eternity from the privacy of their bedrooms. Houses tended to be colorfully painted, ill-heated gargantuans, often sheltering several generations of a single family and many more children than would be the norm today. Houses of a dozen or more rooms were not at all uncommon. The wealthiest built mansions, immense dwellings. Despite their size, surprisingly few had indoor bathrooms. Outdoor "water closets" awaited the remains of the day, and in the nighttime people used a commode like Peter Feliz's New Year's door prize.

It was possible to rent a room in a boarding house, but there were no apartment buildings, no trailer or mobile home parks for the financially limited; nor were there convalescent or retirement

---

[17] Among Doughty's other projects were the Behlow Building, St. Mary's Episcopal Church and the Native Sons block on Coombs and First.

homes for the aged. For the penniless, there were few options. August Tonolla, former proprietor of St. Helena's "What Cheer Saloon" and former owner of the St. Helena Hotel, saw others make fortunes in the very places he himself had labored and failed. He had lost everything. His despondent wife had been committed to the Asylum. "Gus" struggled alone against the suffocating cloak of his poverty until the winter of 1900, when he was scooped up in Napa and placed in the County Infirmary on the road to Sonoma.[18] He, too, was declared insane and was sent to the Asylum to join his wife. It was an act of kindness. The Insane Asylum had become a refuge for those who had lost their bearings in modern times, and there were many who believed it to be Napa County's greatest jewel. Plans were afoot to pave Soscol Avenue at taxpayers' expense between the city limits and the entrance to the Asylum grounds.[19]

Not all the depressed found their way to the Asylum, however. Suicides and other unexplained deaths were weekly occurrences, especially in the winter months. Laudanum—a derivative of opium—was the exit route for many, available through doctors and the few remaining Chinese herbalists who still held forth in the local Chinatowns.

Up in Calistoga, Charles A. Carroll was doing his level best to make ends meet. His newspaper, the *Weekly Calistogian*, barely held its head above water. "Wanted," he wrote from his freezing office on a cold winter's day: "Good wood stove in exchange for subscription, advertising or jobwork at the *Calistogian* office." [20] In addition to his editorial duties, Carroll found work as a real estate agent and as the resident representative of the Caledonian Insurance Company of Edinburgh, whose specialty seemed to have been coverage for fire insurance. A regular feature of his well-written weekly was a listing of available properties. Just $4,500, for example, would purchase 190 acres a mile-and-a-half from town.

---

[18] now the site of Napa County's Human Services offices. Today's Old Sonoma Road was the original route to Sonoma County.

[19] It was completed in 1902.

[20] *WC*, 1-5-1900.

For a mere $1,500 one could acquire a 16.5 acre ranch, a 7-room bungalow and a barn. A 1.5 story home on a small, centrally located plot in Calistoga went for $1,000. That particular piece, wrote Carroll in August of 1901, was in good repair, with a sturdy barn and plenty of water. Calistogans still had to pump their own water at the turn of the century.

What news and information there was came by word of mouth, by the mail or through the very opaque filter of editorial prejudice in the newspapers. The same condition existed in most of the modest-sized towns throughout rural America. The radio had been invented but was not yet used for commercial broadcasting. Television was still decades off. There were a few telephones—the larger businesses had them—but there appears to have been only one operator, Mary Stoddard. When she left to take a position with the Sawyer Tanning Company, the citizenry was urged to be patient "until the new operator becomes accustomed to the names of the subscribers."[21]

A nation-wide movement to improve educational standards was already showing signs of success. It was estimated that 89% of the population could read and write,[22] although the figure is suspect because the sampling excluded significant portions of the population. New laws were adopted enforcing school attendance, and as a result the average white child was now experiencing five years of classroom education. A push for high school graduation was gaining momentum, and adults were encouraged to attend evening classes. Napa City was actually quite advanced in its educational offerings as the century turned. A few powerful individuals with philanthropical mind-sets influenced the community in important ways in this respect.

One such man was Abraham W. Norton, a principal in the Sawyer Tanning Company, Napa City's biggest manufacturing enterprise. Gifted with both a powerful position and a persuasive personality, Norton convinced several of Napa's founding fathers to contribute to the establishment of a local institution of higher

---

[21] *NDJ*, 6-7-1900.

[22] Merle Curti, *The Growth of American Thought*, Harper & Row, New York, 1964, p. 584.

learning, "Napa College." After his death, the college relocated to San Jose, where it became part of the new state university system.

Harry Lawrence Gunn was an instructor at Napa College, organizing a "commercial department" there where adult students could learn the elements of business management. When it moved away, he opened Napa Business College, where many of the community's subsequent leaders received their training. He later served three terms as the county's Auditor and Recorder. Napa Business College offered courses at night. Men and women who could keep their eyes open after their 10-hour-a-day, six-days-a-week jobs could take the entire six-month business course for only $30 and a complete shorthand course for the same price.[23] A program in penmanship—outmoded now, but helpful before the invention of modern office equipment—was available for $15.

The education movement, the large number of children per household and the difficulty people had getting around in the winter resulted in the building of a plethora of small schoolhouses throughout Napa County, some of which have survived. The schools were organized into eight districts. The Superintendent of Schools, John Imrie, was in charge of spreading the budget—about $17,000 in all—to each of these districts. The little schools tended to be poorly insulated, poorly heated and poorly supplied

There were more little schools than there were schoolteachers qualified to teach in them. Teachers made next to nothing per annum. A case in point was that of the unfortunate Mr. C.C. Swafford, who was hired to teach high school students in St. Helena from all 13 sectors that comprised its school district. He was to be reimbursed for his labors at the miniscule salary of $1500 for the year. It turned out that Swafford's high school failed to meet the new state standards for education, however, so it had to close before he was paid. It reorganized the next year as a private school, using the local Presbyterian Church as its campus. The private school failed, too, mainly because hardly anybody wanted to go. Throughout it all, Mr. Swafford never got remunerated. He sued the board that hired him. James Mitchell, the popular Presbyterian

---

[23] *SHS* 4-20-1900. One suspects the full business course was for men only.

minister, was the head of the board and became the principal defendant of Swafford's suit. Swafford lost.

Another teacher, John Laughlin Shearer, had quite a different experience in his career as an educator, perhaps because he focused his attention on the elementary level. He was a classroom teacher in 1900, but in the years to come he would stand out from his peers as a great administrator. One of the innovations he would introduce was the idea of elementary school graduation, which gave young students the motivation to continue at least through the sixth grade. The *Journal* reported that he, Miss Kate Ames (the former Superintendent) and John Imrie had spent most of the 1900 holiday weekend at a teacher's convention in Sacramento. Imrie had defeated Miss Ames for the post in the last election. Ames completed her own education at Berkeley, and in 1902 she would run for her old position unopposed. Besides the telephone operator, she was one of the best-known women in the Valley.

Miss Ames' fame was minor, however, compared to that of another former Napa Valley teacher: Theodore Arlington Bell, whose name would become known in the new era not just in the Valley, but throughout the State and even nationally. Handsome, bespectacled Theodore Bell was born in Vallejo in 1873, and in 1877 he moved to "Bell Canyon," just north of St. Helena, where his parents had a 40-acre vineyard. He attended a one-room schoolhouse about a mile from his home until he was in the eighth grade, and after that he was left to continue his studies on his own, an option most of his peers declined. Theodore breezed through the not-very-difficult requirements for a teaching credential, and at age 18 he became the teacher of the little schoolhouse of his childhood. During recess and after school he studied law, and on his 25th birthday he sat for and passed the Bar exams. By 1898 he had been elected District Attorney of Napa City.[24]

During his first term of office he had an experience that practically guaranteed stardom. A sharp-shooting, stage-robbing murderer named Buck English had been on a crime spree at the Up-Valley quicksilver mines with R.N. Breckenridge, a younger

---

[24] *NDJ*, 9-6-1922.

11

accomplice.[25] They eluded a posse and made their way on foot to the tiny farm town of Monticello in Berryessa Valley. Just south of town they hailed down Johnnie Gardner's stage, which was getting ready for its return trip to Napa. A local farmer recognized them, though, and as soon as the stage left he telephoned the sheriff's office that English and Breckenridge were on their way down Monticello Road. Undersheriff Robert Brownlee quickly threw together a four-man posse that included Bell. They all crowded into a surrey and raced out of town as fast as the horse could go.

The Napa posse met the Monticello stage head-on near the Wooden Valley turn-off, with the terrified Gardner at the reigns next to English, who was now brandishing a rifle. Breckenridge was inside. Undersheriff Brownlee raised his rifle and ordered the bandit to stand down, but English blew the gun out of his hands.

Bell, still armed, took aim and fired, launching a load of buckshot into the outlaw's side. Stray shot may also have winged Johnnie Gardner, but Gardner was able to drive the stage down to town, where he deposited Breckenridge and the bleeding English, who was now unconscious, into the arms of Sheriff George McKenzie.[26] Undaunted by any possible conflicts of interest, Bell himself then prosecuted the case to a jury of his admirers, and the bandits went to Folsom Prison.

They probably got there by train. Travel to any distant point in Northern California was still extremely difficult, especially in the winter, because the major by-ways were subject to turning to mud in the season's rains. There was a movement to at least pave all the main thoroughfares with crushed, macadamized rock rather than the gravel that had given it a thin, not-very-effective cover since the 1850's.

In the meantime, travelers contended with the same miserable, rut-ridden, muck-bound roads they had always known. Even in the summertime it took three hours to get from Napa to Calistoga by

---

[25] Ken Stanton, *Mount St. Helena & R.L. Stevenson State Park*, Illuminations Press, Calistoga, 1993, pp. 81-86.

[26] Louis Ezettie, "Looking into Napa's Past and Present," *Napa Register*, 1-21-1978.

buckboard,[27] which was how most Valley folks traveled if they had to go any significant distance within the county. Buckboards commonly had at least two wooden boards for seats, which were often backless, like the seats in a rowboat. The rear ones could be removed to accommodate cargo. Buckboards were the minivan/SUV's of a century ago. Householders might also have a buggy, a light, hooded carriage with a single bench seat, not unlike a compact car; or they might own a surrey like that in which Bell's posse rode, a hooded carriage with two rows of bench seats that was the forerunner to today's four-door sedan. The more daring could drive a cabriolet, a fancy but rather delicate carriage with a curved bottom and a removable leather top, the convertible sportscar of the pre-automobile era. None of these attractive vehicles offered the durability, however, of the buckboard.

All of them were powered by the family horse, which meant that not only did everyone need a horse, but they needed a barn, oats and hay, tack and horseshoes. Horses were available for hire at any livery stable. All the towns in Napa County had at least one of these. Napa had several. "Fashion Stables" at 42 North Main Street in Napa City did a lot of business. Clarence Newcomb ran the livery stable at the Palace Hotel, the biggest hotel in the City of Napa after the turn the century. His "Palace Stables" had separate waiting rooms for men and women and a barn big enough for 45 horses and their equipment.[28]

Two big livery franchises in St. Helena and Calistoga played important roles in the history of their respective towns. A pioneer named William Elgin had planted a 15-acre vineyard and settled into a nice home on Main Street in the 1860's. When uncertainties in the wine market made his investment seem questionable, he sold the vineyard and used the cash to start a livery business. It did so well he was able to set up a branch at the popular nearby resort, White Sulphur Springs. He brought his son into the business and

---

[27] Fred Hutchinson, *T.B. Hutchinson of Napa*, unpublished, 1950, p. 3
Buckboards may have gotten their odd name from the fact that they were
so receptive to bumps in the road that they could actually eject riders from
the wagon. Hutchinson speaks of such an instance.

[28] Gregory, Op. Cit., p. 665.

passed it on to him when he retired in 1890. The energetic senior Elgin then became postmaster and town treasurer, occupying the latter position throughout the early part of the 20th Century.

William Spiers dominated the transportation industry in Calistoga. He was born on a plantation in Kentucky, where his family raised thoroughbred racehorses. The Civil War and its aftermath ended that, and he and his family fled west. Bill continued on to California and eventually found work at the quicksilver mine in Pine Flat, Sonoma County. Determined to reconstruct the life he once knew, he saved his earnings and founded a freighting company that connected the mines with the railroad terminus in Calistoga. With his business acumen and knowledge of horses, Bill's enterprise grew to become one of the largest livery and stage companies in California.[29] By 1910 he employed 20-30 men and ran as many as 150 horses and 60-70 vehicles.

Horses needed blacksmiths. Old John Gerlach was the main blacksmith in Napa City for many years. He started in a building on First Street near Clay, but as his business grew he moved to a much bigger location on Brown Street, between Third and Fourth.[30] Many men who later opened shops of their own began their careers under his wing.

The blacksmith's shop was a smoky, sooty place that smelled of horse, singed hoof and the forge. The blacksmith's forge was a brick or metal furnace that housed fiery coals. An air pipe beneath the fire and the smith's bellows above it kept the coals red hot. Vital though it seemed, it was a fixture in the community that, like the gristmill, would all but vanish in a few decades. The instrument of its demise, the "horseless carriage," actually appeared in the Napa Valley before it arrived anywhere else in the west. In 1891, John Money and Henry Lewelling, buddies who lived in Oakville and then in St. Helena, built a motor-driven buggy that tore through the streets of Napa, terrifying the citizens and spooking their animals. The constabulary ordered the young men to take their toy

---

[29] Ibid, p. 840. Gregory contends that Spiers' was in fact the biggest in the state.

[30] Ibid, p. 485.

14

elsewhere.[31] Unlike the machine developed by Henry Ford, the Money-Lewelling-mobile attracted neither buyers nor investors, perhaps because it vibrated so intensely that it was virtually undriveable by all but the young and exceedingly hale.[32]

All the farmers in the Valley used horses to work the plows and pull the wagon, the buggy, the surrey and the occasional cabriolet. Most of them kept a portion of their land in pasture for their animals. Thus did householders not only need big houses, but they needed large lots, as well.

The horses themselves did not always comply with their masters' property lines. Visiting horses and their owners were even more of a problem, especially in the vicinity of the racetrack on old Isaac McCombs' property near Union Station, the Southern Pacific depot northwest of Napa.[33] In April of 1900 the Grand Jury found

> that the practice of permitting transient horses and stock
> traders to pasture their stock upon the public highways of
> Napa County very often works as an   inconvenience to
> the traveling public as well as an annoyance and injury to
> adjoining property owners.[34]

Ever since Napa's founder, Nathan Coombs, raised thoroughbreds, race horses had been a Napa County passion. Fred Loeber, who lived about a mile south of St. Helena, was one who turned his attention toward the breeding of fast steeds. He sold one of his stallions, Hornstead, to San Francisco *Examiner* publisher William Randolph Hearst, and he set records. Edward Payson Heald, founder and President of Heald's College, raised prize-winning trotting horses on the stock farms he owned in North Napa and on Howell Mountain near St. Helena.[35]

---

[31] *NJ*, 8-18-1940. In 1902 the Automobile Club of San Francisco put cars on some SF street-corners to sensitize horses to them. Napa followed suit shortly afterward.

[32] *SHS*, 5-12-1939.

[33] Near today's intersection of Trancas and Route 29.

[34] *SHS* Supplement, 4-13-1900.

[35] Heald was a land speculator. He bought and sold property in many places in Napa County.

An Irish immigrant named Patrick Lennon was a popular Napa horse breeder whose rags-to-riches story must have been an inspiration to his peers. Lennon was born in 1842, at the beginning of the calamitous Irish Potato Famine. His mother died of starvation. In 1849 his father gathered what he could and bought passage for himself and Patrick, age seven, to emigrate to Quebec, where he hoped to start farming again. Perhaps weakened by years of hardship, Patrick's father fell ill and died during the voyage, and when the ship docked in Canada the young boy was "homeless, friendless and penniless."[36] He was taken in by a family in upstate New York, where he worked for wages. Eight years later he was finally able to afford to strike out on his own. He sailed to the Isthmus of Panama, made the jungle crossing, and eventually arrived in California, reaching St. Helena as a 16-year-old in 1858. He bought and improved upon a small farm there and sold it for a profit in two years. He went to Napa and rented a ranch at the end of what is now South Minahen Street. Rather than raise crops, which he knew from sad experience could fail, Lennon decided to raise horses. His "roasters"—non-racing utility steeds—went for big money.

In 1898 Lennon sold the ranch to Adolph B. Spreckels, an heir to the C&H Sugar Company, and the "Spreckels Stock Farm" became an intriguing part of the Napa City social landscape. It was to the stock farm that "A.B." stole away for intimate *rendezvous* with his paramour, Alma Emma Charlotte Corday le Normand de Bretteville, a six-foot-tall model with a powerful personality and a questionable past.[37] Alma would eventually marry A.B., and the couple would raise eyebrows in both Napa and Sonoma counties.

Poultry raising was also a common family affair at the start of the new era. For some, it was a source of income. There was spirited debate over the relative merits of White Orpingtons versus Leghorns. Competition for prizes in poultry-breeding contests was keen. St. Helena's Reverend Mitchell often walked away a winner for his fine fowl. Even Alma Spreckels tried her hand at it,

---

[36] Gregory, Op. Cit., p. 1001.

[37] See Bernice Scharlach, *Big Alma*, Scottwall Associates, San Francisco, 1990.

16

although she was also known to have cavalierly served up a couple of champion layers when there happened to be nothing else around for dinner.

Most of the farmers had at least one cow. After Bossie got milked, they put her white liquid in a "milk safe"—a screened shed where great pans of it stood on shelves until the cream, yellow and leathery, rose to the surface. The pans were then placed on a table and the cream pulled off in a sheet that was too thick to pour unless it was beaten. Further beating produced butter.[38]

Farmers could dispense with the chore of doing their own separating by selling their milk to the dairy of their choice. The Ambrosia Dairy was the biggest one around. Ambrosia was the brain-child of a young entrepreneur named William Watt, who arrived in Napa in 1906 and purchased what was once part of the land grant of Salvador Vallejo. Watt called his 250-acre holding "Longwood Ranch." At first he raised hogs and thoroughbred horses there, but then he decided there would be great profit (not to mention fun) in establishing an ice cream manufacturing company to provide frozen treats to nearby resorts. He put in a plant to manufacture ice and installed 26 six-horsepower electric motors. Business boomed. He produced thousands of gallons of ice cream every summer and even arranged for its export to China via the Pacific Mail Steamship Company. His business soon expanded to include the distribution of all dairy products, including eggs. Watt's creamery wagons made daily runs throughout Napa, Sonoma and Solano counties, and dairymen as far away as Dixon sold him their products. Manuel Almada was one of his largest suppliers. Almada's dairy farm was in Soscol, the region south of Napa that had once belonged to Generalissimo Mariano Vallejo, military commander of Northern California before the Bear Flag Revolt. The Almada family would resist, but their dairy farm would eventually be appropriated by the County of Napa for use as an airport.

Oakville was another prime dairy region. The Dos Reis brothers owned 260 acres there and had a dairy they called the "American Creamery." They also owned the Jurry ranch in Cordelia and a

---

[38] McCormick, Op. Cit., p. 10.

number of other properties. The Dos Reis brothers were Portuguese.

Several Swiss immigrants entered the dairy business, among them Joseph Kiser, Braghetta & Cantoni, James Pedrotti (who came to Napa via Duncan Mills and Bolinas) the cheese-making Neuenschwander family, and the Salminas, who switched from dairying to running a hotel[39] to winemaking.

The Salmina family's venture into viticulture came at a critical time. The industry was fighting for its life against a quarter-inch-long giant, the phylloxera louse. Billions of these had hatched and lodged themselves in the root systems of premium grapevines. Many wineries had given up the ghost because of the tiny pest. Others, like Salmina's newly acquired Larkmead, changed hands as their founders retired, went broke or moved away. Yet California wines were just beginning to catch on with consumers, as were the wines of New York State, Missouri, and Ohio. There was a market out there, but it wouldn't be easy.

---

[39] the William Tell in St. Helena near the corner of Spring and Oak Streets

Few likenesses remain of John Walden or Charles Carroll, editor/publishers of the Napa Journal *and* Calistogian, *respectively.*

Raymond Ewer, a St. Helena High School student, drew these around 1910. Ewer left the area after graduating and moved to New York City to study art. He died of pneumonia within a few years.

WALDEN WRITES AND LOOKS WISE

FINAL PUFF BY CARROL BEFORE EING CALLED DOWN.

Napa had comprehensive educational offerings at the turn of the 20th Century. Children at tiny schools like the one at Soda Canyon (above) could eventually gain useful adult skills at Napa Business College (below).

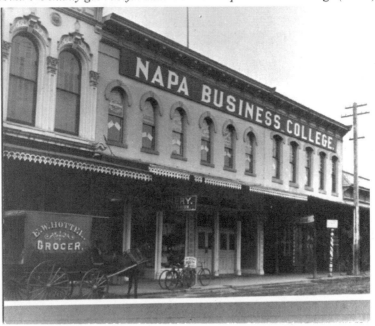

Photo courtesy of the Napa Valley Museum

GRAND BALL

UNITY HOSE CO No. 1

FOURTH of JULY, 1903
NAPA . CALIFORNIA

Courtesy of Napa Firefighters' Museum

The first fire departments in Napa were volunteer units. Pioneer Engine Company No. 1 (above) was the first. The Napa Hook and Ladder, Unity Hose Company, Reliance Hose Company and East Napa Hose Company also fought fires. They raced each other to the scene. The one that got there first could hook up to the closest hydrant and had the best chance of impressing the onlookers who always came to cheer them on. The fire companies held fund-raisers to pay for their equipment. Unity sponsored holiday balls like the one advertised on the dance card, left.

Napa architect Luther Turton designed the Eagle Cyclery on Coombs Street, a club for bikers (men only) which offered exercise equipment, a "shower bath," three billiard tables, ping pong, a reading room and a card room. Turton, like the men in the photo below, was an avid cycler and nearly died when he was broadsided by another biker near his home on First Street in 1901.

Blacksmiths heated iron bands until they glowed and shaped them to the contours of the horse's hoof. Horses pulled the cars of yesteryear.

The Spreckels family raised racehorses (and sometimes eyebrows) at their handsome stock farm south of Napa.

Men and horses ploughed the orchards in spring. In the summer, women sorted the fruit and prepared it for packing. Heatstroke was a problem.

Above, five tons of prunes stand in the noonday sun while the men and horses relax. Below, acres of prunes rest at the Napa Fruit Dryer.

Chapter Two

Pruning

Despite its many chickens, horses and cows, the Napa Valley was not really a typical California agricultural area. The premium wine industry continued to be a major part of the scene as the new era dawned. It imparted an ambience of sophistication and elegance that still drew tourists, as it had beginning in the 1860's. The deadly phylloxera infestation that had ravaged the Valley's vineyards during the last two decades continued to spread, however. Yield went way down. Less than half the Valley's grapevines bore fruit in 1900.[1] The price of grapes went way up. In 1901 Napa Valley vineyardists were getting from $30 to $35 a ton for premium grapes, while south state grape growers only received from $12.50 to $15.00.[2]

Consumers were not willing to pay very much for good California wines. Passengers dining in style on the Southern Pacific, for example, could buy premium dry wine for only 30¢ a pint. Champagne was $1.00.[3] High grape prices and low retail value made it hard for many small wineries to stay solvent.

R.N. Wood, editor of the the prestigious *Pacific Wine and Spirit Review*, noted that

---

[1] Gregory, Op. Cit., p. 148.

[2] George C. Husmann, "Grape, Raisin and Wine Production in the United States." In *Yearbook of the United States Department of Agriculture*, Government Printing Office, Washington, 1903, p. 417.

[3] *SHS*, 12-13-1901.

19

> in some instances prices paid for grapes....have been too high—the prices commanded by our wines in the markets of the east, not warranting the figure paid for the grapes.[4]

At least the product was selling, especially back in New York City. The *St. Helena Star* reported with delight in November of 1901 that the *Henry B. Hyde* had taken nearly 500,000 gallons of wine around the Horn and that a cargo of nearly the same amount was making its way across the Isthmus of Panama. Much of it was being shipped not in puncheons and casks, like before, but in bottles with labels that proudly advertised their origin.

Mounting stress may have prompted more than a few wine enthusiasts to turn to their own products for solace. This was certainly the case for a Calistoga winemaker named John Hiltel, who had a winery, home, stable and tank house on the Silverado Trail about two miles southeast of the town. He and his wife had separated due to his "habitual intemperance," and she had been awarded a portion of their property. Hiltel was unable to cope with this. He demanded she turn over her share of the property to him, and he began making drunken threats. One warm June night in 1900 his remonstrances became so intense and so scary that Mrs. Hiltel sought shelter at the home of her neighbors, the Bolands. The drunken Hiltel went to town and banged on the door of Calistoga's Constable Grauss,[5] insisting he rouse himself from his bed and help settle things with Mrs. Hiltel, once and for all. Grauss tried to calm down the inebriated winemaker and managed to extract a promise from him that he'd go home and sleep it off.

Instead, Hiltel drove his buggy to the Bolands', "and made such a demonstration," reported the *Napa Daily Journal*, "that Boland threatened to horsewhip him."[6] In a rage, Hiltel went to his own

---

[4] Quoted in *NDJ*, 6-22-1900.

[5] Hiltel might have expected Grauss would side with him, because the Constable was also divorced. The Grausses reconciled a few months later, however, and were remarried.

[6] *NDJ*, 6-14-1900.

property and removed from the house everything he believed was his. He then grabbed a can of kerosene and saturated the buildings and their remaining contents. He ignited them all. The neighbors saw the flames and were able to save the horses and the stable, but the house and winery were destroyed. Later the man next door[7] testified that he found Hiltel behind the house, standing guard over his own things. Hiltel was convicted of arson and went to San Quentin, briefly.

The tough times were hard on almost everyone, especially the oldest. Several of the industry's aged pioneers died around the turn of the century, among them Edward Mee, Frank Sciaroni, James Dowdell and one of the most influential of all, Frederick Beringer. "Fritz" Beringer became ill with a condition known as "Bright's Disease," a kidney disorder that, in the days before dialysis and antibiotics, was incurable.[8] He succumbed in July of 1901. Despite the heat of the day, hundreds came to the Rhine House parlor, where his casket was on display. A San Francisco wine merchant, Charles Bundschu, delivered the eulogy.[9] The service was conducted both in English and in Fritz's native tongue, German, a common occurrence in the Up-Valley, where persons of Teutonic descent comprised a significant part of the population.

Balance and patience were required if the industry were to prosper. The *Wine and Spirit Review* warned against "overenthusiasm as to the capabilities of the market." Before phylloxera, there had been too much wine and too little market. Overflowing inventories had to be converted into brandy, a substance that improves with age. Little wineries with big cash flow problems had neither the time to wait nor the space to store brandy, so they sold it, raw and harshly unpalatable.

---

[7] R.U. Bennett

[8] Joyce M. Black and Esther Matassarin-Jacobs, *Medical-Surgical Nursing*, Harcourt Brace & Company, Chicago, 1997, p. 1630.

[9] Lorin Sorensen, *Beringer: A Napa Valley Legend*, Silverado Publishing Company, St. Helena, 1989, p 70. Bundschu's son would be prominent in the industry 30 years later.

It was important, the *Review* said, "not to go into excess in the planting of new vineyards or the replanting of old ones."[10] The *St. Helena Star*, long a champion of the industry, concurred. "Let vineyards be planted on suitable lands," wrote editor Mackinder, "and then on soils or lowlands where alfalfa can be grown to better advantage let dairying be followed."[11] The *Star* buttressed its point by printing glowing articles about the progress of the Taplin Brothers' dairy just east of town. It wrote positively about the dairying enterprise of the Channing Mansfield family of Napa, who had put in two big silos to store corn for their cows near Union Station.[12] It faced the railroad, and its rear entrance opened onto Edgington Lane, a little road that is no more.[13]

But while grain grew fairly well in the Napa Valley, the soil was even better suited to another California specialty, prunes. Shortly after the turn of the century, orchards of lithe young prune trees began to proliferate in the Valley. Dried and carefully prepared for shipment, prunes had no problem at all surviving the trip back to the eastern markets that the vintners had already opened up.

Henry Harrison Harris of Rutherford was among the first to plant them. Harris was profoundly respected. He had arrived in Napa County in 1853 and had married another Valley pioneer, Lurinda Stice. He built a good-looking, two-story stone winery and planted a vineyard but seems to have made little if any wine when the century turned; the *Star* reported in 1902 that vintner Georges de Latour was using the Harris facility to store Beaulieu's wines.[14] By 1903 Harris had harvested enough prunes to realize a $3,000 profit from them, prompting him to proclaim his Rutherford estate the "finest prune land in the valley."[15] Eight years later he had resumed grape-growing, but he was also bringing in $11,000 from

---

[10] Idem.

[11] *SHS*, 11-15-1901.

[12] Local architect William Corlett designed it, and local contractor C.H. Gildersleeve poured the concrete.

[13] *NDJ*, 11-28-1900.

[14] *SHS*, 1-10-1902.

[15] Gregory, Op. Cit, p. 377.

22

his prune orchard.[16] Henry's cousin, William M. Harris, moved in next door, renting the winery of a man named C.P. Adamson.[17] He, too, put in a farm and a vineyard, and his children married into well-known local families. Rutherford began to develop into a prestigious address.

Balthasar Darms was one of many who removed their extensive vineyards altogether and planted orchards, in his case peaches, pears and cherries in addition to the popular prunes. He probably bought his fruit trees from his neighbor, Richard Tyther, who planted many of the trees and vines at Oak Knoll. Tyther went into the nursery business and called his 50-acre place "Dry Creek Orchard."

It became clear that while the alternative of dairy farming may have had its attractions, prune ranching might be even more lucrative. The biggest employer during the fruit-picking season was the Napa Fruit Company. It became famous for its "Napa Pack," a selection of locally grown fruits and nuts (but mainly prunes) that graced the tables of families all over the country. The Butler family ran the place, and several prominent Napans served on its board, among them a young lawyer, Charles E. Trower, and a popular physician, Dr. M.B. Pond. Dr. Pond was well-known in his time, but it is Trower's name that is best recognized today, for the street that was named for him. Trower arrived in the community in 1893 and quickly found his way to the school board, the library board and the Board of Trustees of the First National Bank of Napa.[18] He would remain an important figure in the community for the next 30 years, sometimes behind the scenes on boards, and sometimes very conspicuously in the public eye. Both he and Ralph Butler eventually served as mayors of Napa.

William Fisher installed a fruit dryer on his place near Union Station, preparing the harvest from his own orchards and those of his neighbors. Other fruit dryers cropped up throughout the county

---

[16] He had the capital to purchase the Sonoma Road dairy farm of another pioneer, the old Bear Flagger Harvey Porterfield.

[17] Gregory, Op. Cit., p. 833.

[18] Ibid, p. 587.

over the next several decades. Ernie Peters had one at the Y where Congress Valley Road and Old Sonoma Road intersected; the Lewelling family had two of them, one on Main Street and the other on Spring Street in St. Helena. C.D. Mooney erected one on Henry Harris' place in Rutherford.[19] The *Star* revealed in 1902 that F.L. Alexander and some associates thought they could install "a first-class plant" for under $7,000 at the Barro train station on Lodi Lane in St. Helena.[20] Alexander was cashier of the Carver National Bank, St. Helena's main financial concern, and would continue to be a community leader for decades. The Knipschield Company established a dehydrator-building business on the County Road on the banks of Sulphur Creek in St. Helena. As long as there was fruit to dry, Knipschield's would flourish. Napa Valley farmers had no way of knowing that down the road, the drying and packing of fruit would become about the biggest thing going in the wine country, at least legally.

Mackinder of the *Star* did not give raisins the respect he granted prunes. When the Southern Pacific Railroad sponsored a National Raisin Day, Mackinder responded with satiric disdain:

> Don't pay any attention to seeds or even a little grit. Just grittily eat away. If appendicitis should follow, never mind that there are plenty of surgeons who for a few hundred dollars would be delighted to remove a troublesome appendix. Those 20,000 tons of raisins down in Fresno must be disposed of before the next crop comes along...[21]

Many of those who chose to remain in the wine business preoccupied themselves with eliminating the tiny phylloxera louse that continued to embed itself in the roots of their grapevines. Researchers so far had determined that the parasitic bugs preferred to entrench themselves in the root system of *vinifera* vines (the kind that make the best wine) but not in the roots of varieties that were native to the area. Winemakers had long ago discovered,

---

[19] *SHS*, 1-5-1900.

[20] Ibid, 3-28-1902.

[21] *SHS*, 4-23-1899.

24

however, that native grapes made poor wine. The simple solution was to graft premium-quality grapes to louse-resistant native rootstock. There was vigorous debate among the growers as to which roots to use and how the grafts should be effected.

A native-born St. Helenan with the unlikely name of Bismarck Bruck[22] led the side that favored "bench grafting," a technique where shoots were grafted onto selected rootstock cuttings. Bruck's credibility was impeccable. His uncle was the Valley's first commercial vintner, Charles Krug. Both his mother, Isadora, and his aunt, Carolina, were daughters of Edward Turner Bale. Following in the footsteps of his father, Louis Bruck, Bismarck was the manager of the Charles Krug winery. He was dark-haired, handsome, a forceful speaker and devoted to the wine industry.

Bruck felt that the trick to survival would be to replant vineyards with bench grafts from *Vitis rupestris St. George*, a native vine whose grapes were nothing special, but whose roots were, mercifully, unappetizing to phylloxera. In 1902 George Schonewald replanted his phylloxera-ravaged vineyard on Hudson Street in St. Helena with *St. George* and went into the rootstock business. With the help of his Italian assistant, Edward Bellani, Schonewald sold 300,00 resistant root cuttings that year, at $4.50 to $15 per thousand. Georges de Latour of Beaulieu bought 10,000 of them, and 20,000 went to Calistogan M. Holji, who bought "Walnut Grove" from the old pioneer William Nash.

In bench grafting, the work is done indoors, at a table or a workbench, using cuttings of healthy, phylloxera-resistant rootstock and good prunings, or "scions," from vigorous *vinifera* vines. Matching incisions are made in both the root and the scion. The two are bound together, bark-to-bark and notch-to-notch, with a fungus-resistant ligature. (For this, Bruck recommended Italian raffia that had been dipped in copper sulfate.) The new graftings

---

[22] His German father named him after his hero, Otto von Bismarck, former *reichschancellor* of the German Empire. Father Byrne of St. Helena Catholic Church refused to Baptize him with that name, so the baptism was conducted at the Episcopal church. In childhood, he was sometimes called "Pete" and in adulthood, "Mark."

are stored somewhere warm and moist, like sand, until a "callus" forms. New scion shoots grow from the callus, supported by roots that could thumb their noses at bugs. Like Schonewald, Bruck planted resistant rootstock and sold bench grafts at $12 to $20 per thousand. He sold 250,000 of them in 1902, mainly to people outside the Valley. Bench grafting had the practical advantage of being exportable and mass-producible.

A chief spokesperson for another school of thought was George C. Husmann.[23] It was Husmann's opinion that it was safer and better to graft onto resistant rootstock that was already growing in the vineyard. He called this method "field grafting." For rootstock he was partial to the Lenoir grape, and he bitterly resisted the notion of using anything else.

As it turned out, both sides were right. St. George, Lenoir and a few other varieties proved to be dependable root sources, and both methods of grafting had their place. Bruck's bench grafting technique was especially helpful at a time when large quantities of starters were needed to remedy the devastation done by the phylloxera.

On August 2, 1901, a pruning of a different and entirely unexpected kind occurred in Calistoga.[24] It started behind John C. Wolfe's wood frame grocery store a few minutes after 5:00 in the afternoon. It had been one of those hot, wilting summer days, the kind that sucked the moisture out of all living things. With a sudden boom, the gasoline that J.C. had been storing in cans

---

[23] George's father, also named George, was a professor at the University of Missouri where he authored, in 1868, a pioneering article entitled "Grapes and Wine," the first to treat the subject of winemaking in a scholarly fashion. The senior Husmann arrived in Napa County in 1881 to manage J.W. Simonton's Talcoa Vineyards in the Carneros area. Both of his sons, Frederick and George C., were also respected authorities. Frederick became the viticultural superintendent of the US Department of Agriculture.

[24] See *NDJ*, 8-3-1901, *SHS*, 8-9-1901, *WC*, 8-2-1901.

erupted into bright orange flames, and before folks knew what was happening, the entire north side of Lincoln Avenue was smoking.

Volunteers emerged from everywhere in the tiny town to fight the blaze. They managed to attach a hose to the hydrant in front of Captain W.T. Simmons' Furniture Store & Mortuary nearby, but the fire was already so hot it burned the hose off and soldered the hydrant into the open position. Water gushed out uselessly, reducing to a trickle the pressure available to the town's other hydrants. Simmons' store erupted in flames, too. People tried pulling smoking furniture out into the center of the street, but it burned up anyway.

The Wells Fargo office attached to Simmons' went up in flames, and burning embers quickly spit over Washington Street to the roof of Charles M. Hoover's brick grocery store, which turned into an oven. Fiery debris flew across Lincoln Avenue to Mrs. Bounsell's Restaurant and the Rochedale Hotel, both of which ignited like matchboxes. The wind, blowing sharply from the northwest, buffeted glowing ashes high into the sky, starting more fires everywhere.

Bill Spiers and his men got the horses out, but soon their entire building was involved, the flames fed by the hay. The "Fresh and Salt Meats, Lard, Sausage, and Balogna" advertised at the Peoples' Meat Market next to Spiers' roasted. The soda water cylinder at Cora Fowler's ice cream parlor became rocket-powered and shot through the roof, landing in J.F. Gerber's house, starting a fire the bucket brigade rushed to extinguish. Another part of the fountain, also airborne, crashed through the roof of T.B. Hutchinson's house and landed, red hot, on a bed.

The office of the *Calistogian* went up in flames. Editor Carroll had just enough time to haul out the prior years' issues of the newspaper, but not the ones already printed in 1901. Although he supplemented his income by selling fire insurance, his newspaper and press, valued at $2,000, were only insured for $600. Many others had no insurance at all, and virtually none had insurance equal to the worth of their property.

The Magnolia Hotel, with its tiny, airless rooms, "Hot Sulphur and Moorish Mud Baths" and kerosene lamps, became a bonfire, taking The Railroad Exchange bar along with it. Ed Largey's bar across the street went up in flames, as did Dave Willis' saloon. Charles Armstrong's Telephone Office & Pharmacy, crusty old Calvin Stevens' Hardware Store & Bank and Badlam's Opera House all caught fire and burned to the ground. All three blacksmiths and harness-makers and all the doctors and dentists lost their places. John Hiltel's new winery, a converted barn that had once housed the horses of Sam Brannan, also went up in smoke. Those Calistogans who appreciated irony might have seen some strange justice in this.

Tiny, frail Mrs. Margretha M. Spreen was trapped in her burning house on Cedar Street. Mrs. Spreen had an excellent survival instinct: She had outlived 10 of her 13 children. One of them now owned and operated the burning Magnolia Hotel. With great effort the elderly woman was able to kick off the screen that was nailed onto her second-story window. She lept out into the arms of some passers-by.

Miss Josie Hopkins fainted onto her smoking bed and was rescued just in time. Postmaster Grauss (brother of the town constable) and Judge Wright both suffered heat exhaustion. A little boy named Powell reeled in the flaming American flag from the pole next to the burning Town Hall. Town Hall wasn't saved, but the flag was.

Nobody died, and they all called it a miracle.

The fire would have taken off down the Valley had the wind not changed later in the evening. Not even the little gasoline engine from Stevens' Hardware Store & Bank could have stopped it, although it might have helped in saving the Odd Fellows' Hall from destruction. In the end, only the Odd Fellows building, Grauss's store and the Railroad Depot survived the conflagration.

Calvin Stevens quickly bought the Odd Fellows building from long-time owner Lovina Graves Cyrus and re-established his vitally needed hardware store and bank.[25] The Spreen family hauled away the rubble that was once their hotel, and in June of 1902 political

---

[25] Lovina Cyrus was no stranger to disaster. She was a survivor of the Donner Party and one of the Valley's earliest pioneers.

aspirant Raymond Benjamin led a "grand march" around its replacement, the much nicer "Hotel Calistoga." The parents of the flag-saving Powell boy helped cater the gala opening.[26]

Sam Brannan, promoter, businessman, entrepreneur and rascal, had built Calistoga back in the 1860's. It was to be a playground for the wealthy, the American version of a European resort spa. He conspired with local politicians to have a railroad line lead straight to it up the Valley. Originally called "Brannan's Hot Springs," Calistoga got its odd name via a slip of Brannan's inebriated tongue, when he tried to toast "The Saratoga of California" and came out instead with "The Calistoga of Sarafornia." He spent most of his considerable fortune on Calistoga,[27] and when it failed, so did he. He sold out and left the country, dying of a heart attack in Mexico around 1880. The townspeople he left behind had to get along without him, which many were all too ready to do, since Brannan wasn't especially popular. Judging from the difficulty editor Carroll had keeping his office warm and by his comments after the place burned down, Calistoga may have needed some form of cautery in order to heal its morale. Before the coals had cooled, the women of the town had elected Mrs. William Fowler[28] to be chairman of an effort to canvass the community and determine which individuals had specific needs caused by the fire, and who had the wherewithal to meet those needs. Mrs. Fowler established a steering committee composed of one representative from each ladies' group in town—each church, each sewing society and quilting circle, each literary and whist group—and one woman who was not affiliated with any organization. This concentration of woman-power did much to get the town back on its feet. The ladies met nightly to sew clothing for those who had escaped with only the shirts on their backs.

---

[26] *SHS*, 6-13-1902.

[27] Brannan made most of his money bilking the Mormons, of whom he was a leader back in 1846, and then the Gold Miners. See Lin Weber, *Old Napa Valley*.

[28] The Fowlers were also original Valley pioneers. William had participated in the Bear Flag Revolt.

Publishing from the *Star* office the week after the horror, Carroll remarked that he was surprised and happy to see the men—Calistoga's burned-out shopkeepers—gathering in groups on the ash-sticky street corners, speaking congenially to each other. He called it "almost promiscuous."

Women had their social groups; men did, too. Most men in the Napa Valley belonged to some kind of fraternal organization, and many belonged to several. The Masons were the largest, but other popular groups included the Odd Fellows, the Druids, the Foresters, the Redmen, the Knights of Pythias, the Elks, Knights of the Golden Eagle, the Maccabees, the Loyal Order of Moose and Woodmen of the World. Some orders came into being for certain origin groups, like the Knights of Columbus for Italians and the Native Sons of the Golden West for men born in California. The "Royal Arch Masons" was for Catholics who wanted to be Masons but could not because of that group's pro-Protestant bias. It was mainly composed of men in the alcoholic beverage industry, although Charles Carroll was a member. Some of the fraternal orders engaged in beneficial projects for the community at large. They varied in their methods, but most of them featured secret initiation rituals, mutual assistance in time of trouble and a lot of socializing. They provided instant fellowship for newcomers to communities and thus were a means of guaranteeing a certain amount of continuity within middle-class society. Many fraternal societies still function, but they were in their heyday during the first half of the 20th Century.

Men went to their fraternal societies once a week; those belonging to several orders would make several meetings a week. On other nights some of them went to the saloon, attended lectures or rallies or played baseball, cards or other games. Women also attended numerous evening meetings away from home, leaving small children in the care of older siblings or with grandparents. Without the diversion of television or movie theaters, adults tended to entertain themselves in groups segregated by gender, class and ethnic background. When something exciting happened—a fire, for example—folks dropped everything and ran out to watch.

30

There were ethnic neighborhoods in the city of Napa. East Napa was heavily Italian and experienced rapid growth during the first quarter of the 20th Century. A few Italian families acquired a modest degree of wealth and achieved positions of leadership in the community (the Cavagnaros, Migliavaccas, Carbones and Silvas, for example), but many still worked very hard for very little reward. They gathered after work at saloons like those at the Brooklyn and Roma Hotels. Unionism was a spirited, driving force in other Bay Area communities in the early decades of the 20th Century, but it did not directly impact Napa until much later, and even then its influence was feeble compared with other places in the North Bay.

Chinatown occupied the area near the intersection of First Street and the Napa River. Its population dwindled steadily. "Spanishtown" was north of Chinatown, encompassing the blocks between today's St. John's Catholic Church and Clay Street. The number of Hispanic families in Napa around the turn of the century was also relatively small. Both Spanishtown and Chinatown were susceptible to flooding.

Those with a great deal of money traveled in their own small circles. The family of San Francisco's former mayor, James Phelan, for example, owned property in Berryessa Valley. The Phelans' ranch was not far from the holding of another powerful political family, the heirs of silver king James G. Fair. [29]

Beautiful, tranquil, sparsely populated Berryessa Valley was once the rancho of a high-ranking Californio family, the Berryessas. Little by little, their grant had been stripped from them and their heirs by the political machinations of the 1850's and '60's. Now the golden, gently undulating countryside was divided among an assortment of local and absentee owners, many of whom ran cattle there. A robust stream or small river, Putah Creek, ran through the center of it. Putah Creek (pronounced "Pewter" by the

---

[29] Fair had been the US Senator from Nevada when Leland Stanford was there as Senator from California, but he actually lived at the Lick House in San Francisco.

old-timers) was named for the original Berryessa rancho "Las Putas." It flowed down the Middletown side of Mount St. Helena, meandered a bit through Lake County, then took a right turn and crept down through the center of Berryessa Valley.

Putah Creek provided water for the little ranching town of Monticello, where there were, at the start of the 20th Century, a little hotel, a nice hot springs resort and some pretty homes. Abraham Clark had owned most of the little valley's farming land for many years; indeed, he was the largest single land owner in all of Napa County for decades and lived in a palatial home on what finally totaled 13,000 acres. He died in 1892, but his wife and many of his numerous children were still around. His daughter Alice married G.S. McKenzie, who ran the general store and was Napa's sheriff when Bell shot English. Another daughter, Henrietta, married Berryessa rancher Joseph Harris. Like his brother-in-law, Joe would also be sheriff one day. Son Alonzo raised cattle and horses. Reuben Clark ranched there, too. They were all Democrats, and most of them were strict Prohibitionists.

Monticello had a stable community. The Dardens, for instance, had been there since '67, growing grain on their 52 acres. Mary Sweitzer had been there even longer than that. Her husband, Lowery, had passed away back in 1878, but she carried on the ranch and owned a block of 12 lots in town. Her house was near R.H. Pithie's masterpiece, the "Big Bridge," reputed to be the largest stone bridge west of the Rockies.

Beneath the Big Bridge ran Putah Creek. It crossed the Yolo County line and wandered along a path followed in part by today's Route 128; headed toward Winters, then rolled its way east to "Davisville," today's college town of Davis. It gradually found the Sacramento River, with which it conspired, in rainy winter months, to flood the growing suburbs of the State's capital. That would all come to an end, and so would the farmlands of the Berryessa Valley, before the 20th Century was done.

The Phelans' property bordered on Joe Harris's. And it was on Joe Harris's that a curious discovery had been made recently: oil.

In October of 1900, Theodore Bell, Charles Trower, George Allen and a professional surveyor went prospecting for oil in

32

Berryessa Valley. They returned with several full bottles that they said came from springs on Harris's place. A well should be drilled, Bell told the *Napa Journal*, to find the source somewhere in the sandstone and shale below. Whoever drilled that well would be welcomed to half of the claims resulting from the strike, and Bell and his company would own the other half.[30] Three days later, the *NDJ* reported that an "expert" from the Mt. Shasta Oil and Development Company, Thomas Finnell, was going to develop what suddenly became the "Berryessa Oil Lands." He would run a "drift," or tunnel, into a hillside where a strong seepage of gas had been detected. There was so much gas, the article said, that the shaft couldn't go much deeper than 12 feet.

The very next day, the *NDJ* said that the Monticello Oil Company had just formed, with Theodore Bell as the primary owner. He was reported to have invested $40,000. Trower, Allen, Theodore's brother Edward, A.J. Raney, and four other men also invested. Meanwhile, Joe Harris leased his 1,559 acres to Mt. Shasta, with the stipulation that the lease would terminate in a year if no oil was found.[31]

Finnell's Mt. Shasta Company leveled the ground at the site where they planned to drill and had lumber hauled up from Napa. They also bought a 1,000-gallon tank to store what they claimed would soon be gushing from the well. They could double the output, they said, by drifting into the hillside another 12 or 15 feet.[32] The oil they had found so far, they said, was of the highest grade, and they were using it to run their machinery. "This oil is so pure a lubricant and of such an excellent quality," Mt. Shasta crowed, "that it is being used in buggies, bicycles, etc., with better results than are attained by the best lubricating oil sold in the market. The oil is simply brought to the boiling point and strained to eliminate the sand."[33]

---

[30] *NDJ*, 10-23-1900.

[31] *NDJ*, 10-27-1900.

[32] *NDJ*, 10-31-1900.

[33] *NDJ*, 11-10-1900.

Walden ran an editorial quoting authorities who promised that there would be an oil rush in California that echoed the great gold rush 50 years earlier. "Theodore A. Bell has found more vacant land and is preparing to file location on it," the paper exclaimed. "Those who wish to 'get in on the ground floor' had better move lively."[34] Indications for oil were popping up on the Gosling ranch in Berryessa and in Wooden Valley, on the ranch of Thomas Moore. Another article hinted that "a large portion of the Finnell ranch" had just been bought by an unnamed sugar company, although everyone guessed it must be the Spreckels family's C&H.

So much oil, of so fine a quality, so near the surface, so close to home! Better get some before the Spreckels grab it all! In November a third oil company formed, this one including on its Board some of the local heavy hitters: John T. York, H.P. Goodman, E.H. Winship, Henry H. Harris, T.H. Stice, Robert P. Lamdin, A.W. Barrett, A.M. Gardner and W.B. King.[35]

Simpson Finnell, who was not a wealthy man, financed the Finnell Land Company with under-the-table help from George Goodman, President of the J.H. Goodman bank. Without the knowledge of his board of directors, George "borrowed" almost half a million dollars from the bank to finance the Land Company's prospecting operations and erase a large indebtedness that Simpson had incurred. In return, Goodman became sole owner of the land company. He stood to make another fortune.[36]

The *St. Helena Star* followed the Berryessa Oil Rush too, although with not quite the enthusiasm of the *NDJ*. "An excellent quality of oil," it announced, had been found by M. Swift 14 miles north of Monticello, toward Knoxville. With Swift were L.G. Clark, Fred Ewer and Walter Sink. Traces had been found, too, in Calistoga, it added. Other members of the Swift family also bought into the oil craze. W.T. Swift and G.P. Swift founded the Zem Zem Oil & Development Company in January of 1901.

---

[34] *NDJ*, 11-21-1900.

[35] *NDJ*, 11-23-1900.

[36] *NDJ*, 7-03-1909.

Oil strikes were making news all over the country. It was oozing out elsewhere in Northern California and positively bursting from the ground in the state's south. That very same week drillers in Texas had hit a stupendous gusher called "Spindletop," which prompted an equally stupendous land rush. Land that had gone for under $10 an acre was now worth $900,000 an acre.[37] Texas pig farmers became millionaires overnight. Few in Berryessa would have objected if this fate became theirs, as well.

Now practically everyone with any cash in the bank made a bee-line to Berryessa. Theodore Bell and his brother Edward, also a lawyer, collected several others to form the Monarch Oil Company on Joe Harris' Berryessa land, including John Imrie (the Superintendent of Schools), Henry Meacham (the City Assessor), George Gardner (Treasurer of Napa County), David Dunlap (the new Sheriff), H.P. Goodman (bank owner) and James Daly (an undersheriff). Also on the roster were businessmen C.W. Armstrong, W.E. Deweese, J.H. Schuppert, L.B. Arnold, J.G. Johnson and N.W. Collins.

Not to be left out, E.H. Winship, E.D. Beard, J.E. Beard, D.L. Beard and Raymond Benjamin created the Bald Eagle Jr. Oil Company. Winship, David Kyser and others also created the Hunting Creek Oil Company west of Knoxville, a tiny mining community in the county's extreme northeast.

The San Francisco *Bulletin* reported in February, 1901, that Bald Eagle sold its portion of formerly cheap Berryessa land for $35,000. The Napa & Berryessa Oil Company took out a full page advertisement in that paper later in the month. In March there was also an article there describing the oil in Berryessa as "unusually fine;" an inducement, said the paper, for someone to build a railroad in that direction. The San Franciscio *Post* observed that the Zem Zem region was attracting investors from the East Coast.

In early April, the *NDJ* quoted a Colonel Crane, President of the Miners' Petroleum Association: "I consider the oil indications

[37] Daniel Yergin, *The Prize*, Simon & Schuster, New York, 1991, p. 85.

in Northern California," he said, "superior to any that I have seen in any part of the world."[38]

In mid-April, A.W. Pieratt of Capelle Valley struck oil after drilling down 125'.

After that...silence. There were no more big stories in the local papers about oil strikes. There may have been oil there, but somehow most of it vanished before it could come to the surface. The drillers and drifters, surveyors and investors quietly packed up their things and went away. A lot of money had changed hands for nothing, much of it going in legal and professional fees to attorneys like former schoolteacher Theodore Bell.

The value of this new form of gold was only beginning to be recognized. As a replacement for whale oil and tallow, "rock oil" or "coal oil," as it was once called, illuminated homes around the country in the form of kerosene. Gasoline was used as a cleaning solvent. Oil was converted to light whole buildings as well as city streets. It lubricated the moving parts of bigger machines, like the locomotives and cars of the Southern Pacific. But by far the most significant use of oil would prove to be as a fuel in a contraption called the "internal combustion engine." Fuel oil already powered small machines like the inadequate little engine from Stevens' Hardware Store & Bank that the volunteers used to fight the fire in Calistoga. But when Henry Ford quit his job at the Edison Illuminating Plant in 1893 to make gasoline-powered vehicles, he started a demand that transformed the world. Ford's first automobile was completed and ready to go in 1896. The horseless carriage had become a rare but impressive sight on the streets in many American cities by 1902, and as described above, Money and Lewelling had already driven a motored vehicle through Napa. Prompted by the invention of the automobile, oil production in California had grown from 470,000 barrels in 1893 to 24,000,000 by 1903. [39]

---

[38] *NDJ*, 4-3-1901.

[39] Yergin, Op. Cit., p. 82

The trains of the Southern Pacific, however, did most of the serious people- and produce-moving. The Southern Pacific owned all the railroad track in Napa County in 1901; it controlled more than 85% of all the track in the state. It also controlled the California state legislature, the judiciary, the Board of Equalization, the Railroad Commission, the Republican Party and most of the local newspapers. It even determined the price of food and wine, and people were starting to complain.

Chapter Three

Moving People

Just one week ago today while in the Temple of Music at the Pan American Exposition at Buffalo holding a public reception, an anarchist coming in the guise of one desirous of shaking the president by the hand, fired two bullets into his body in a hellish desire to lay low the chief executive, thinking thus to achieve the fiendish desires of a society whose mission is one of death and ruin.[1]

When Leon Czolgosz shot President William McKinley, no one in the Napa Valley could have been more aghast than Frank Mackinder, editor of the *St. Helena Star*. His emotions came through loud and clear in the 72-word sentence he wrote to announce that McKinley had succumbed to the two bullets Czolgosz fired into the big man's body. Mackinder editorialized about it again a week later in a second 72-word sentence:

How a being, which bears the name of a man, could have so base a heart and so weak a brain as to stoop to such a dastardly deed as to deliberately take the life of so good and great a man as our President William McKinley in such a Judas-like manner, is beyond the understanding of every American citizen, no matter what party he belongs to or what denomination or creed.[2]

---

[1] *SHS*, 9-13-1901
[2] *SHS*, 9-20-1901

When McKinley ran for his second term in 1900, Mackinder had endorsed him strongly, asserting that during the administration of the President's Democratic predecessor, Grover Cleveland (1885-1889, 1893-1897), 24 citizens of Napa County went bankrupt, eight of whom were farmers. During McKinley's term, bragged Mackinder, only four people in Napa had gone bankrupt, and none of them were farmers.[3]

Johnny Walden of the *Napa Daily Journal* was not nearly so florid in writing about the shooting as was his peer up valley. During the two weeks of the President's decline, he wrote brief updates on his condition, one of them dwarfed by an energetic write-up about a big meeting of the Women's Christian Temperance Union (WCTU) that took place in St. Helena, upon which the *Star* did not report.[4] When the President died, Walden rimmed the obituary in black, and wrote a long, sedate article about McKinley's many achievements as a soldier and statesman.

In contrast, Napa Mayor J.H. Fuller outdid even the *Star*. After the President died he issued a one-sentence proclamation of the city's grief that was 138 words long. It may not have been enough, though. All the businesses in the county closed their doors to honor McKinley, but it was to St. Helena and not Napa that Republican Congressman Frank L. Coombs went to deliver his address to the people of the Napa Valley.

Congressman Coombs spoke to an apparently adoring crowd that had gathered in Hunt's grove, a lovely park at the end of Hunt Street. "There has been no excuse for murder here," he told the St. Helenans. "There have been no examples like our own. Men are well clad and not oppressed. The air they breathe is liberty itself."[5] Whatever his oration may have lacked in clarity was more than compensated by its length. He went on for 45 minutes praising McKinley as a soldier, congressman, governor and president, and when he finally finished, the crowd, baking in the heat of the day, joined together in a rendition of "Nearer, My God, to Thee."

---

[3] *SHS*, 11-2-1900.

[4] *NDJ*, 9-8-1901

[5] *SHS*, 9-27-1901.

Lieurene Greenfield recited "Crowning Our Martyred President," and Josie Forni placed a ceremonial wreath on the slain man's picture, which was supported by an easel. Councilman Owen Wade proposed that a monument be built at the school grounds, and St. Helenans dropped more than $200 into the fund that was established on the spot. (There might have been more, perhaps, had not the hat so recently been passed to help the burned-out Calistogans.)

The nation lost no time in avenging the murder. On November 1, 1901, the *Calistogian* ran this headline:

M'Kinley's Murderer Goes
To His Doom
Had a Sound Sleep and Dies Without
Any Indication of Failing Courage

Son of Napa City's founder Nathan Coombs, Frank Coombs was a hero to many in the Napa Valley. He had been US Ambassador to Japan under President Harrison back in 1892 [6] and was a prime mover behind national legislation that restricted the number of Chinese laborers who could be permitted to enter the United States. Unsatisfied with merely banning them from American shores, he also put forward laws to forbid the Chinese from populating the newly acquired territory in the Philippines.

His Sinophobia especially ingratiated him with St. Helenans, who had been complaining about the Chinatown at the south entrance of town for almost two decades. As it had in the past, the *Star* continued to express anti-Chinese sentiments. "For the past ten years," smiled Mackinder a few months later, "this State has been practically free from invasion by coolies."[7]

The prejudice seemed nearly universal in the Napa Valley. Henry Lange, a Democrat, won the hearts of his contemporaries by opening a "white laundry" on St. Helena's Main Street to compete

---

[6] Gregory, Op. Cit., pp. 576-77.

[7] *SHS*, 11-15-1901.

with one of the few forms of private enterprise in which the Chinese engaged, "thus giving the public a chance to show where they stood," said the *NDJ*'s Walden,[8] who was not exempt from bigotry, either.

The few citizens with the courage to oppose public opinion did so at some peril. The Wheeler family allowed a number of Japanese workers to live on their ranch on Zinfandel Lane. Threats were made, and it was feared that "strong sentiment in certain corners" would result in violence to "rid the community of the Japs."[9]

The intensely sinophobic Coombs was so steeped in anti-Asian bias that he missed the truly pressing issue that was on most voters' minds.[10] Public resistance to the Southern Pacific Railroad was very much alive, and Coombs appeared to some to be too friendly with what novelist Frank Norris called "The Octopus." He made use of the free passes SP officials issued to candidates of their choice so that they could canvass their districts for votes. He may not have paid much attention, at first, to his Democratic opponent, a young man the *Petaluma Argus* called "a beardless youth and school boy philosopher."[11] Theodore Bell, Napa's 29-year-old former District Attorney and would-be oil magnate, had caught the eye of the Democratic political machine, most likely during the Berryessa Oil Rush, and most particularly, perhaps, through his dealings with San Francisco's former mayor, James Phelan. Phelan may have profited from Bell's work in increasing the value of his Berryessa oil land. The Ukiah *Dispatch-Democrat* floated a story describing the young politican as good "Congressional timber," a "young man of force." "This district needs some young blood infused into it," the article said. [12]

Despite growing up only a few miles apart, the two men were very different. Frank Coombs was laconic to the point of seeming

---

[8] *NDJ*, 10-18-1902.

[9] *NDJ*, 2-14-1904.

[10] Donald W. Wheaton, *Quarterly of the California Historical Society*, V, No. 3, September, 1926, p. 287.

[11] Quoted in *NDJ*, 10-16-1902.

[12] Ibid, 6-26-1900.

aloof. His manner was deliberate, cautious, perhaps even shy. During the campaign he sought to impart a sense of stability by portraying himself as a native Californian with the deepest possible roots in the *status quo*. His parents, he told an audience in Sacramento, were married right there at historic Sutter's Fort.[13]

Bell was quite different. He was, he said, a friend of labor, and he demonstrated this by going everywhere and shaking hands with everyone—something the more austere Coombs did not seem to enjoy.[14] He drew much attention to the sorry state of the rivers in the District, specifically the Sacramento, Napa, Petaluma and Russian. His opponent, he complained, was only able to eke out $25,000 from Congress to improve the very flood-prone Sacramento. He would, he promised, not only better that paltry sum, but he would also secure government funding to straighten the ox-bow in the Napa River, which would, he believed, remove the yearly threat of inundation that kept residents of Napa on edge all winter.

Unlike Coombs, Bell spoke out against the "trusts," monopolistic industrial power blocks, but most particularly he assailed what to many Californians had become Evil Incarnate: the Southern Pacific Railroad. It took a bite out of practically every business in California, because it owned virtually all of the transportation, much of the land, and had interests in most of the financial institutions and media in the state.

Speaking out publically against the omnipotent railroad was not a safe thing to do. The last of the Big Four, Collis Huntington, had died in 1900, but his ghost lingered and haunted Golden State politics through its Political Bureau, which was headed by SP crony/San Francisco attorney William F. Herrin.[15] Henry E. Huntington succeeded his uncle as head of the railroad, but even after he retired and sold out to E.H. Harriman, the squid's tentacles

---

[13] *San Francisco Examiner*, 10-3-1902.

[14] Idem.

[15] W.H. Hutchinson, "Prologue to Reform: The California Anti-Railroad Republicans, 1899-1905," in *Southern California Quarterly*, Historical Society of Southern California, September, 1962, p. 197.

Photo courtesy of California State Library

Theodore Bell

Photo courtesy of the Napa County Historical Society

Frank Coombs

The great Calistoga fire of 1901 burned down nearly every business in town. Saloon-keeper Ed Largey rebuilt his establishment as soon as the ashes cooled.

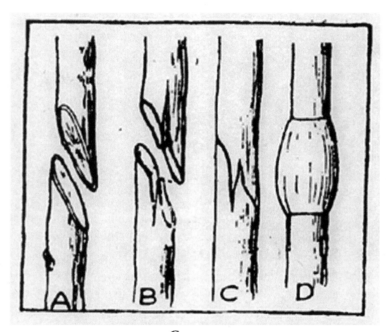

GRAFTING

A. MATCHED INCISIONS ON ROOT AND SCION
B. NOTCHES ON ROOT AND SCION ALIGNED
C. ROOT AND SCION JOINED
D. SECTIONS JOINED WITH RAFFIA SOAKED IN BLUESTONE

intruded everywhere. Perhaps most ominously, its ink appeared in the press, both in major newspapers and smaller, local ones. Fremont Older, publisher of the San Francisco *Bulletin*, had received $250 per month from the railroad, but in 1900 he stopped taking it and turned on his benefactor, becoming a powerful critic of the monopoly.[16] Frank Pixley, editor of the *Argonaut*, got $10,000 a year[17] before he became a railroad opponent. The *Examiner* was on the dole for $30,000 and had a contract with the SP to provide both advertising and "fair treatment," i.e., positive reporting and favorable editorials. Hearst's vituperations against Huntington and his trains cost him the $30,000 but won him the respect of many.[18]

Berryessa's James D. Phelan, friend of labor and former Mayor of San Francisco, threw the force of his blessing behind young Bell. The *Examiner*'s Hearst, who himself would be the Democratic nominee for President in 1904, did so as well. Bell, the *Examiner* reported, "preached sound Democratic doctrine couched in language that could not offend the most sensitive Republican."[19] But for the most part, Theodore Bell was a lone Democrat in an inky sea of Republicans.

As November, 1902 drew close, the big election was on everyone's mind. The *Napa Daily Journal*, one of the few small dailies not under the thumb of the SP, entrenched itself firmly in the camp of Bell. Carroll of the *Calistogian* stood behind Coombs and the Republican ticket. The *Star*, of course, vigorously supported Coombs. Just before the voters went to the polls, Mackinder threw the spotlight on the newly completed bronze bust of the slain Republican hero, President McKinley. It was unveiled, with much fanfare, at the St. Helena Elementary School. Both candidates had their nights at Crowey's Napa Opera House

---

[16] Oscar Lewis, *The Big Four*, Alfred A, Knopf, New York, 1966, pp. 296-297.

[17] William Deverell, *Railroad Crossing*, University of California Press, Berkeley and Los Angeles, 1994, p. 131.

[18] Ibid, p. 132.

[19] *San Francisco Examiner*, 10-3-1902.

(Raymond Benjamin served as master of ceremonies for Coombs' big rally), and their backers lit a great bonfire at the junction of Main and Second Streets in Napa.[20]

Bell won. He was one of only three Democrats in the entire state to do so.[21] When all the votes were counted, he had 628 votes more than Coombs, and he beat the incumbent by only 11 votes in Napa County. Coombs took it hard. The flabbergasted *Star* revealed that the scion of Napa City's oldest family had "deep regret over the defeat."[22]

The Republican Raymond Benjamin was elected to Bell's old position as DA. His big wedding and public visibility had paid off.

Shortly after the election, some of the newspapers pointed to possible errors in how the votes were counted. Bell's name was at the top of the list, and a mark for "No Vote" could be mistaken, perhaps, for a vote for Bell. The *Star* and other Republican organs tried to persuade Coombs to demand a recount, but Coombs declined. "That sort of contest I would not resort to for a seat in Congress," said Coombs.[23]

But it was the Republicans and not the Democrats who had cornered the market in dubious politics. The governmental corruption that had been a feature of the Golden State in 1850 was still alive and more than well. Sacramento was a hotbed of disrepute. Persons with no qualifications other than their loyalty and financial dependence on the Railroad were rewarded with jobs in the corrupt Sacramento bureaucracy. Napa itself made a notable contribution to the senatorial stenographers' pool. J.A. Vaughn, whom District Attorney Bell had forced from his position as official reporter in Napa's Superior Court because of habitual drunkenness, was now making $5.00 a day as stenographer to the

---

[20] The bonfire was actually carried on the back of a big wagon, which had been lined with fireproofing for the event. The fireproofing didn't work, however, and the wagon caught fire. The driver was severely burned trying to keep the terrified horses from trampling the spectators.

[21] Olin, Op. Cit., p. 31.

[22] *SHS*, 11-7-1902.

[23] *SHS*, 12-5-1902.

State Finance Committee.[24] Vaughn had once boasted publically that "his influence with the Court was such that he could decide cases."[25] Walden tried for months to expose not only Vaughn, but Napa City's entire judiciary, in blasts like this:

Judge Ham's Pet Forced to
Resign Office as Reporter

...[Judge] Ham, naturally, would not like to have the
acts of his protegee given "publicity"...And then there
is Justice Marois, one of the Judge's lickspittle, and
Justice Caldwell, another of Vaughn's champions. This
honorable judiciary might be brought into bad light,
by reflection.

The Napa Valley had been among the first to feel the effect of railroading's mighty power. Back in the 1860's, State Senator Chancellor Hartson of Napa managed to lay tracks to Sam Brannan's resort, even though the county's residents had voted the project down. The Napa Valley Railroad soon went bankrupt; Southern Pacific bought it, and Leland Stanford bought Brannan's resort.

Stanford was also drawn to the wine industry. He plunked down $1,000,000 for 55,000 acres near Corning in the northern part of the Sacramento Valley and planted nearly 3,000,000 grapevines. It was by far the biggest vineyard in California at the time.[26] The Central Valley town of Vina came into being to support it. Stanford intended to produce the greatest quantity of the highest quality wine in America, but as it turned out, neither was possible. Unlike the thousands of human beings whose livelihoods depended on Stanford's good will, neither the soil nor the climate would obey him. Many of the young vines curled up and died in the dry heat of summer, and much of the low quality juice he did manage to

---

[24] $5.00 a day was good money. The per diem for elected officials was only $7.00.

[25] *NDJ,* 7-7-1900.

[26] Lewis, *Ibid*, p. 126.

extract had to be converted into brandy.[27] Had Stanford actually succeeded in his plans, the consequences for the Napa Valley could have been serious. Unable to obliterate the Napa Valley wine industry, the Railroad had to be content with merely tormenting it by charging impossibly high freight rates.

Freshman Congressman Bell tried to make good on his campaign promise by tugging at political strings to get money to straighten the Napa River.[28] The river demonstrated its need for straightening by flooding parts of the city twice in February of 1904, and at the end of that month he was able to introduce a joint resolution to at least have the river professionally surveyed.

He authored legislation that greatly interested California vintners. He sought to bring the wine industry under the control of the Internal Revenue Service so that a tax could be imposed on it. The tax that he sought would be slight on pure wines but harshly punitive on wines that had been adulterated. His proposed "pure wine bill" was an attempt to drive East Coast and Midwest vintners out of business. The growing season in the more northern latitudes was much shorter, and winemakers there regularly resorted to adding sugar to their product. Bell's "pure wine" tax would be so stiff that it would make cool-climate winemaking unprofitable. It had no hope of passing the heavily Republican Congress.[29]

Bell was well received by the other Democrats in Washington and attracted the attention of William Jennings Bryan, who ran many times for President. Among other things, Bryan was a Prohibitionist, and, perhaps misinterpreting the intent behind Bell's taxation scheme, he took Bell under his wing.

Bell only served one term in Congress. District voters went Republican again, and when his term was up in November of 1904, he was defeated. His great opponent, the Southern Pacific, was stronger than ever.

---

[27] Stanford aged the brandy in barrels that he stowed as ballast in sea-going ships.

[28] *NDJ*, 1-6-1904.

[29] *NDJ*, 3-27-1904.

The population of California had increased 22% between 1890 and 1900. Sea-bound Hawaii had grown a whopping 41.2% in only four years. Napa County's population at the turn of the century was virtually the same as it had been for the past 10 years. Its 1900 census counted 16,451—only 40 more souls than in 1890.[30] It was by far the slowest growing of the Bay Area counties, and many feared that its incipient decline would escalate into a mass exodus. Hundreds came for the weekend, especially in the summer, to spas like Napa Soda Springs, but many thousands more traveled straight through and spent their time and their dollars in the newly opening resorts of Lake County.

The high land prices about which many liked to boast were part of the problem. Few could afford to purchase farms or vineyards large enough to support their families, especially in prosperous times when the cost of land was at its peak. Most of the Valley's ranchers were actually tenants, renting their fields from old-time residents who could then retire to nice houses in town. In times of economic hardship, however, even the land owners were often unable to keep up with costs. They had to sell out and become tenants themselves.[31]

What few people could detect at the time was that almost all of the nation's rural communities were emptying out. Everyone was moving away. The children of pioneer Joe Chiles were an example. His daughter Dixie married Alfonso N. Bell, a prosperous St. Helena shopkeeper (a cousin of Theodore Bell's) and remained in St. Helena. His son Henry married a young lady from Davis and moved to her hometown. J.B., Jr. hung around the area for a while and ran a butcher shop in sleepy Calistoga, but in 1900 he relocated to the much larger community of Napa, where he and a partner set up a shop on Main Street. The partnership dissolved, though, and by 1903 J.B. Chiles was operating a streetcar for the Southern Pacific in busy, exciting San Francisco.

---

[30] *NDJ*, 10-25-1900.

[31] See Stephen Birmingham, *California Rich*, Simon & Schuster, New York, 1980, p. 44.

Up-Valley businesses were small, family-owned, family-run concerns. The wineries that had survived phylloxera lacked the capital to employ much staff. Only in the city of Napa were there industries of the size that could support a growing middle-class. Even in Napa, though, the numbers looked bad.

To promote growth and stimulate the county's economy, Napa's city fathers turned to a new solution. They would accept with pleasure the invitation of an SP foe named John Wesley Hartzell to build an interurban railroad. It would be powered by electricity, and its rates would be only a fraction of the Southern Pacific's exorbitant fee. It would link together the communities of the Valley and make travel a pleasure rather than an athletic event. Its presence would both encourage growth and determine what shape the healthy new demographics would take. Everyone would want to own land near the clean, convenient, low-cost public transportation, and a real estate boom would make the well-placed ones wealthy (or so they all hoped).

John Hartzell was a high-tempered railroading genius from the Midwest. He had built electric railroads in Illinois and Kansas. He came to California and successfully lobbied the state to legalize the use of electricity for street railroads. He had installed an electrically powered line from Market Street in San Francisco to the San Mateo County border, and had thus acquired much practical California experience. He bought cheap land in the Vallejo area in 1901 and got franchises to run an electric railway in Benicia, Vallejo and Napa. The Napa city council congratulated itself for having wrested $5,000 from Hartzell for his franchise; Vallejo only received $500.[32]

Hartzell saw that he needed outside backers to help fund his "Vallejo, Benicia & Napa Valley Railroad." After a fruitless search in SP-dominated San Francisco, he found takers in Los Angeles. John Cross, who had built and profited from a line between Sacramento and Stockton, came on board, as did W.F. Botsford, president of America National Bank in Los Angeles. John

---

[32] Ira L. Swett and Harry C. Aiken, Jr., *Napa Valley Route: Electric Trains and Steamers*, Interurbans, Glendale, CA, 1975, p. 32.

Hartzell's brother also joined the team. Thus fortified with investors, Hartzell announced his intention to build an interurban line from Benicia to Vallejo and then on to Napa, with a side line to Napa Soda Springs.[33] It would bisect the Valley by following the County Road (Highway 29) through the center of St. Helena, sending another side line to the White Sulphur Springs resort. It would proceed to Calistoga and then on to Lake County. While he was at it, Hartzell also secured a franchise for Solano County. Using Napa Junction as a central hub, he would go west to Cordelia, Rockville, Manka, Fairfield, Suisun, Vacaville and Dixon, and then into Yolo County, ending in Woodland.[34]

To power such an elaborate route, he would install overhead lines with alternating current. Direct current lines would have demanded the construction of numerous substations; AC was a more economical choice for a system that would cover so many miles. Each car would sport a pantograph, a diamond-shaped structure with a metal bar on top that maintained constant contact with the network of live wires above it.

Hartzell's plan was ambitious. It was so ambitious, in fact, that he knew he either needed more money or had to modify his grand scheme. By the spring of 1903 the project still hadn't begun, and the Napa City fathers were growing impatient. Hartzell decided to drop Benicia and the side-lines from the initial plan, and finally, in August of that year, the first load of railroad ties was delivered to the pier in Vallejo. Work commenced immediately, and a roadbed with shiny new rails started inching its way up toward Napa.

Since the interurban line would be in direct competition with the Southern Pacific, Hartzell felt it would be necessary to make a statement that indicated he would not be intimidated by the giant monopoly. In November he sent an advance crew into Napa to lay tracks across the SP rails on Soscol Avenue, just south of the SP depot. A week later the SP freighted in a crew of its own to lay tracks in the direction of the VB & NV's line, and when the SP's track touched that of its young competitor, the SP's men began to

---

[33] *NDJ*, 4-4-1902.

[34] Swett, Op Cit., p. 32.

tear up the electric line. The VB & NV's chief engineer ran to the home of Mayor Fuller to protest, and Fuller quickly consulted with the City Attorney, John T. York, grandson of the old pioneer. York, a Democrat in neither the pay nor fear of the Southern Pacific, informed the SP crew that city regulations forbid cutting into the street without a permit. The SP stopped laying track, but it failed to remove the track it had just put down.[35] The situation was dramatically tense. Violence was avoided, possibly because York possessed good negotiating skills. [36]

One way the SP's Big Four secured their profits was by eliminating outside contractors. They were their own construction company. Their lumber came from their own forests, hewn by their own employees. They even owned their own food franchises and occasionally went to lengths to discourage their employees (and their passengers) from sampling the wares of non-SP purveyors. Alcoholic beverages of any kind were expressly forbidden to railroad employees, although as mentioned above, wine was apparently available to passengers. When the Daglia family built the Depot Restaurant and Saloon on Soscol Avenue, the SP strung wire around its perimeters to discourage people from quaffing its liquid fare. Determined drinkers (or possibly the Daglias) cut the wires with regularity, and the SP finally resorted to erecting a tall wooden spite fence to conceal the place from view.[37] These little sabotages did not interfere with the saloon's popularity, especially among the Italians who lived nearby.

Hartzell eschewed the SP style. He inspired local pride and interest in the VB&NV by hiring local firms to handle different aspects of the project. He chose Napa's Corlett Brothers to manufacture the wooden cross-arms to be used on the electric

---

[35] Ibid, p. 51.

[36] A similar confrontation occurring about two years later in front of the Grapevine Winery Santa Rosa would result in bloodshed. See Paul C. Trimble, *Interurban Railways of the Bay Area*, Valley Publishers, Fresno, 1977, pp. 98-99.

[37] Swett, Op. Cit., p. 54.

supply poles, which gave employment to many in their plant just beyond the Third Street Bridge in East Napa. Napa Gas & Electric Company, a privately owned utility, received the franchise to provide the power.

The Migliavacca family purchased the land around the Depot Restaurant and Saloon in 1902. Two years later they sold it to Hartzell for triple the price, for it was there that the line would build its main station. Napa's premier contractor, E.W. Doughty, was tapped to erect the new facility.

The electric line went up Soscol to the intersection of Third, which was becoming a major hub of activity. (The very imposing Palace Hotel stood on the southwest corner.) The line then turned west at the intersection and proceeded down the center of Third as far as Seminary Street. It made a short northwest diagonal, across the property of a family named Simmons, until it hit Jefferson at Second Street. It followed what is now Jefferson (but was Calistoga Avenue back then) to a terminus at Lincoln Avenue.[38]

Winter and its accompaniment of rain, mud and minor flooding halted the VB&NV's progress for several weeks. The difficult problems of sending cables under the Napa River and building functional voltage transformers also had to be overcome, but at last, on May 10, 1905, the line was ready to receive its first jolt of electricity. Mayor Fuller stuck his neck out and accepted the challenge of pulling the switch that sent the 6,000-volt current through a transformer, which converted it to 3,300 volts. The electricity passed through a thick, well-insulated copper cable that had been sunk into the Napa River and emerged again at the substation. There it powered a large motor that passed the current through a generator and sent it sparking over the network of overhead trolley wires. The electric lights in Doughty's new depot lit up festively, and that was the end of the ceremony. The interurban cars themselves had not yet arrived.

---

[38] The tracks of the Southern Pacific continued up a few blocks, past the Soscol/Third Street intersection, then veered to the northwest, slicing diagonally across town (the path taken by the Napa Valley Wine Train).

It was almost a full month before the much-heralded first coaches came to town. Newspaper reports spoke of commodious new cars that could seat 80 in comfort. What actually came were reconditioned open excursion cars, No.'s 9 and 10, nicely painted in dark red and gold and bearing the inscription "VB & NVRR." The cars came in pieces, the wheels on one flatcar, the cabins themselves on two others. They seated only 60, and they were hardly new. They had been built in the 1880's for use in something called the "Park & Ocean Railroad," a San Francisco line that never really came into being. Pacific Electric of Los Angeles, a Southern Pacific company, purchased them and sold them to the VB & NVRR.[39] Each had its own electric motors and airbrakes and could operate without the locomotive. Unfortunately, due to an unforeseen glitch they were unable, at first, to be linked together.

To eager Napa eyes, they were beautiful. Engineer Charles Frederick Otterson, a big, burly young man with a genius for managing both machines and men, dispensed with formalities and gleefully took the cars on their first round-trip run to Vallejo as soon as the welding cooled.

The new locomotive arrived some time later, also in pieces. It was too tall to fit through a tunnel in Cordelia on its passage from Los Angeles and had to be disassembled. When Otterson and his men put it back together, it turned out to be an odd-looking thing. It resembled a flatcar with an upright rectangular cab in the center of it. It was 45' long and may have reminded some of a barnyard animal, because people called it "The Pig." What it lacked in grace it made up for in practicality and durability. It boasted four 50-horsepower Westinghouse motors and, although it found its way off the track quite a few times, it was virtually indestructible, lasting as long as the system itself did.

Two more passenger cars arrived over the next several weeks, as did two trailers, six freight cars and a mail car. Much of the equipment came from Los Angeles, accompanied by some of the railroad's new staff, including an experienced motorman and most of the line's management team.

---

[39] Swett, Op. Cit., p. 69.

There was more to the electric line than the Vallejo-Napa run. It also had a link with its own, non-SP-affiliated ferry, the Monticello Steamship Company, which plied the Bay between Vallejo and the Market Street Ferry Building in San Francisco. Among its ships were the *Monticello,* the *Napa Valley* and later the *General Frisbie* and the *Calistoga.*[40] They ran in competition with the Napa Transportation Company's fleet, which for years had consisted of the *Zinfandel* and the *Napa City.* In May of 1902, perhaps sensing the competition that was waiting in the wings, Napa Transportation had added a new ship, the *St. Helena.* Like the others it was a sternwheeler and almost square: 36' long and 31' wide. It had 25 staterooms with two beds each.[41]

The VB & NVRR was an immediate success. It took about 10 minutes for the interurban to make the run between the East Napa Depot and the terminus at Calistoga Avenue (Jefferson) and Lincoln, with many stops along the way. Most days there were 13 runs. Cars left Calistoga and Lincoln at 6:05, 6:45, 8:20, 9:45, 10:05, 11:20, 3:40, 4:30, 6:20, 7:25 and 9:50. Cross-town trips cost 5¢. A complete round-trip ticket to San Francisco and back from Napa cost only $1.10. Despite the low fares, the company's profits exceeded its most optimistic predictions within the first few months.

Napa's Unity Hose Company, which engaged in a friendly competition with the Alert Hose Company over which volunteer fire fighting company could throw the best parties, hosted a big Fourth of July bash with a celebration of the new interurban as its centerpiece. Many people came up from San Francisco to join in the festivities. Several weeks later, on August 11, Vallejo's "Twenty Thousand Club" sponsored a banquet to fête the new train and the people who brought it to life. Vallejo's Mayor Roney called

---

[40] See George H. Harlan, *San Francisco Bay Ferry Boats*, Howell-North Books, Berkeley, 1967, pp. 103-104.

[41] *SHS*, 5-30-1902. Few commuters would have wanted to sleep on the brief trans-Bay trip, unless, perhaps, paid companionship was available. Prostitution was one of the relatively few professions in which women of the time engaged.

it a "marriage feast between Vallejo and Napa" and spoke favorably of the good work Theodore Bell had done in Congress to assure a prosperous future for the Mare Island Navy Yard there.[42] Napa's Republican Mayor Fuller claimed illness and was unable to attend. John T. York took his place.[43] The chumminess that the two cities enjoyed would sour, unfortunately, mid-way through the century.

Success bred competition. Another line, an SP-backed enterprise called the "San Francisco and Napa West Side Steam Railroad," declared its intention to run trains from Napa to Tiburon using the Southern Pacific's westside Union Station in Napa as its terminus. There were to be four stations, beginning with a place called Wingo, followed by Ignacio, San Rafael and Tiburon, where it connected with a ferry. A round-trip ticket would cost $1.25.

To impede the competitor's progress and insure that future spans of the VB & NVRR had the right-of-way, John Cross purchased the old racetrack on pioneer Isaac McComb's place by Union Station. He let it be known that the area would be subdivided into homes.[44] He then laid VB & NVRR track over the likely path the steam railroad would be taking. The Westside Railroad opened for business in May of 1905 and probably had to pay the VB & NVRR access fees.[45] Later that year Cross approached the Napa City Council, seeking an injunction to prevent the steam line from crossing his little subdivision, which was bounded on the north by Myrtle Street, by Sacramento Street on the west and Sonoma Street on the east.

Cross also sent a crew to St. Helena early in 1905 to lay about 65' of track near the SP depot on Railroad Avenue. He fully

---

[42] Bell had been helpful in supporting a bill that brought a small collier to Mare Island, the first step in making it a port for the Navy. Others were probably more directly responsible for the bill's success, but Bell was happy to accept the credit.

[43] Swett, Op. Cit., p. 84.

[44] NDJ, 2-17-1904.

[45] Swett, Op. Cit., p. 57.

believed that at some future date the interurban would, as it had promised, extend its service up the Valley.

The City of Napa did in fact experience a growth spurt as a result of the interurban, and the line prospered. They both flourished despite the fact that the Napa River flooded again in the winter of 1905-06. The train arranged for wagons to convey its passengers across stretches that were under as much as three feet of water.[46]

The enticing scent of money wafted its sweet way past the noses of several who had been watching the interurban prosper. One of those noses apparently belonged to W.F. Botsford, a primary stockholder in the VB & NVRR. He bought or maneuvered out Hartzell and Cross, and a new corporation formed, calling itself the "San Francisco, Vallejo & Napa Valley Railroad," the SF, V & NVRR. Also on the board of directors were John T. York and L.J. Perry of Napa, I.J. Hatch of Oakland and O.N. Hatch of Vallejo.[47] The Yorks, Perrys and Hatches were all related. W.J. Botsford was the new president.

Two new electric railroads also announced their intention to build interurbans across the Napa Valley in March of 1906. The "Napa and Lakeport Railroad Company" and the "Clear Lake and Southern Railroad Company" both brought franchise requests to the Napa City Council. A railroad rush seemed imminent, reminiscent of the Berryessa Oil Rush of 1900.

Hartzell refused to admit defeat and found backers as far away as France to finance his plans for extending the interurban beyond Calistoga. Because of the premium wine industry, the French were becoming familiar with the Napa Valley, and although it may have seemed risky to invest in a place so very far away, some were willing to do so.

Investors were also on the mind of Frank Mackinder. He knew it wouldn't be long before the electric railroad would find its way up the Valley, and he was determined that St. Helena would be more than just a view from the window for travelers en route to Lake

---

[46] Ibid, p. 99.
[47] The Hatches owned the Monticello Steamship Company.

County. Mackinder was well aware that tourist dollars were also slipping away to the southern part of the state. What the town needed, he believed, was a first-class hotel, something in the style of Monterey's Del Monte, creation of the SP's Charles Crocker; or perhaps like San Diego's Del Coronado, the work of John D. Spreckels. Northern California hotels were drab and shabby compared with the new tourist palaces in the south:

> They are way behind the times in every respect. Quarters
> are small and cramped; accommodations for bathrooms
> are entirely inadequate; kerosene lamps or candles are
> used to light the guest to bed.[48]

It took several years of spurring on by Mackinder, but finally, on April 6 of 1906, the *Star* excitedly announced that plans were to be unveiled for the creation of a huge, innovative, first-class hotel in the center of St. Helena's modest downtown area. It would be the dominant feature of the town. Many of the local movers and shakers were behind it. Vintner/banker Charles Carpy, Sr., would subscribe $2,500 to it, and Mrs. Sarah Esther Bourn would also contribute generously. George Schonewald, "whose name...[is] synonymous with success when used in connection with a hotel enterprise,"[49] would be involved from the start. It would transform the place, bringing hordes of visitors; it would be to St. Helena what White Sulphur Springs had been 50 years earlier. By the middle of April, investors had earmarked $18,000 for the massive project.

Sadly for the local movers and shakers, their plans for the new resort were completely outclassed by an act of God. April 18, a Wednesday, dawned warm and clear, but just a few minutes later all hell broke loose. The most destructive earthquake in the history of California rolled in from the north at 5:12 AM. In the Napa Valley it began with a noisy, rolling jolt that stopped the pendulums on the clocks and rang the church bells. Trees swayed as if in a strong breeze, but there was no breeze. Houses groaned

---

[48]*SHS* , 1-24-1902.

[49] *SHS*, 3-30-1906. Schonewald helped create the Del Monte.

NAPA CITY, 1906

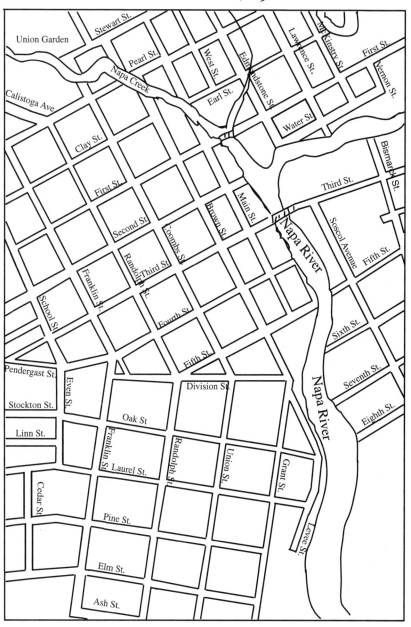

The Courthouse lawn in the heart of Napa was a community gathering place.

The earthquake of April 18, 1906 damaged buildings in the Napa Valley, but there were no deaths.

Above, Uncle Sam's Winery in Napa went out of business after the great jolt. Gifford's Department Store (middle) occupied the ground floor of the Migliavacca Building on First Street West of Brown and received heavy damage from the story above.

St. Helena's brick and stone buildings felt the temblor, too. The Beringer Winery (below) went out of plumb.

The steamer Zinfandel ferried passengers from San Francisco to Napa.

with the dry shear of wood on wood. The Bunces' home on 147 Grant Avenue (now South Brown Street) in Napa lifted up off its moorings and jerked north three feet. Its neighbor down the street at Number 59 did the same, bucking W.R. Lockard and his family out of their beds. For 48 seconds the sickening motion continued, progressing from a roll to a lurching twist that toppled chimneys, broke glass, crumbled plaster into fine dust. Wine barrels rumbled off their skids in Oakville, as their contents sloshed over onto cracking concrete floors. A 30,000 gallon water tank belonging to the Southern Pacific lifted up into the air and crashed to the ground.

The front of D.O. Hunt's stone building on Main and Hunt Streets, St. Helena, separated from the rest of the structure by as much as two inches. Cracks appeared in the walls of the Beringer winery, and the big old stone building went out of plumb. Four gables at the Charles Krug winery fell off the barn, and the winery walls cracked.

It was much worse in Napa City. The fanciful tower that Luther Turton a had built for the Semorile building on Main and First Streets collapsed into itself, tipping over the type cases at the *Napa Daily* and *Weekly Journal*s, blanketing the office with plaster and bricks. Across the street, the southern wall of the Napa Opera House dislocated and crashed onto the Napa Hotel, plunging through the roof and onto a bed, partially burying a terrified guest in bricks and masonry. The old Goodman Bank building on Main near Second fractured. Part of Turton's Migliavacca building collapsed, and the metalwork on the drawbridge on Third Street twisted and locked in place. Some of the stone bridges in town crumbled loose.

The west wall of the Hayes Theater separated from the rest of its structure, leaned over the street and crashed, as did the second story of the W.W. Thompson building, also made of brick. The roof at the Revere House Hotel caved in, and what was only moments earlier a semi-gracious verandah became rubble. The roof beneath the cupola at the Courthouse on Second Street gave way, dropping into the chambers of the Superior Court and demolishing the office of Henry Gesford, whose wife was away visiting friends in Redwood City. The Christian Science Church was totaled, and J.A.

McClelland's very nice brick residence on Coombs Street between Fourth and Fifth clattered to the ground. Cracks split open some of the Gothic towers at the Napa Insane Asylum, panicking the inhabitants.

Twenty homes in all were destroyed in Napa. Not a single chimney in the entire town was left standing. Many were injured, but nobody died, and despite the snapping of electric wires there was no great fire, although the following day S.M. Tool's fruit packing and drying business near Union Station went up in smoke.

The earthquake struck San Francisco in two prolonged, wrenching rips, very loud, sounding like the cacophony of an orchestra of mad cellists. Buildings rocked and fell and hundreds died in one tumultuous minute, and then there was sudden silence, followed by human groans and the hissing of gas.

General and Mrs. F.M. Clark of Yountville's Veterans' Home were asleep at the Golden West Hotel in San Francisco when the temblor hit. The elderly couple groped their way through the heaving building and out onto the street seconds before it collapsed. Rosalia Sherman, wife of D. Sherman of Calistoga, was not so lucky. When her home on Turk Street collapsed she was pinned beneath the rubble, and a week later she would succumb to the injuries she sustained. A popular St. Helenan, Henry Siess, had come to the big city for a special meeting of the grand chapter of the Royal Arch Masons. He died when the home in which he was staying on 12th Street collapsed. The building caught fire, and his charred remains were removed days later.

Willis Mackinder, brother of Frank, was in San Francisco with Jacob Beringer and George Schmidt. They hastened to the wharf, boarded the first steamer out of the city and were back in St. Helena by late afternoon with eyewitness accounts of the disaster. Fires had started, they said, and they predicted that hundreds of homeless refugees would be making their way across the Bay within the week, seeking shelter. Willis convinced four more of his friends (Alfonso Bell, Frank Alexander, W.S. Brownlee and Philo Grant) to climb into an automobile with him and drive over to Santa Rosa to check on the fate of the folks there. The *Star* could thus post this early scoop on the horrors on the other side of the western hills:

> [T]he business section of the city [is] entirely destroyed. There is but one small building standing on Fourth Street, (the principal thoroughfare) from the Athenaeum to the California Northwestern depot, a distance of at least a mile. All the hotels collapsed and many residences are destroyed. Flames completed the ruins. Forty bodies had already been removed and the debris from the hotels has not yet been touched. The loss of life will be great, as the hotels were crowded with guests.[50]

Homes and hotels alike in Santa Rosa were noted for the poor quality of their construction,[51] and they proved to be death traps for more than 60 victims in all, including Joseph Bayes, a Napan who happened to be spending the night there. With only one hose company and a limited water supply, Santa Rosa burned to the ground.[52]

Other cities also suffered. Like a giant mole going two miles per second, the earthquake churned up the ground under Fort Bragg and Fort Ross, knocked over a lighthouse at Point Arena and a train at Point Reyes, destroyed the towns of Bolinas and Tomales and killed 19 citizens in San Jose and 110 inmates at Agnews State Hospital, most of them crushed to death. Favoring no one, it tore apart Leland Stanford's university in Palo Alto and Rudolph Spreckels' sugar refinery in Salinas.

The Heath sisters of St. Helena were staying at a resort in Inverness. They staggered from their cottage before it collapsed, to find that not only had nearly every other building there been flattened, but that wide fissures had opened up in the earth. They walked and ran seven miles to the little community of Ross in their bare feet.

---

[50] *SHS*, 4-19-1906.

[51] Gordon Thomas and Max Morgan Witts, *The San Francisco Earthquake*, Dell Publishing Company, New York, 1972, p. 97.

[52] Ibid, p.97.

George R. Curtis was sound asleep in his home in Windsor and was hurled from his bed by the force of the quake. As he and his neighbors picked their way through the destroyed town, they noted that every brick building in Windsor was demolished. He made his mind up then and there to leave Sonoma County and within weeks purchased acreage in Napa County.

Spared but dazed, many of the people of the Napa Valley wanted to help. A group gathered on the steps of the Courthouse at 9 PM in Napa to organize a relief committee. There were speeches, of course; present and past politicians immediately made themselves available. Mayor Fuller presided over the meeting. Frank Coombs and the Catholic priest, Father Joseph Byrne, addressed the crowd, as did big Charles Otterson, formerly of the VB & NVRR and just elected chief of the Napa Fire Department, a new union of the city's three volunteer hose companies. He volunteered to go to San Francisco to locate missing loved ones and help bring them to Napa. Several of the town's prominent ladies gathered at the Presbyterian church and elected officers to interface with the Red Cross.[53] A relief committee also formed up-valley. The Women's Improvement Club and the Board of Trade pooled their leadership and members and agreed to coordinate their efforts with those in Napa.

Becoming organized was an antidote to the extreme sense of disorder almost everyone felt. Among the first measures instituted by the mayors of all the Valley's municipalities was to close the saloons. After an innkeeper in Yountville was arrested for defying the emergency measure, the closure was taken seriously.

While the good citizens of the Napa Valley were struggling to compose themselves, the hissing of gas in San Francisco had turned into roaring rivers of flame. Building after building was engulfed in fire. Flames consumed the 449 O'Farrell Street, home of the late vintner Frank Sciaroni's widow. Ada Atkinson, widow of vintner

---

[53] Mrs. Frank Bush was President and would remain so for 43 more years. The other officers were Mrs. Wilder Churchill, Mrs. William Fisher, Mrs. Edward Winship, Mrs. William Evans and Mrs. Herbert Sawyer.

J.B. Atkinson, had already fallen on hard times and was running a boarding house at 1329 Leavenworth. It, too, fed the fire. Ethel Baxter, the future Mrs. Otto Beringer, was staying in the city with friends. She had just bought a lovely new hat, quite expensive. After the earthquake she located her purchase and walked primly away from her hotel with it carefully secured in its hatbox.

Much less prim was East Napa's Dave Cavagnaro, who happened to be spending the night in the unsavory part of town known as the "Barbary Coast." He later told friends that he witnessed San Francisco policemen purposely setting fire to some of the buildings there. He slipped away, unharmed.

Charles Carpy's French-American Bank and all his other San Francisco enterprises turned to ash within hours. The large inventory of George Fuller's San Francisco-based paint company caught fire and exploded, and his San Francisco home burned down, exiling him for a time to his house in St. Helena. Weirdly, the glass stored in one of his warehouses remained unscratched. Frederick Hess of the La Jota winery lost the printing press, cases of type and most other assets of his *California Demokrat* newspaper. He also lost his San Francisco home. Vintner W.F. Keyes of La Jota's neighbor, Liparita Winery, suffered heavy losses. J.H. Wheeler's side business, a cream of tartar works, was destroyed. John Benson escaped injury when his suite at the Pacific Club burned down; he had to return to Oakville and his *Far Niente* winery, where he lived the remaining four years of his ultra-private life without the luxuries of up-scale urban living.

All the papers, contracts and legal documents in the possession of John Wesley Hartzell went up in smoke, and with them went his dreams of extending the electric railroad line through the wine country to Lake County. As soon as his French investors got word of the disaster, they pulled out, deeming California to be too hazardous. Ruined, Hartzell would die of a stroke before the year was out.

Residents of the big city, already traumatized, were gripped with panic. Fights broke out. Twenty people were shot dead within the first 24 hours, some accidentally, others not. Governor Pardee telephoned Napa's Sheriff David Dunlap and ordered him to organize a militia to help patrol the streets of San Francisco. Pardee elevated First Lieutenant George Wright of Napa's Company H to Captain. Captain Wright was authorized to arm 50 men with clubs, and they boarded the steamer *Zinfandel* early Friday morning to start a tour of duty in the burning metropolis. They brought with them 1800 loaves of bread from Napa, St. Helena and Napa State Asylum, plus beans, coffee and 11 hogsheads of fresh water. Company H remained in San Francisco for weeks. They camped at Haight Street near Golden Gate Park and helped distribute food to long lines of suddenly homeless San Franciscans. They were soon joined by 1,000 sailors and marines, who helped enforce martial law in the city.

Theodore Bell and two friends[54] boarded the steamer *St. Helena* the morning after the quake, along with Chief Otterson and other volunteers, including Judge Gesford, who was agonizing over the well-being of his wife. They brought with them 13 teams of horses, some wagons and a few mules. Two men went out with each team and wagon, picking their way through the bricks and glass down Van Ness Avenue and Eddy Street and on to Golden Gate Park. After depositing food and other items, they filled the empty wagons with survivors and carted them to the landing at Fort Mason and the ferries at the foot of Market Street. Bell and his crew worked so hard that they soon wore out their shoes and had to send to Napa for replacements. At night they slept on deck with the animals.

Relief workers from St. Helena and Calistoga turned their efforts toward helping quake-stricken survivors in what little remained of Santa Rosa. St. Helenans gathered at Turner Hall[55] at 9PM on Monday. They elected J.H. Steves, owner of the hardware store, to be in charge of directing the relief work from up-valley. The greatest immediate problem for Santa Rosans was the lack of food. By the weekend Steves and the Committee on Supplies were shipping 350 pounds of cooked meat, 50 sacks of flour, a large

---

[54] George Secord and Robert Corlett

[55] site of today's Lyman Park on Main Street. Originally built as an athletic and social center, Turner Hall was a large wooden building that also served for a time as a school.

quantity of potatoes, canned goods and matches. A similar group from Napa arranged through the Southern Pacific to send bread, coffee and beans. San Franciscans, Steves discovered, had plenty of food but needed bedding for the thousands who were sleeping in Golden Gate Park. The local Knights of Pythias organization answered Steves' call by purchasing 18 new mattresses and 18 new blankets.

The newspapers did their best to publish reports about others with ties to the Napa Valley:

> Mr. and Mrs. Robert Brownlee and Mr. and Mrs. A.A.
> Gardner came up from San Francisco yesterday morning.
> Their places of business were destroyed in the great fire
> and they lost everything except for a few personal
> effects. They were glad, however, to escape with their
> lives. [56]

> Mr. and Mrs. H.E. Roper received the sad news Sunday
> night that their two-months-old baby had died last
> Wednesday at the Children's Hospital in San Francisco.
> During the conflagration it was temporarily buried
> in the city, but the body will be disinterred and brought
> to Napa for final interment. [57]

Seven hundred refugees crowded aboard the steamer *St. Helena,* and the *Zinfandel* brought 500 more, most of whom stayed in Vallejo. Some of the travelers were on stretchers, including two Napans, Mrs. F.M. Cassell and Mrs. H. Lathrop, who had been in San Francisco hospitals recovering, the *NDJ* reported, from appendectomies.[58] They came to Napa via the electric train.

Other stretcher cases were also delivered to Napa. On Sunday two unconscious women and one unidentified man were carried off the steamer *Monticello.* The *Journal* followed the cases of the two women. The first was a dark-haired, apparently middle-aged person

---

[56] *NDJ,* 4-20-1906.

[57] *NDJ,* 4-24-1906

[58] "Appendectomies" could have been a euphemism. It was common at the time for ladies to be rather delicate about body parts.

of "moderate means" thought to be suffering from nervous exhaustion and shock. She was taken to the County Infirmary on the road to Sonoma, where she lingered for several days, comatose. The second, a younger woman, was discovered to be what doctors described as "a morphine fiend" who appeared to have an active case of smallpox. After the first woman died the distraught family, who had been searching for her for days, identified her as a Mrs. Castiglione, in her 60's. She had been sick with the flu. The second woman, finally identified as Margaret Wendt, also died. Fears of smallpox, cholera, typhoid and similar epidemics spread through Napa, San Francisco and other communities, not only because those who had been in quarantine were now mingling with the general public, but also because the integrity of the water supply was in question.

The SF,V & NVRR moved male refugees to its depot, the "East Napa Pavilion." The electric road also brought women and children to the Westside's depot at Union Station. The Westside's service was temporarily knocked out, because the quake had twisted the metal on the drawbridge over Petaluma Creek.[59]

Dave Cavagnaro invited burned-out San Franciscans of Italian descent to stay at his Brooklyn Hotel in East Napa. Among those to take him up on his offer were two sisters recently arrived from Italy, Theresa and Rosie Curti, who had lost what little they had. Alone, frightened and strapped for cash, both were soon rescued from their plights by young Napa men. Fortunato Martini, owner/proprietor of the Union Hotel on East First Street, married Rosie; Joseph Tamburelli snatched up Theresa. Before long it became apparent to the entire community of East Napa that the sisters possessed unusually sharp business skills, as will be seen.

The great earthquake and fire also revealed the acumen of another Italian. Amadeo Peter Giannini had utilized an unusual method for attracting investors to his little Bank of Italy, launched in 1904. He sent representatives out into the Italian community to solicit stockholders, limiting investors to not more than 100 shares

---

[59] Even after the bridge was repaired, people were afraid to use it. The train tried to lure back commuters by lowering its rates.

each. Little by little, targeting regular people like artisans, laborers and merchants, he drew in many small investors. He made small loans to people whose credit had not yet been established, a practice that saved them from the clutches of loan sharks. "Real" bankers from the big financial institutions looked down on him. They called him the "Dago Banker."[60]

When the quake hit, Giannini was at his home in San Mateo. He immediately went to San Francisco and, with the help of two employees, hauled away $80,000 in hard cash from the bank, as well as most of its chairs and tables. Fearing robbers, he buried the currency under crates of oranges. It took them most of the night, but they managed to carry it all back to Giannini's house. He hid the money in his fireplace. San Francisco's "real" bankers, meanwhile, piled all their assets into the fireproof vaults beneath their banks, which, like the Bank of Italy's modest frame structure, were clearly in the path of the continuing conflagration. All of the banks burned down. The money and documents within the vaults were intact, but the chambers were too hot to open for weeks.[61] It was therefore impossible for anyone to draw out cash.

Giannini set up a desk at the Washington Street wharf and affixed a sign that said, "Bank of Italy."[62] He parceled out fractions of the $80,000 as small emergency loans. Those who had been able to rescue their own money from the disaster needed somewhere safe to put it. They entrusted it to Giannini, who carefully recorded every penny. His representatives then circulated throughout San Francisco and the Bay Area, including East Napa, accepting currency from customers for safekeeping and making small loans to help people get by. The Italian population breathed easier, and

---

[60] See Julian Dana, *A.P. Giannini: Giant in the West*, Prentice Hall, New York, 1947.

[61] Officers at the Firemen's Fund Insurance Company at California and Sansome Streets tried to open the firm's upper vaults on Tuesday the 24th, but with the sudden introduction of air a fire started immediately in the superheated chamber and the contents were destroyed. *NDJ*, 4-25-1906.

[62] Dana, Op. Cit, p. 58.

Giannini quickly went from being a moderately wealthy man to a rich one.

Governor Pardee, meanwhile, declared legal holidays, first day-to-day on the 20th, 21st, 24th and 25th, and then through the end of the month. All the banks in Napa County closed. The Napa Savings Bank and Goodman Bank ran ads reassuring people that their funds were secure, but concern mounted by the day as people ran out of money. On the 21st F.L. Alexander of St. Helena's Carver National Bank sold his dehydrating plant to a man from Oakland for the cash it would bring. On the 24th all the bankers in the county formed a committee to go to Oakland, where a consortium would be held on how to proceed.

The Napa Valley's financial institutions finally opened on May 1, and there was an immediate run as patrons withdrew cash for expenses and to pay their taxes, which had been due on April 30. Most of the banks in San Francisco remained closed, their vaults still too hot to open.

Throughout it all there were aftershocks. There were three moderate shakes, one each in the early morning hours Friday and Saturday and one at 3 PM on Sunday. A sharp aftershock hit at 3:15 on the 26th, rattling windows and nerves and killing a woman who was standing at her kitchen sink in San Francisco. Another sharp aftershock came on the 29th about a half-hour after midnight.

A general increase in violent crime persisted for several months after the shaking finally stopped. Two former residents of the Veterans' Home, both working as woodcutters, got into an argument; one of them hacked the other to death with an axe. A prostitute named Carrie Clark got into a disagreement with her paramour, Roy Spurr, in the brothel at 1 Clinton Street in Napa. He ended up killing her. An unknown arsonist set a series of fires in several places in the Valley. One of his victims was the White Church in what is now Bothe State Park. Erected in 1853, it was the first place of worship built in the Up-Valley and a much-loved reminder of the old days. Pioneer George Tucker, who lived nearby and owned the property on which it was built, watched sadly as it burned to the ground.

Within a week of the disaster, the SF, B & NVRR railroad started laying track to St. Helena. There would be no huge hotel in the center of town now, but at least there would be modern transportation.

Chapter Four

Favorite Son

T he influential wine merchant C. Schilling of San Francisco and St. Helena revealed that the California Wine Association had suffered greatly in the quake. The CWA lost 10,000 gallons of wine in Cloverdale, 25,000 gallons in Windsor, 100,000 in Forestville, 100,000 in Oakville and several millions of gallons in San Francisco. Even worse, they lost a large cache of ultra-premium blends they had stored away in a special area to be released within the next few years, well aged and superior, they hoped, to anything produced in California so far. The special collection was to be their ace in the hole.[1]

Despite its thin inventory, the CWA launched a price war against their Eastern competition. It began in New Orleans, where the wines of Oakville's Franco-American Winery[2], a CWA contributor, were very popular. Red wines would sell for 30% below their standard price.

---

[1] Thomas Pinney, *A History of Wine in America*, University of California Press, Berkeley and London, 1989, p. 360.

[2] Brun & Chaix

The CWA told the San Francisco *Call* that it was a means of gaining market share from producers in Missouri.[3] Many Bay Area newspapers wrote with an obvious journalistic bias that cast scorn on wineries from other parts of the country. They relished opportunities to disparage the "brick vineyards" back east. When the US District Court confiscated some adulterated wines fermented in Sandusky, Ohio, for example, the concoction's contents were listed in the *Chronicle*.[4]

Newspapers saw themselves, for the most part, as spokesmen for the businesses that supported and/or dominated their communities. Most newspapers in California were basically organs for the Republican Party, which was the political voice of Big Business (mainly the Southern Pacific railroad).[5] Businesses could assure favorable coverage by contributing generously to the newspapers.

There were exceptions, of course, like John E. Walden's *Napa Daily Journal*. When Carroll of the *Calistogian* hinted that it might be all right for voters to split their ticket in the 1906 elections, Mackinder of the very Republican *Star* took him to task in an editorial.

Newspapers had the power to make and to break. The career of one Napa Valley celebrity revealed the full extent of journalism's role in shaping the course of California history. The celebrity was Theodore Bell.

After Bell lost his second bid for Congress, he returned to practicing law but remained active in the Democratic Party. He continued to oppose the Southern Pacific's monopoly on transportation. There would be a gubernatorial election in 1906, and Bell's fellow Democrats wanted to nominate former San Francisco Mayor James Phelan for Governor. Phelan declined. His term of office had been marred by crippling strikes, bloody rioting and frustrating encounters with a genteel gangster, Abe Ruef, who

---

[3] *SHS*, 11-16-1906.

[4] It contained fermented commercial dextrose, artificially colored and preserved with benzoic acid.

[5] Deverell, *Op. Cit.*, p. 90.

controlled a well-developed underworld of prostitution, graft and other forms of corruption. Instead, Phelan, Rudolph Spreckels (brother of A.B.) and Fremont Older, publisher of the *San Francisco Bulletin*, started a campaign to investigate Ruef.

Portraying himself as the champion of Labor, Ruef had more or less bought the mayoral post for his puppet, Eugene Schmitz, in 1901. Ruef and Schmitz ran San Francisco. After handpicking nearly every member of the San Francisco Board of Supervisors, they distributed lucrative franchises and other favors to their friends, and they extracted protection money from nearly everyone else. They were greatly assisted in this by the "Royal Arch," the fraternal organization so popular with men from East Napa. Royal Arch henchmen forced selected brands of champagne, beer, whiskey, brandy and cigars upon the city's restaurants and saloons.[6] Those who wanted to work outside the Arch were told to pay Ruef up to $5,000 for their franchises.[7] Ruef and Schmitz also controlled the very busy prostitution trade that flourished in San Francisco, espcially on the Barbary Coast. On the street level, many such houses featured "French restaurants"—up-scale dining palaces offering European-style cuisine (usually prepared by Chinese chefs) and wine. Jessie Hayman, madam of San Francisco's popular Nymphia and Municipal Crib, for example, sold approved wine at 500% above cost.[8] Upstairs and in other rooms, she sold time with her ladies, also at high rates.

Some saloons in Napa also offered female companionship, as they had back in the 19th century. Without naming names, the Napa

---

[6] Robert Glass Cleland, *California in Our Time*, Alfred A. Knopf, New York, 1947, p. 12.

[7] Franklin K. Hichborn, "The Party, the Machine, and the Vote," in *California Historical Society Quarterly*, XXXIX, No. 1, March, 1960, p. 19.

[8] Curt F. Gentry, *The Madams of San Francisco*, Doubleday & Company, New York, 1964, p. 190. What percentage of that wine came from Napa is not known, but it is probable that restaurateurs had to accept a portion of bad vintages along with the good, and Napa had plenty of both.

City Council warned "that unless some of the saloon men mended their ways as to certain infractions of city ordinances, they would suddenly find themselves without a license."[9]

The publisher of the *San Francisco Examiner,* William Randolph Hearst, responded to the obvious need for reform by bolting from the Democratic Party to start his own, the American Independent Party. He nominated San Francisco's District Attorney William Langdon as his candidate. Hearst knew what many others also sensed: that the Ruef/Schmitz coalition had a secret partner...the Southern Pacific railroad.

The Octopus continued to wield great power in all levels of government and was particularly successful in blocking legislation intended to curb its hegemony. When Governor Pardee lost favor with the Railroad,[10] it tapped the shoulder of another man, James Norris Gillett, a lumber dealer from Humboldt County. The SP was so powerful and apparently felt so immune to censure that it made little attempt to conceal its part in the Republican convention in Santa Cruz in September of 1906. When the convention was over, gubernatorial nominee Gillett and several top SP executives posed for a group photograph. In it, Gillett's hand rested amiably on the shoulder of Abe Ruef.

The Democrats held their convention the next week in Sacramento. Rumors circulated at first that the party's pick for Governor would be Marshall Diggs of Yolo County. As the week went on, however, a career legislator named Anthony Caminetti started a groundswell to nominate the young Napan, Theodore Bell. Both Bell and Caminetti were pro-labor and pro-union, but Caminetti had inside information that the powerful *Los Angeles Express*—the oldest Republican newspaper in Los Angeles—would support Bell for Governor.[11] Both publisher E.T. Earl and editor Edward Dickson were strongly anti-SP, and Bell's defiance of the

---

[9] *NDJ*, 6-25-1913.

[10] for criticizing a similar monopoly, Standard Oil. See Cleland, Op. Cit., p. 29.

[11] George E. Mowry, *The California Progressives*, Encounter Paperbacks, Chicago, 1951, p. 61.

Railroad in 1902 had won him favor in their eyes. Delegates from Los Angeles started a fad that would persist for the next two months, that of wearing bells, any kind of bell, pinned to their lapels. Bell, however, had promised Diggs that he would not interfere with Diggs' hopes to head the ticket. Diggs and Bell had a late night meeting on September 11, and when they emerged from the hotel room, Diggs had agreed to withdraw from the race.[12] Theodore Bell won the Democratic nomination for Governor by acclamation.

His first order of business was to help the Party frame its platform. It included the introduction of a number of innovations. Among them were:

- Support of a direct primary by voters, rather than in-house Party primaries;
- Election of US Senators by popular vote rather than by appointment of the legislature;
- Public ownership of utilities;
- Control of monopolies through legislation;
- Laws to protect and also limit labor strikes

The convention voted to condemn Hearst for deserting them and officially read him out of the Party. Most of its collective venom, however, was reserved for the Southern Pacific. The Democratic Party and its Republican allies assailed the monopoly for tampering with the law on every level of government and financially molesting the citizenry.

John Walden was ecstatic. The *Journal* followed the convention and Bell's campaign in fine detail. It ran the full text of Bell's acceptance speech and printed much of what other papers in the state had to say about his nomination.

The *Los Angeles Express*, *Woodland Democrat*, *Solano Democrat* and *Vallejo Times* came out for Bell, as did other papers throughout the state. Organized labor (except the group supporting Ruef and Schmitz) also stood behind him. The *San Francisco*

---

[12] *NDJ*, 9-12-1906.

Examiner, of course, did not. Bell and Hearst exchanged insults throughout the campaign.

Said Bell, bravely:

> I care not what Hearst does. I've declared war on him to the death, and, even should he support me, I would denounce him from one end of the state to the other. If the good people of the State will back me we will drive him from the politics of this State."[13]

Bell's nomination for Governor was the most significant political event to arise from Napa County. Nevertheless, the staunchly Republican *Star* firmly opposed him. He was "impulsive," it said, and "possessed of poor judgment."[14] The *Calistogian* also rejected him, although less forcefully. The *Napa Register* simply observed (accurately, as it turned out) that Bell and the Democrats might have blundered in treating Hearst so harshly.[15]

Another significant event also occurred in the election year of 1906, one that went without much comment from the press. Miss Kate Ames, Napa's very able Superintendent of Schools, was on the slate of potential nominees for State Superintendent of Schools at the Santa Cruz Republican convention. It was an important position. Hearst's candidate, William Langdon, had served in that post before becoming District Attorney in San Francisco, and much was happening in education. She did not receive the nomination. "Well," she sighed, in an interview afterward, "I found that the machine was too much for me…It is most discouraging for a woman to seek recognition in a State that has long resisted the advocates of woman suffrage."[16] In contrast, the Democrats did nominate a woman to run for Superintendent on their ticket. She eventually lost. Women had not yet won the right to vote, and the issue of suffrage was a hot one.

---

[13] *Napa Weekly Journal*, 10-5-1906.

[14] *SHS*, 11-2-1906.

[15] *NDJ*, 9-15-1906.

[16] *NDJ*, 9-8-1906.

The Republican President, Theodore Roosevelt, did not support Gillett and was well aware of the corrupting influences of the Southern Pacific and Abe Ruef. Older of the *Bulletin* had appealed to Roosevelt for help in cleaning up the political mess in San Francisco, and by the summer of 1906 the President had seen to it that William J. Burns, a well-known Secret Service agent, was assigned to the case.[17] By mid-October, Burns and his associates had collected enough evidence to begin prosecuting Ruef, Schmitz and scores of others in San Francisco for police graft, the granting of special privileges and illegally manipulating utility rates. The *San Francisco Call* broke the sensational news that the SP's chief strategist[18] had paid Abe Ruef $20,000 to "deliver" San Francisco votes to Gillett at the Santa Cruz convention. The *Call* and dozens of other newspapers across the state ran the infamous group photograph of Gillett surrounded by SP executives, with his hand on Ruef's shoulder.

This obviously damning material may have been too potent. Gentlemen of finance began to perspire under their starched collars as investigators broadened their inquiry to include Pacific Gas and Electric, Parkside Realty, the San Francisco cable car system, the Home Telephone Company and Pacific States Telephone and Telegraph.[19] Three San Francisco supervisors were caught in the act of offering bribes, and soon 15 other members of the board confessed to bribery, as well. The chicanery was uncovered, but so was corruption among many of the leading industrialists and financiers of the state's largest city. Many of these had additional interests in other parts of the state and had their own leverage, on a more modest scale, with the press.

Some of the threatened businessmen applied social pressure on Phelan, Spreckels and their supporters to stop the investigation. Alma Spreckels' rather risqué past was brought up for public review in the newspapers, and family quarrels within the Spreckels clan gained notoriety.

---

[17] Gordon Thomas and Max Morgan Witts, Op. Cit., p. 32.

[18] William F. Herrin

[19] Mowry, Op. Cit., p. 33.

When the election came down to the wire, newspapers throughout the state shied away from Bell. The only big Republican daily to stay with him to the end was the *Los Angeles Express*. Bell lost by little more than 8,000 votes. Langdon came in a poor third, tallying only 45,000 to Bell's 117,000 and Gillett's 125,000. (There was also a Socialist candidate who received 16,000 votes.) Hearst's candidate and fears spurred by the galloping scandals rustled away votes that would surely have gone to Bell and cost Bell the election. Inconsolable, Walden of the *Journal* could not bring himself to actually admit that his favorite son had lost the race. He ran big headlines announcing that Bell had carried Napa County by a wide margin, barely referring to the fact that Gillett and the Railroad had won the war.

Far from weakening the SP's stranglehold on California legislators, the immediate result of Bell's unsuccessful anti-Octopus campaign was an increase in corruption in Sacramento. The SP was nothing less than a third house within the government. One of its chief henchmen actually had an office in the Capitol right across the hall from the Speaker.[20] A final collection of SP plantings, the state judiciary slapped down practically every scrap of regulatory legislation that survived the congressional gauntlet.

The trend toward superfluous, inappropriate appointments within the state bureaucracy grew even worse. As payoffs for various favors, 83 men were hired as doorkeepers for the Capitol's three doors. Thirty-three "women of dubious reputation"[21] had access to senate chambers as "committee clerks." Thirty-six sergeants-at-arms, 18 watchmen, 18 porters, seven postmistresses and 98 other assorted employees drew pay on taxpayers' money.[22] The Republicans raised their per diem pay to $25 in the Senate and $13 in the House.[23] They actually passed a bill to move the capital from Sacramento to Berkeley, a measure that was pressed by a knot

---

[20] Mowrey, Op. Cit., p. 81.

[21] *Fresno Republican*, quoted in Cleland, Op. Cit., p. 33.

[22] Mowrey, Op. Cit., p. 63.

[23] Idem.

of Berkeley real estate agents who were friendly with the SP's top executives.[24]

1908 was a presidential election year. Bell attended the Democratic convention in Denver and made the nomination speech for the Party's perennial contender, William Jennings Bryan, who had run and lost in 1896 and 1900. Bryan was a gifted orator, a religious fundamentalist and a Prohibitionist. The wine country's favorite son served him loyally, touring the nation and making campaign speeches on his behalf. William Howard Taft defeated Bryan handily.

1910 was another gubernatorial election year. In great favor with the Party, Bell became the Democrats' candidate once again, and this time William Randolph Hearst supported him.

Many Republicans knew that it was critical that something be done to reform the party. The scattered few who were not in the grip of the railroad began to find each other. Inspired by Chester Rowell, publisher of the Fresno *Republican,* a group evolved that called themselves the "Lincoln-Roosevelt League," invoking the names of two Presidents whose work, they believed, exemplified the Party's ideals. This small cluster of reform-minded leaders began what has become known as the "California Progressive Movement." For their platform they adopted and built onto many of Bell's innovations. They called for:

- a direct primary;
- regulation of utility rates;
- an Emancipation Proclamation of the Party from SP dominance;
- voter initiatives, referendum, and recall;
- workmen's compensation;
- women's suffrage;
- a minimum wage law for women;
- conservation of forests;
- outlawing of gambling at racetracks

---

[24] Ibid, p. 65.

The Progressives also had a moral message. Disturbed by what they believed to be the disintegration of public and private behavioral standards, many in the movement called for the abolition of prize fighting, gambling, prostitution and alcohol. The use of slang and colloquialisms like "ain't" was also added to this list. Some Progressives were ready to censor literature in general, drama and public dancing, as well.[25]

They chose as their candidate a hot-tempered, florid-faced firebrand named Hiram S. Johnson. Embracing part of the platform that Bell had actually fathered, Johnson proclaimed in February that he was ready to "redeem the state" from the influence of the Southern Pacific. Johnson revealed himself to the people of California as incorruptible, courageous, cantankerous and tireless. His running mate, a self-made businessman named Albert Wallace, was a Prohibitionist, but in his campaign speeches Johnson steered away from most of the peripheral Progressive issues. He pounded relentlessly at the evils of the Railroad, as if Bell had never existed.

Having had the main plank of his political platform stolen from under him, Bell addressed a broad variety of topics in addition to the Southern Pacific. The main area in which he differed from Johnson was in his support of labor and the unions. Few cities in America were as pro-union as San Francisco in 1910, and the Bay Area in general followed its lead. Bell's liberal message appealed to many in the state's north.

It did not appeal, however, to Bell's old supporter, former Berryessa landowner James Phelan. Phelan was a principal backer of the Progressive movement, and he did all he could to promote Johnson. Included in his helpfulness was a letter to Henry Morganthau of New York, where he said that Bell was "affiliated with the...United Railroad 'machine' and therefore "lost the confidence of right-thinking Democrats and independent men of California."[26]

---

[25] Mowrey, op. Cit., p.100.

[26] From *James D. Phelan Papers*, Aug. 29, 1910, quoted in Olin, Op. Cit., p. 199.

Indeed, given a choice between Bell and Johnson, the Railroad chose Bell, probably deeming him easier to work with. Johnson was able to make hay of Bell's unpopular backer. He accused Bell and Hearst—former bitter enemies—of uniting to collaborate with the Octopus. Johnson won the election, defeating Bell 177,000 to 155,000. There were numerous other contenders, but they did not have nearly the votes Bell did.

"Si," the average Northern Californian farmer, knew that Hiram Johnson borrowed heavily from Bell in preparing his campaign platform.

Many in the Napa Valley viewed the Southern Pacific (above) as an enemy of the people that charged back-breaking rates for freight. The electric trains of the Napa Valley Route (below) carried passengers from the ferries in Vallejo to Calistoga, with many stops along the way.

Chapter Five

Writing on the Wall

Corruption of all sorts chewed away at America's social fabric in the early years of the 20th Century. It was so endemic, so much a part of the *status quo*, that most people had trouble identifying just what, exactly, was wrong with the world. People worked hard, but most of the money seemed to be in the hands of only a lucky few. It was common for folks to look back fondly to an earlier age when life seemed simpler, more just, easier to comprehend. Ed Kelton, for example, campaigned for Sheriff of Napa County in 1910 on an anti-automobile ticket. He canvassed the Valley in a cart pulled by mules and won by a large majority.

This tendency to glorify the past was nothing new. It was fashionable in the 1830's, for example, to imagine that the American lifestyle of the 1730's was a time of great moral rectitude. To many, "moral" implied "sober," in all meanings of the word. A myth developed that the Bible-based Puritan society eschewed the partaking of such things that would enhance merriment—like strong drink. The truth was that America's earliest settlers had a robust thirst for fermented beverages, and that the Bible is replete with positive references about the beneficial effects of alcohol, along with warnings about its abuse.

Nevertheless, mid-19th Century reformers who were obsessed with fixing what was wrong with society hit upon a theme that connected many of society's ills with Demon Rum. Alcoholism was identified not as a medical or social dilemma but as a spiritual and moral failure.[1] A person going to an American church in the three decades before the Civil War would be very likely to hear a sermon on the evils of drink.

By 1850 anti-alcohol organizations had formed all over the country, including in the Napa Valley.[2] The American Civil War and the problem of human slavery diverted the reformers' attention from the alcohol issue for a time, but it reappeared in the 1870's. Once again, many mainstream Protestant clergy took aim at alcohol, but this time their ranks were swelled by a new force: women.

One of the first of these new reformers was a 60-year old housewife from Ohio named Elizabeth Thompson. "Mother" Thompson reasoned that if drinking were a spiritual problem, then the cure for it was prayer. She organized a militia of local women to stand outside the business of a local merchant and publicly pray him into stopping liquor sales.[3] When they succeeded, she and her followers did the same outside a busy saloon, adding hymns to their spiritual arsenal. Inspired by Mother Thompson, "Women's Crusades" took place in various other Ohio villages.

The post-Civil War temperance movement gained momentum when the Presbyterian Church in Cleveland rallied around the idea of declaring war against liquor, and in 1874 their efforts led to the formation of the Women's Christian Temperance Union. The WCTU was not really interested in temperance (moderation) but in banning alcoholic drink altogether. It was effective from the outset, thanks mostly to the driving genius of its first president, an enthusiastic spinster named Frances Willard. Willard managed not

---

[1] Edward Behr, *Thirteen Years That Changed America*, Arcade Publishing, New York, 1996, p. 26.

[2] It is one of the great ironies that the town of St. Helena got its name from the local chapter of the Sons of Temperance.

[3] Behr, Op. Cit., pp. 36-37.

only to establish chapters in every state, but also to get the Prohibition message into the curriculum in public schools. From the 1880's on, children in American public schools were inculcated with the doctrine that alcohol in all forms is evil.[4]

Other things also fell under the WCTU's disapproving gaze. Fashion, always the cause of raised eyebrows, was a popular target. The short sleeves, slit skirts and lowering neckline of ladies' dresses in the years around 1910 were condemned as "sensuous."

Frances Willard's name is all but forgotten. Much more familiar is that of an early member of the WCTU, an imposing, wild-eyed crackpot whose weaponry included not prayers and hymns, but a well-sharpened axe. Carry Moore was born in 1846, the same year the Napa Valley's earliest pioneers started the Bear Flag revolt and brought California into the Mexican American War. As Carry Nation, she would become the symbol of a social revolution that would bring the Napa Valley to its knees.

Carry grew up in the South. The Civil War was a disaster for her slave-holding family.[5] They fled their Kentucky plantation and eventually made their way to Kansas. Carry revealed at an early age her penchant for uphill battles. To the complete outrage of her parents, she befriended the local African Americans. She steeped herself in African mysticism and had numerous paranormal experiences. She might have gone on to do significant humanitarian work, had she not, in 1867, married a doctor named Charles Gloyd. At that point her life's path took a sharp turn. Shortly after the wedding it became clear that Gloyd was an alcoholic who was also addicted to tobacco. Carry never forgave him for these shortcomings, and in her lifelong pursuit to undo Charles' foibles, she vowed to purge the world of drink and smoke. [6]

Even more poignantly, she blamed Charles and his habits for the fact that their daughter was born with birth defects. This last blow

---

[4] More than 100 years later, the WCTU still functions in some regions of the country.

[5] Behr, Op. Cit., p. 40.

[6] Ibid, p. 41. Like so many of his peers, Gloyd was a Mason. Masonry was also a target of her assault.

might have pushed her over the edge, and for Carry, the edge was perhaps closer than it was for many of her peers. Her mother appears to have suffered from a serious mental disorder. She rejected Carry, and later in life she believed herself to be Queen Victoria,[7] a delusion that caused her to spend her final years locked away in a psychiatric facility.

Carry separated from Charles, who died shortly thereafter. She married a second time, to a preacher-cum-lawyer in Medicine Lodge, Kansas, and she found sorority in the WCTU. It was in the quiet village of Medicine Lodge that Carry began to wreak havoc. She bullied her way into the local drugstore—one of the town's major liquor distributors—and destroyed the place with her axe.

Her campaign against alcohol and smoking spread to other communities in Kansas, and soon the telegraph wires were humming with media hype about her escapades.

"Mrs. Nation launched her crusade against the joints at an early hour this morning," wrote the *Napa Daily Journal*, one of hundreds of small newspapers to be fascinated by her exploits. "She arose at 4:30 and soon afterwards started a tour of joint-smashing." On that particular occasion in February of 1901, Carry happened to accidentally strike herself in the right temple with her axe. Six feet tall, of ample frame and dripping with blood, she "turned over two large slot machines and smashed the glass in front of each. She soon made a wreck of a large refrigerator, and after that turned her attention to the liquor and the fixtures behind the bar. A keg of beer then came in the way of her hatchet..."[8]

All over the country, individuals with grudges against drink emulated Carry Nation. In Napa, for example, "Dr. C.H. Farman 'carrie-nationized' the Revere house bar Saturday morning" and was on the way to do the same to the Oberon bar across the street when he was arrested.[9]

Carry Nation's zeal was easy to lampoon. Far more potent in terms of real effectiveness were the propaganda and politics

---

[7] Ibid, p. 40.

[8] *NDJ*, 2-6-1901.

[9] *NDJ*, 2-24-1901.

coming out of the Anti-Saloon League, founded in 1895. The ASL promoted any candidate for political office who publicly declared himself Dry.[10] The brains behind its strategy of lobbying and political endorsement were two Ohioans—Wayne Wheeler and Ernest Cherrington. Wheeler focused on disseminating information about the League's activities to newspapers across the country and, later, on seeing to it that ASL personnel became part of the establishment that enforced Prohibition laws. Cherrington was in charge of the League's official organ, *American Issue*, as well as its other publications—*The American Patriot, National Daily* and *New Republic*. He also headed up its fund-raising and education programs.[11] Both men reported to a hard-driving, retired Methodist minister, Purley Baker. Handsomely funded, the ASL was able to employ a large support staff.

The ASL drew most of its money and membership from mainstream Protestant churches. Many of its hardest workers were women. Its principle targets were saloons, and virtually all the patrons of saloons were men. Men ate lunch there, congregated there after work, and went there in the evening after dinner or after their fraternal meetings to socialize and drink beer. Often they spent much too much of their paycheck there, and in some saloons in some cities, they patronized the secondary businesses of gambling and prostitution. The presence of these technically outlawed enterprises implied anything from police laxity and laissez-faire to widespread political corruption.

In small Midwest townships, where the ASL began and saw its first successes, many saloons were actually owned by breweries.[12] Many breweries were owned and operated by Germans—a large, recent immigrant group, heavily Catholic. Thus the first opponents in what eventually became a life-and-death struggle over the beverage choice of all Americans were largely Protestant Midwestern women who were at least second-generation

---

[10] Pinney, Op. Cit., p. 434.

[11] K. Austin Kerr, *Organized for Prohibition*, Yale University Press, New Haven and London, 1985, p. 121.

[12] Behr, Op. Cit., p. 58.

Americans; and the beer industry, which was dominated by German-American males, mostly Catholic.[13]

Few brewers saw the coming storm as clearly as did Gustav Pabst and Adolphus Busch, both of whom owned major Midwest companies. They urgently petitioned their peers within the alcoholic beverage industry to unite against the peril that Wheeler, Cherrington et al posed. Their trade group, the United States Brewers' Association,[14] fought back against the Prohibitionist message by portraying beer as a wholesome, natural, low-alcohol beverage: "liquid bread."[15] The German-American Alliance—a lobby supported by thousands of Americans of German descent—gave the USBA a lot of financial support.

American hard liquor distillers heeded the cry of Busch and Pabst and in 1908 formed the National Model License League, whose aim was to establish a regulatory agency that would assure consumers of the pureness of their products, not unlike today's Food and Drug Administration. They urged the brewers to join them in their public relations effort, but the truth was that with a few exceptions like Pabst and Busch, it was beyond the imagination of most brewers to imagine a world without beer.[16] Rather than uniting with the spirits industry and forming a pro-active "liquor trust," the brewers tried to dissociate themselves from the distillers, touting their own wares as healthy and good. They insisted beer was a "temperance drink."

Having just emerged from a maddening battle against lice in the rootstock, vagaries in the market and ignorance in the public about the merits of their product, the men and women of the wine industry suffered no such lack of imagination. The sudden popularity of Prohibition might be transient, and it might not. The *Star* kept its readers abreast of the developments in the issue by

---

[13] Another enterprise condemned by the ASL was professional boxing, also an activity associated with males.

[14] The USBA was established in 1862, when Prohibition was also an issue.

[15] Kerr, Op. Cit., p. 27.

[16] Ibid, 160-163.

following temperance legislation closely and by printing letters and other materials by men in the industry.

St. Helenan L.J. Vance, Secretary of the American Wine Growers' Association, published a warning to his fellow growers shortly before he died. Professional agitators, said Vance, were on a mission

> to destroy the vast property and capital represented in the grape and wine industry in California. [Wine growers] should understand...that the so-called prohibition craze or crusade is directed at them...If the wine maker cannot sell his wine he does not want the farmer's grapes.[17]

Andrea Sbarboro, President of the California Grape Growers' Association, published a book called *The Fight for True Temperance*, richly illustrated with pictures from the Napa Valley. Its theme paralleled that of the beer industry's—that wine is a temperance drink.

As part of an overall effort to portray wine as salubrious, C.S. Crowninshield, the American consul in Naples, wrote a letter to Sbarboro describing the scene in Italy, where wine was a staple in the diet. The *Star* published part of it:

> [D]runkenness is almost unknown here...wine is taken freely among all classes; most workers drink from a pint to a quart each day, but there is almost no strong liquor. [18]

The California State Board of Health lined up behind the wine industry. California wines, wrote its Secretary, Dr. N.K. Foster, are "pure and wholesome."

> It strikes me, as a professional man, that it would be well for the people of the United States, as well as other countries, to take cognizance of the fact that the board of health considers that the wines of California are not only healthful but pure and unadulterated.[19]

---

[17] *SHS*, 9-18-1908.

[18] *SHS*, 11-13-1908.

[19] *SHS*, 10-2-1908.

Thanks to the ASL, Congress began to pass anti-alcohol legislation. Among the first was a law in 1908 that forbade the time-honored but unhelpful practice of selling adulterated sweet wine as cough syrup, pep tonic and other medicinal remedies. The California Grape Growers' Association (CGGA) lobbied the Department of Commerce and Labor to overturn this ruling, since it allowed foreign wineries to market these compounds without restriction. The Department's Assistant Secretary wired Pietro Rossi, President of Italian Swiss Colony and a member of the CGGA that the regulation would be "materially modified."

The next year the US Department of Agriculture revived and extended the idea that Theodore Bell had promoted when he was in Congress. It ruled that fermented grape juice that had been adulterated with sugar would no longer be considered "wine" and could no longer be sold as such. California vintners saw this as a triumph. CGGA head Andrea Sbarboro's callous reaction however, did nothing to promote industry harmony:

> When asked if this ruling would not severely cripple
> Eastern grape growers and wine makers, who were
> making the best wines possible from their grapes by
> the use of sugar, Mr. Sbarboro said that could not be
> helped. If they could not produce grapes from which
> wine could be made without the use of sugar, they
> should go to where they could grow them or cease making
> so-called wine.[20]

Despite the rising tide of Prohibition, the California wine industry continued to betray its eastern counterparts. To further distinguish California wines from eastern competitors, Governor James Gillett signed into law AB 494, stipulating that all wine from California must be prefixed with the letters CAL or CALA, resulting in such strange-sounding words as "Calclaret" and "Calburgundy." The California Wine Association complied with Gillett's odd law by marketing a number of Napa Valley wines under its "Calwa" label. Its brochures advertised Hillcrest's "finest

---

[20] *SHS*, 9-10-1909.

old cabernet claret;" Greystone's "good light Hock type" and Vine Cliff's "finest Riesling," all Calwa wines.

Virtually all of the CWA's wines were blended in its immense Winehaven facility in Benicia, which was a technological masterpiece for its day. Its 50-ton crusher could handle up to 1.5 tons a minute. Grapes came in by rail, on special sidings that allowed four cars at a time to deposit their loads. Conveyor belts took the grapes to the crusher. The resulting juice and pomace were then pumped to fermenting tanks through large galvanized pipes. Later, cellar workers drew wine from tanks selected by the winemaker and funneled it into a large blending machine. The wine was bottled, capped and labeled, all by machine. The process was far more sophisticated and expensive than that used by individual independent Napa Valley vintners.

The CWA hedged its bets, beginning in 1907, by experimenting with the production of non-alcoholic grape juice, mainly with grapes grown in the Fresno area. Several vintners in the eastern states also began bottling grape juice around this time.

St. Helena's Bismarck Bruck, who had championed the technique of bench grafting St. George vines and was now a major voice in the wine industry, established Bruck's Grape Juice Company in 1909. Using premium grapes from the Moffitt Vineyard near St. Helena, Bruck crushed both red and white grapes and marketed them with attractive labels in quart- and pint-sized bottles. Advertised as "absolutely non-alcoholic," Bruck's juice was touted as "not only a delightful beverage, but...absolutely pure, and unlike most temperance drinks, a health-giving tonic."[21]

But the unfermented grape juice industry did not take off in California as it did in the East. Eastern growers cultivated concord grapes, which had a distinctive tart flavor. California grapes were sweeter, and without the kick of fermentation they tasted rather bland. Of the 15 grape juice manufacturers in California in 1909, only four were still in business by 1914 and sold only 75,000

---

[21] *SHS*, 2-26-1909.

gallons, in contrast to the 50,000,000 gallons of California wine that went to market in 1914. [22]

Diverging from its usual reportage about wine and winemaking, the *St. Helena Star* devoted a column in 1909 to the merits of growing table grapes.[23] For the *Star*, as for most voices connected with the industry, however, the notion of outright Prohibition was just too massive to comprehend. Wrote Mackinder, in April of 1909: "Prohibition will never become general and will come and go, as agitators are concerned by conditions."[24]

Several states had already gone Dry. Maine, the very first Prohibition state, entered the Union Dry back in 1851. Kansas was Dry when it was a territory and continued that way into statehood in 1880. North Dakota followed Kansas' lead in 1889. Georgia and Oklahoma went Dry in 1907; North Carolina and Mississippi followed in 1908 and Tennessee went in 1909. Hundreds of individual counties and townships across the nation were also jumping on the wagon, including several in California.

Prohibition and the clamor about it were starting to make a dent in wine sales. The market for wine grew listless, although IRS statistics indicated that sales of beer and whiskey had actually gone up nation-wide.[25]

One of the problems was that Europe—especially Italy—was glutted with wine. California was only just recovering from the phylloxera infestation, and yield was still comparatively low. Moreover, the freight charge from Europe to New York by sea was 2¢ per gallon. From California to New York by rail, the charge was 7 1/2¢ per gallon. European vintners could therefore afford to charge less for their wine in America's eastern markets than could the West Coast vintners. Given a choice between low-priced continental wines of reasonably consistent quality and unpredictable, higher-priced domestic ones, wine drinkers (mostly of European origin themselves) usually selected the foreign brands.

---

[22] *SHS*, 3-27-1914.

[23] Idem.

[24] *SHS*, 4-23-1909.

[25] *SHS*, 6-10-1910.

In September of 1909 the CWA levied a $10 per share charge on its stockholders. Its war-chest fortified, it then went to battle with independent growers in many parts of the state. The tactic was not completely successful. At its July, 1910 annual meeting the CWA announced that it could not cover all of its debts and that a syndicate had formed to buy more of its stock, the proceeds of which would go to cover the company's shortfalls. It was also forced to dismantle and raze its quake-damaged plant in Windsor.

With sales down, grape prices plummeted. The CWA could only offer its growers $10 a ton in 1910. The Migliavacca Wine Company, an independent firm in Napa, was able to give its growers $12 a ton. This was a far cry from the $30 to $35 vineyardists had commanded back in 1901.

The huge CWA combine collected another major infusion of money in 1913 by doubling its capital stock from $10,000,000 to $20,000,000. When Congress threatened to raise the tax on brandy from 3¢ a gallon to $1.10, the CWA dug into its now reinforced reserves and hired Theodore Bell to go to Washington to lobby. Along with him went State Senator L.W. Julliard to represent the California Grape Growers' Association and M.F. Tarpey, representing the Southern California Wine Association.[26]

Prohibition itself found its way into the Napa Valley in its milder form, that of temperance. When the City of Napa granted liquor licenses to "the keepers of houses of ill-fame," many were outraged—not about the brothels, but about the licenses. "Men may differ as to the necessity of the so-called social evil," wrote Carroll of the *Calistogian*, "but there can be no defensible excuse for permitting liquor to be dispensed at such places."[27] After a flood inundated parts of east Napa, some of the local whores went out and swam in the floodwaters. No one seemed to complain much.

In May of 1910 the St. Helena city council voted to suspend for 10 days the licenses of three bars that had stayed open a few minutes past 12:00 AM, the curfew. In November of that year,

---

[26] *NDJ*, 7-22-1913.
[27] *WC*, 1-1-1909.

W.C. Grimes' saloon was shut for good, the city councilmen describing it as a "disgrace." Mrs. Mary Selowsky, proprietress of the "Stone Bridge Saloon" on the hill across from St. Helena's Pope Street Bridge, received a huge fine—$250—for selling liquor without a license. The license with which she and her girls sold themselves also came to trial, and her brothel was shut down for a while.[28]

Most of the township of Yountville became Dry because of a new law prohibiting the sale of booze within 1.5 miles of the Veterans' Home. The county hired W.S. Hardin to snoop about in "blind pigs"—places suspected of breaking temperance laws. (The odd slang was a not-so-secret password. Everyone knew that when the proprietor of a place asked if you wanted to see the "blind pig," he or she really meant, "Do you want some alcoholic refreshment?") Frank La Coste ran a blind pig in Yountville. Three customers ratted on him, and he was sentenced to 180 days in the county jail and forced to pay a $500 fine.

Elderly Mrs. Mary Ghirendi's bar was well within that radius, yet she persisted in selling liquor. When she was arrested she bravely asserted that rather than pay the $500 fine, she would spend 100 days in the county jail. She was incarcerated. Once the novelty wore off, Mrs. Ghirendi wanted to be released. She petitioned the Governor to have her sentence commuted because of her advanced years. The request was denied; she could be released only if she paid the fine for the remaining days.[29]

Hardin nabbed another erstwhile Yountville saloonkeeper, Peter Guillaume, whose establishment was quite popular. Theodore Bell's brother, Edward, defended Guillaume in court and helped him beat the rap, scoring his victory against the young new District Attorney, Nathan F. Coombs, Frank's son. Within another week or so a similar case came to court, that of Yountville saloonkeeper Madge Righly. Ed Bell won that case as well, but during the trial an eruption burst forth between Bell and Coombs that nearly ended

---

[28] Mary had a branch office in Napa, which she leased to another woman of similar enterprise.

[29] *NDJ*, 7-3-1909.

in a courtroom fistfight. In the family feud of Bell vs. Coombs, public sentiment at that time may have favored the Bells.[30]

Some Napa Valley saloons were very rough places and deserved the bad reputation the ASL attributed to them. Soon after the Stone Bridge Saloon reopened, for example, Peter Cesari shot Dominic Decarlo there over a disagreement in a card game. Jules Maggetti's Oakville establishment was frequently a setting for drunken brawls, and even Bismarck Bruck was moved to testify that the place was "disgraceful." Patrons in Peter Guillaume's (supposedly) Dry Yountville establishment had to duck for cover when Edward Fortier, exceedingly drunk, staggered about brandishing a knife, insane with jealousy over his wife and another man.

Some places tried hard to distance themselves from the saloon element. The G&G movie theater in St. Helena announced that it was "doing their utmost to put on the screen nothing but moral and highly entertaining pictures." They offered a weekly raffle, the prize being a case of Bruck's Grape Juice.

The WCTU organized a chapter in St. Helena, and immediately, with little or no publicity, it had 20 members. The Presbyterian, Methodist and Seventh-Day Adventist churches held an ecumenical "Union Temperance Meeting" with entertainment provided by the choir of the St. Helena Sanitarium. Children and young adults read original essays and poetry, and the Presbyterian minister, the indefatigable Reverend James Mitchell, awarded prizes to the most worthy. Somewhat surprisingly, the *Star* reported on the lecture given by the keynote speaker, a Dr. Abbott:

> Dr. Abbott, speaking as a physician, informed the audience that the latest scientific research proved alcohol to be always and only a poison, and showed how, in the minutest doses, it had an injurious effect on the human system, never promoting, but always destroying, health.[31]

Economically, it was not a good time for California in general. Money was hard to get, and some people had none of it at all. An

---

[30] *NDJ*, 1-17-1914.
[31] *SHS*, 7-15-1910.

"Army of the Unemployed" numbering more than 1,000 collected from various parts of the state and began a slow march up the Sacramento River Valley.[32] In larger cities like San Francisco and Stockton, laborers staged strikes to improve their often wretched working conditions.

As always, it was hardest for the elderly and for single mothers, who tended to suffer quietly. The Droste family on Napa's South Randolph Street was among the poorest of the poor, a fact that was discovered by officer Lafe Smith when he received a call to find a missing child. Five-year-old Johnnie Droste had wandered away from home. Smith found him and shared his lunch with him, but when he brought him home he discovered that his mother had three other children under five, no money and no food in the house. The father, he learned, was a glass blower whose lungs had gone bad. He was in Los Angeles, looking for work. Smith related the family's sad story to Walden of the *Journal*. Walden printed it, and immediately enough donations came in to feed and clothe the children, provide passage for the family to LA and finance temporary lodging for them after they arrived there.

Elderly people—especially those who had been locked into Napa State Hospital[33]—had few, if any, to advocate for them. Some were even put into the institution against their will by scheming relatives. Such a fate befell Mrs. Chloe F. Tilton, the white-haired widow of a former San Francisco City and County Supervisor.[34] When Charles S. Tilton died in 1904, he left her an 18-acre estate near the asylum. The main house was nicely appointed and boasted of an extensive library. Its total value was about $40,000, a large sum in those tight times. Mrs. Tilton's first cousin, Ida Killey, had herself made legal guardian of Chloe's person and property and immediately threw the widow into NSH. Killey rented out the estate to a female friend for $25 a month.

Other than chronic worry about the well-being of her possessions outside the hospital's walls, Chloe showed no signs of

---

[32] *NDJ*, 3-12-1914.

[33] It changed its name about this time.

[34] *NDJ*, 2-5-1910.

mental illness whatsoever, according to a hospital matron[35] who had known her since she arrived. The matron testified, moreover, that Killey failed to supply Chloe with "the necessaries she should have had in the hospital." A Sonoma attorney[36] tried to get Chloe released in 1908, but failed.

In 1910 a member of Napa's Odd Fellows club, Louis Hammersmith, learned of Chloe's plight, and, with the backing of his fraternal organization, managed to get a hearing for her with a judge in San Francisco. Judge Coffey interviewed all the parties involved including Chloe and found her to be entirely mentally competent. No one at the hearing had seen signs of mental illness in her during her six-year confinement at the institution. He ordered her to be released and removed Killey from her guardian position.

Abuses of individual civil liberties took place at Napa State Hospital regularly, but it was rare for anyone to challenge its medical hierarchy. It was so difficult to leave NSH that for many, the only way out was to escape. One such example was the situation of Frank Lux.[37] Lux once lived in Oakland with his wife and two children. One evening on his way home from work, he happened to see two drunk men abusing a neighborhood child. When he attempted to intervene, one of the men hit him on the head with a bottle. He soon began experiencing severe headaches and irritability, and under the duress of this pain he consulted a doctor. He was told that he had suffered brain damage and that his condition would deteriorate. Lux made comfortable accommodations for his family and went to NSH to recover, which he evidently did. Deeming him still a danger to his family, however, the staff refused to let him go. He was allowed no freedom and was confined to a single building, although he could walk about and get sunshine for two hours each day inside a walled enclosure. Lux put himself on a rigorous exercise program, where he dramatically increased his physical fitness. One night in the spring of 1909, after he had been incarcerated at the hospital for a

---

[35] Marion Eaton

[36] R.F. Crawford

[37] *NDJ*, 2-6-1910.

long time, he was allowed to attend a dance that was being held for the patients. He used that occasion to get away, running as fast as he could all night. His absence went unnoticed for hours.

Lux made his way to Fort Bragg, where he got a job and made enough money to book passage to Mexico. He worked without incident as an accountant at a mine in Mazatlan for several months and then decided to return to San Francisco. He had, perhaps, let his identity as an escaped mental patient slip, because when the steamer came to port, a detective and an NSH official arrested him and returned him to the hospital, despite the fact that he was symptom-free, had gone nowhere near the family he supposedly wanted to kill and was well able to care for himself.

People knew bad things were going on at the state hospital, not only in terms of patients' rights, but in its financial dealings, as well.[38] It took a combined effort by the State Board of Control and a special grand jury in 1912 to bring the guilty to justice. Interrogation by DA Coombs revealed that Dr. Elmer E. Stone, the medical director, had been scamming the State of California for years. The ploy that finally got him caught had to do with hay, which he ordered more often and in greater quantities than the hospital needed. He set up a dummy account at the James H. Goodman bank and had a clerk there write him checks from it to cover the cost of hay deliveries and their attendant freight charges. He then wrote reimbursement requests to the State for more than the amounts actually charged. The State reimbursed Stone, and he deposited this money in the dummy account, keeping for himself the difference between the reimbursement and the real cost. Sometimes the hay went to the state hospital, but often Stone kept that for himself, too. Over the years he made quite a bit of money this way.

Isaac Enright, the hospital's plumbing foreman, skimmed a dollar an hour from each employee on the padded payroll of his department and resold for his own profit the plumbing supplies the State provided for him. The purchasing agent, Franklin W. Bush,

---

[38] See "Report of the Grand Jury, 1912," Napa, 1912.

awarded contracts to favored businesses at inflated prices, providing them with lucrative monopolies. Sometimes these businesses used the hospital as a place to dump inferior products. Stone was aware of and promoted these and other misdoings. Stone was charged with embezzlement. The 519 pages of transcripts from the court phase of the investigation reveal a deeply corrupted system that proffered unfair advantages to upper-echelon staff and their friends and withheld opportunities for fair competition among Napa County businesses. Stone pled for mercy, but Walden of the *Journal* would have none of it. "He is without honor, is cunning and crafty and is now endeavoring to save himself from the penitentiary,"[39] he snarled.

It was not that rare for people who should know better to try solving their financial problems by less than honorable means. In 1909 the County Coroner/Public Administrator, C.C. Treadway, left town "in a big automobile" with a new set of undertaker's instruments. He passed bad checks at a number of saloons on the way up the Valley and disappeared from sight. He was not, according to the *Star*, "by his lonely." "Chester has showed these inclinations to wander from home for several months past," explained his embarrassed father, "in fact ever since he took charge of Napa Soda Springs property as Public Administrator."[40]

Treadway's defalcation provided a portion of gossip upon which the locals could chew; it was not nearly as destructive, though, as the scandal that erupted in Calistoga. The town's only bank crashed, and its president, Harry Harding Brown, was charged with felony embezzlement. Deputy DA Raymond Benjamin was the bank's lawyer, and he urged depositors to be patient. The money was all there, he claimed, and everyone would be reimbursed. Benjamin knew full well, however, that the money was in fact not there. He then bailed out as the bank's attorney.

It was revealed that around the time of the great earthquake, when the banks had been closed for weeks, Brown had forged promissory notes for loans in various sums, using the names of

[39] *NDJ*, 1-30-1912.
[40] *SHS*, 9-1-1909.

depositors. One was that of a relative, a sign painter named F.B. Camm, and it was this case that exposed his chicanery. Camm supposedly signed for a loan of $2,361. A sum for that exact amount was deposited into an account of Brown's.

Just as his dubious transactions came to light, Brown decided to take a trip, and a detective from Napa followed him. Brown went to his hometown in Illinois to seek money to cover what he had skimmed, and, failing that, went to New York trying to get passage to sail to Honduras. Perhaps lacking the funds for the voyage, he traveled to Washington, DC, where he had powerful friends. He was arrested there, and Sheriff Dunlap went out to bring him back to Napa County.

Had Frank Silva, the prosecuting attorney, chosen to use the Camm case as the hook on which to hang Brown, he might have won. Instead, he chose that of an Oakland man who had bought a certificate of deposit at the Bank of Calistoga when the bank had no money in it. Theodore Bell was Brown's defense lawyer and got Raymond Benjamin to testify on behalf of the defendant. Benjamin presented the jury (seven farmers, a laborer, a drayman, a cooper, a horseshoer and a grape-grower) with a convoluted story involving land transactions and Brown's juggling of the bank's status from a national bank to a state one, a practice that was not uncommon in the days before banking reform. His word and Bell's ability to confuse the jurors was intimidating enough to stop the judicial process in its tracks.

The trial lasted two days and ended with an acquittal. Carroll of the *Calistogian* was disgusted.

> Nothing in the history of Calistoga has hit the town as hard as the bank failure. The biggest fire the town ever had was a blessing compared with the loss wrought by the bursting of the only financial institution in town. But the people of Calistoga are brave; they can stand the shock; they will do it, and everybody will continue to do business at the old stand. It may be that the people have the pleasure of

seeing more than one man don felon's stripes before
this matter is over.[41]

Brown had used some of the bank's funds to purchase land in
Oakland within days of the institution's failure. When Calistoga
grocer (and bank stockholder) Charlie Hoover made a racket to get
his money back, the bank's new attorney, E.L. Webber, offered
Hoover the mortgage on the Oakland property, which Hoover
accepted. Papers were filed. Other people got wind of this and
demanded their pounds of flesh, too. Webber was finally
subpoenaed to explain how Hoover got this sweet deal, "and also to
explain many other things [the bank's] Receiver [Harry L.]
Johnston thinks he has a perfect right to know."[42] Webber
complained that he was being jabbed with pointed questions that
really should have been aimed at Raymond Benjamin, whom
Carroll called "slippery Ray."

The Bank of Calistoga was a prestigious operation before
Brown's indiscretions were uncovered. Its Board of Trustees was a
local Who's Who that included men from Napa as well as from
Calistoga: George S. Beach, Raymond Benjamin, John S. Brown,
W.F. Bornhorst, C.L. Armstrong, H.M. Meacham, J.A.
McClelland, H.P. Goodman, John R. Rutherford, Ephraim Light,
William Spiers, C.M. Hoover, Jacob Grimm, R.H. Walsh and G.
Iaacheri. The Cashier was G.S. Cutler, Brown's brother-in-law.
There were 370 depositors.

Shadiness on an even grander scale also came to light that year,
when the deal that old George Goodman had cut with Simpson
Finnell back in 1900 (see page 34) became public due to a
complicated lawsuit. The 4,500 Berryessa oil shares that Goodman
bought were valued at $30 each in 1900. Nine years later they
were virtually worthless. Had the wells produced, Goodman would
have realized an enormous profit, especially if he had then decided
not to divide his shares with the unwitting bank. Goodman, who

---

[41] *WC*, 8-14-1908.
[42] *SHS*, 3-19-1909.

had tremendous local prestige, was able to explain away the problem.[43]

Litigation was another popular means of acquiring the riches of others. One of the oldest families in the Valley—the Lawleys of Calistoga—made it their life work to sue each other. Napa pioneer John Lawley was a gold miner who came to the Napa Valley around 1850 and married into one of the region's most influential families, the Kelloggs.[44] He owned one of the Valley's first lumber businesses and had sold to Napa City the site on which the county Courthouse was built. He was an original subscriber to the Napa Valley Railroad, President of the Napa Valley Telegraph Company and a trustee of the Phoenix quicksilver mine in Pope Valley and the Bank of Napa in Napa City. He further improved his fortune by buying[45] and selling land in Berryessa Valley. His greatest achievement, however, was the Lawley Toll Road, a route over Mount St. Helena whose construction he supervised. Much later in his life, he and his daughter, Molly Lawley Patten, operated a tollhouse at the summit of the road. Anyone using the road had to pay a rather hefty fee. The person who used the road most often was Bill Spiers, whose stage line (and later whose tourist cars and busses) conveyed hundreds of people a week to the resorts of Lake County. He paid as much as $5,000 per year in toll fees.

John Lawley died shortly after the earthquake in 1906, at the ripe age of 90. His sons, Charles and Harry, claimed that the rights to the toll passed on to them. Bill Spiers disagreed, as did Molly, who held no fondness for the Lawley "boys." Spiers filed a complaint to make the Lawley Toll Road a public highway, arguing that the franchise could not be passed along to the heirs after the franchisee's death.

---

[43] *NDJ*, 7-3-1909.

[44] Florentine Kellogg had built much of the Bale gristmill. For a complete history of John Lawley, see John Wichels, "John Lawley: Pioneer Entrepreneur, " *Gleanings,* Napa County Historical Society, Vol. 3, Number 1, February, 1982.

[45] or perhaps just taking

Spiers sat on Calistoga's city council and was well regarded. The Lawley brothers may not have experienced the same level of public esteem. When the brothers attempted to charge Spiers for using the route, Spiers complained to the town constable, and they were arrested. They posted bail, and upon their release were informed that every time they asked Spiers to pay a fee they would be charged with misdemeanor extortion and arrested. The Lawley brothers stubbornly continued to charge Spiers and continued to be arrested, jailed and released. Lawsuits around the case proliferated for years.[46]

The plutocratic Spreckels family also bombarded itself with lawsuits. When patriarch Claus Spreckels died it was discovered that he had written Napa horse breeder Adolph and his brother John out of the will. Claus Jr., Rudolph and their sister, Mrs. Emma Ferris, received big bequests. Adolph and John sued for what they believed to be their rightful portions and won. Their mother, Ann Christina Spreckels, then disinherited them, on the grounds that they had already received their inheritance when they won the lawsuit. Her estate was valued at between $5,000,000 and $10,000,000: more than enough to go around.[47]

Another way some people chose to get money was by simply stealing it outright. Three men, only one of whom was masked, held up a Middletown shopkeeper in March of 1914, and when the victim made a move as if for his gun, one of the bandits shot him dead. They tied up his brother, grabbed $52 from his store, stole three tired horses and fled south into the wild scrubland near the Napa/Lake County border. A big posse from Lake and Napa Counties traced them to an abandoned quicksilver mine, where they disappeared. One of the robbers, a man named Jack Crane, slipped out and went to the house shared by the robbers' girlfriends to find

---

[46] *NDJ*, 7-1-1909. Bill Spiers died in April, 1931, at the age of 77. He had just gotten a shave and was feeling fine when he stepped into his car to drive the short distance home. He was hit with a massive stroke, but during the moment he was dying he had the presence of mind to turn off the engine of his car and drift into death.

[47] *NDJ*, 2-20-1910.

food. Crane was arrested there (and so were the girlfriends of the robbers).

The other two bandits (Burt Bell and a man named Fitzgerald) dodged their pursuers and made their way to the remote cabin of Chris Sperling, a German who hadn't heard about the murder and robbery. Sperling fed them and wished them well, a blessing that proved effective, because early in the morning the next day the two boarded the southbound electric train at Dunaweal in Calistoga and enjoyed a pleasant trip into Napa, where they breakfasted with the parents of the aforementioned girlfriends. Thus refreshed, they boarded the train to San Francisco and disappeared forever.

There were also those who chose to forego money altogether and grab dinner on the hoof (or claw). Chicken thieves plagued owners of henhouses, and cattle rustlers operated south of Napa and in the wilds of Pope Valley. Their motivation was hunger. Hunger drove Charles Hall and his young wife to derangement when the plump cow of their neighbor Joseph Yudnich kept wandering onto their property in Butts Canyon through a hole in Yudnich's fence. The cow trampled the frail orchard Hall had planted. Near to starving, Hall shot the cow and butchered half of it, leaving the other half in a creek bed. When Yudnich found the remains, he called Sheriff Kelton, who conducted a house-to-house search for the rest of the animal. He found the missing fore- and hindquarters neatly tucked into a bed at the Hall's, as if asleep.[48]

W.F. Botsford, President of the Vallejo, Benicia & Napa Valley Railroad, became the unfortunate focus of blame in March of 1910, when another reorganization of shareholders, calling themselves the San Francisco, Napa & Calistoga Railroad (SF, N&C) took over the electric interurban line. The train's new owners complained that it was not profitable enough. The diminishing returns, they said, must be due to Botsford's failure as a manager. They sent him packing. The *San Francisco Call* gossiped that the

---

[48] Hall was given a small fine and sentenced to 90 days in the county jail. *SHS*, 4-23-1915.

Bismarck Bruck

*Bismarck Bruck brewed alcohol-free grape juice as
a "temperance drink." The display of bottles above was
a big draw at St. Helena's 1913 Vintage Festival.*

Photo courtesy of the Napa Valley Museum

Doctors at Napa State Hospital lived in mansions like these at the front of the complex. Patients, however, lived in squalid conditions in back wards, with little hope of recovery--or escape.

The tracks of the interurban train ran through the center of St. Helena. The sign at the entrance to town welcomed visitors with the promise of a "ten dollars fine for riding or driving on this bridge faster than a walk."

Among the most influential men in Napa County in the years before World War I were lawyer John T. York (above left), Star *editor Frank Mackinder (above, right) and Napa's ill-fated mayor, Dave Kyser.*

Photo courtesy of Napa Firefighters' Museum

Charles Otterson

real reason Botsford was removed was that he had mishandled a $1,500,000 bond issue.[49]

In July of 1912, SF, N&C superintendent McIntyre was finally able to announce that the line had purchased a site for its Calistoga depot, which would be at the intersection of Lincoln and Washington Streets. It wasn't until September that the electric train finally reached its projected Napa Valley terminus.

Frequent accidents beset both the interurban and the Southern Pacific. Workmen and persons walking along the tracks were accidentally electrocuted, cows wandered into the path of oncoming trains, and on at least two occasions men from the Veterans' Home fell asleep on the railroad tracks and were crushed. On June 19, 1913, the SF, N&C experienced a disaster of the first order. Bad tides on the San Francisco Bay had delayed the arrival of the connecting ferry, so when passengers finally boarded train #6 in Vallejo,[50] the train was running a little late. A number of men—perhaps 20—crowded into the front car, which was the smoker, and unfolded their newspapers for the ride. The conductor that morning was a substitute, Horace C. Richmond. He was given new orders, which he followed. Corresponding orders, however, were not wired to train #5, which had left Calistoga on time but was running slightly late when it pulled out of Napa, headed for Vallejo. Both trains put on speed to make up the lost time.

When southbound train #5 was passing the tiny community of Flosden on a single track just south of American Canyon, its motorman, William Juarez, saw northbound train #6 in the distance.[51] He pulled the emergency brake and screamed for the passengers in the front car to run to the back of the train. The two trains quickly entered a blind reverse curve and met head on.[52] Slowing down and empty of most of its passengers, the lead car of #6 climbed on top of #5. Its heavy wheels and floor ripped through the lower car, mangling the smokers, several of whom were

---

[49] *SF Call*, 3-27-1910.

[50] The *Calistoga Flyer*

[51] *NDJ*, 6-20-1913.

[52] Trimble, Op. Cit., p. 134.

instantly decapitated. Thirteen died in all, and more than 40 were injured. Sheriff Ed Kelton was among the survivors, having escaped with injuries to his mouth that loosened all of his teeth. He nevertheless remained on the scene for the next 24 hours, rescuing some and helping remove the corpses of others.

Hoping to minimize the costly litigation it knew would follow, the train tried to blame Horace Richmond, the rookie conductor, for the wreck. He had not followed company procedures, they charged. The dispatcher, Edward J. O'Leary, was also at fault, they said. He should have known the rules for handling late departures.

The California Railroad Commission began an inquiry. Richmond was hospitalized from injuries sustained in the crash, but O'Leary could testify before the board. "I am train dispatcher, change ticket agent, [and] baggagemaster," he explained. "[I] keep the time of the men and do unclassified clerical work. On the day shift, I work from 6 to 5, with 1 hour off to eat. I received a salary of $65 a month...I was never told to familiarize myself with the rule book until after the wreck."[53]

The SP-dominated Commission ruled that the fault ultimately lay with its competition, the top brass of the electric railroad. Richmond and O'Leary "were but agents of a very lax system," they said, and the line was trying to operate its trains as if they were streetcars rather than an interurban system.[54] Conductor Richmond later sued the interurban for his injuries and won, but even before the ruling had been handed down, other lawsuits over the case began. As a result of these, the SF, N&C Railroad lost the revenue it needed to complete its elaborate plans for laying track to Lake County.

While Sheriff Kelton was recovering from his loose teeth and sore mouth, a carload of Napa dignitaries was returning from a fishing trip at Lake Tahoe. Piled into a Model T with their gear were David S. Kyser, the undertaker who was elected Mayor of Napa in 1907; Charlie Otterson, the fire chief and first foreman of

---

[53] *NDJ*, 6-28-1913.
[54] *NDJ*, 7-22-1913.

the old V, B & NVRR, and Emil Zahler, owner of the popular Owl Hotel on the southwest corner of Main and Third Street in Napa.

A half mile from Emigrant Gap, their road intersected the rails of the Southern Pacific, at a break in a series of snow sheds.[55] They stopped for a passenger train, which was making its ponderous way through the sheds. It was uphill for the car, and Otterson had to climb back into the rumble seat and prepare to jump out with wooden blocks to brake the car if it started to roll downhill. Zahler was driving. When it appeared the train had passed, he gunned the engine to keep the vehicle heading uphill, but to his horror and that of his companions, another train was right behind the first one. Zahler tried desperately to drive the car off the track, but there was no escape. They collided.

Otterson flew about 40 feet from the car, losing his shirt and pants in mid air. He landed in a bush outside the sheds. Unscratched, the big man brushed himself off, redressed, and went looking for his friends. The Napans' auto was deep in the tunnel, imbedded in the train. In the dim light, he could make out the bloody bodies of Zahler and Kyser. The train had tossed them ahead of the car some 70 feet into the snow sheds, slamming them against the pilings there. Kyser had suffered a severe blow to the back of his head, and Zahler's left arm and both legs were badly broken, the flesh nearly ripped off to the bone on all three limbs. Neither man was conscious, and what remained of the car, Otterson said later, could be put in a basket and carried by a child.[56]

Zahler succumbed three days after the accident. He was a member of the Masons and the Eagles, and both fraternal organizations participated in his memorial service, which was held at Kyser's funeral parlor. State Assemblyman James Palmer read a eulogy. A drill team accompanied the funeral cortege to Tulocay Cemetery, which was crowded with mourners. Emil Zahler left behind a wife and seven children, two of whom were married, the rest still at home. Just after the funeral the youngest, 10 year-old Otto, fell or jumped from a rowboat into the Napa River and had to

---

[55] *Placer County Republican*, 6-23-1913.

[56] *NDJ*, 6-25-1913.

be rescued, lest another tragedy beset the family. Dora, Zahler's widow, tried to sue the Railroad for her husband's death, but she lost the case.

Napa's mayor remained in a coma for several days, but eventually he came to and could finally be transported back to Napa. He was never able to regain his health fully, however, and he died of pneumonia within a year. His funeral was even more· elaborate than Zahler's and was the cause of a parade-like procession that featured at least one band. The Napa Ambulance Company led the way, followed by the fraternal organizations in which the mayor had been involved: the Eagles, the Redmen, the Druids, the Elks and the Oddfellows, plus the entire City Council, numerous other city officials and the Napa Fire Department, and finally the horse-drawn hearse itself, accompanied by the Napa Commandery of the Knights Templar, the leading Masons.[57] Napa's saloons were ordered to close, and most of its businesses shut down, probably because there was hardly anyone around that afternoon to frequent them. Everyone was marching in Kyser's parade.

The summer of 1913 was an unlucky, unhappy season for many in the Napa Valley. Shortly after Chief Otterson escaped from the train accident, he was called upon to fight the biggest fire Napa had seen since the 1860's. Like the Calistoga fire, it began behind a hardware store, Young's, on the southeast portion of Main Street near Third. Young's was destroyed, as was Welti brothers' harness store, the Steuck-Bernard Cyclery and F.G. Noyes' lumberyard and wharf on Third Street. Residents and tourists staying at the Berlin Hotel next to Noyes' gathered their possessions and fled in terror. The hotel was spared. Five days later a second fire broke out, this one at the Bon Ton Bakery, which was adjacent to the structures involved in the first fire. The Wylie Building on the southeast corner of Main and Second burned down. What enabled Otterson and his crew to keep the blazes from incinerating downtown Napa was the almost total absence of wind.

---

[57] *NDJ*, 5-13-1914.

The breeze remembered the Napa Valley in mid-September. It caught onto a small fire at the 160-acre farm of Henry March in Chiles Valley and blew it into a major forest fire that swept through Capelle and Foss Valleys, consuming homes and killing two people. The fire split into two sections, one charging northward through Rector Canyon until it almost reached Napa Soda Springs; the other veering south toward Mt. George. The second leg burned its way toward Gordon and Wild Horse Valleys and stopped just short of General Miller's old estate, which had not yet become the Silverado Country Club. It coursed down Hagen Road, and then part of it jumped to Green Valley and marched toward Cordelia. A secondary fire broke out north of the original blaze, destroying parts of Conn and Sage Canyons.

The fires were the result of a blistering, summer-long heat wave. Three people died of the heat on a single day in St. Helena. Hundreds of chickens perished, and there was a rabies outbreak, with at least one mad dog running through the streets of downtown Napa, frothing at the mouth.

Calistogans suffered from the hard times, too. Few people stopped there anymore to partake of the hot springs, and Sam Brannan's once lavish resort was threadbare. The president of a large machinery company looked into buying what remained of the resort, which may have been worth about $70,000 at the time. When the deal fell through, local editor Charles Carroll's sigh seemed almost audible: "Once more Calistoga's hopes have been blighted on springs grounds improvements," he wrote, "but the Calistogian still believes that they will be sold some day and that Calistoga will become famous thereby." [58]

Like many Californians, the people of the Napa Valley sought, as they had in years past, someone or something to blame. While alcohol was the target for the frustration of some, others indulged in intensified racial bigotry, which was never far beneath the surface. When the Webb Bill passed the California legislature, forbidding Asians to lease land in California for more than three

---

[58] *WC*, 1-30-1914.

years, many Napans felt it was too lenient. They agreed with State Senator J.B. Sanford (the "Grey Eagle"), who argued that "California should be maintained as a white man's country."[59] They even protested when Japanese vegetable farmers dared to market their produce under Anglo-sounding names and cried for measures to make this practice illegal. One almost unbelievably ethnocentric California legislator tried to push a proposal that would require Asian immigrants to pass a stringent physical fitness test before being allowed to enter the United States. His measure made sense, he claimed, because in his view they were only suited to do physical labor.

The Napa police conducted a series of raids in the local Chinatown and other places considered to be "Napa opium resorts." The *Journal* ridiculed the suspects scooped up in the busts:

> Two white devotees at the shrine of Madjoun (the opium god), also seven "Chinks" were assiduously trying to get rid of the "yen yen" (craving for opium)...[60]

Fittingly, perhaps, 1913 ended with a devastating flood. The Napa River crested in mid-morning on December 31, inundating Spanishtown, Chinatown and parts of the business section. The flood ran the steamer *St. Helena* into an inlet somewhere between the Stanly Ranch and the Spreckels Stock Farm, where it hit bottom and wouldn't budge until a tugboat finally yanked it from the reeds and mire. Because of the flood, sections of the interurban were under deep water, and there was no way to get to Vallejo.

The roads were as hopeless as always, although some in the Valley tried to argue that the county must be ahead of its peers, because it was the first in the state to vote itself a direct tax for road building.[61] Thanks in large part to County Supervisor Jasper Partrick, a strong advocate of good roads, there were in fact stretches of serviceable pavement here and there in the cities of

---

[59] *NDJ*, 5-7-1913.

[60] *NDJ*, 6-17-1913.

[61] Gregory, Op. Cit., p. 875.

Napa and St. Helena. But for getting out of town, people relied on good weather and the railroads.

Jasper Partrick was a Democrat. In 1910 he stepped down from his position as Chairman of the Board of Supervisors, because the Board was almost entirely Republican, and his replacement was St. Helena's wine industry advocate, Bismarck Bruck. Following Partrick's lead, Bruck went to work on a project to improve transportation options for the people of the Napa Valley. Bruck helped author a proposal to create an "around-the Bay-boulevard" that would extend from Cordelia through Napa County, Sonoma County and Marin.[62] He called the Napa-Marin section the "Black Point Cut-off" for its projected terminus to the west of the mouth of the Petaluma River. Bruck and the supervisors proposed that the land for the route be ceded to the state and that the voters of Napa, Solano, Sonoma and Marin counties approve a bond issue to fund the project. The new road would require numerous bridges, so it would be expensive. Bruck's plan met with great enthusiasm in Napa County. Several "Good Roads Clubs" formed to promote the project's success.

The Napa River's 18 miles of salt water from the Third Street Bridge to the river's mouth had always been a major transportation artery. The River was in sorry shape. Not only was it polluted from the many industries that lined its banks, but it was jammed in places with logs and other debris, and there were several spots where irregularities in the banks narrowed the passageway and caused hazards. Since 1888 professional surveyors had been recommending that the river's usefulness could be at least partially improved if it could be dredged in places to a depth of a minimum of 4' at low tide and uniformly widened to a minimum of 75'. Dredging had, indeed, occurred, and some of the results were tragic. Stripped of the rocks that once lined its bottom, it could no longer cleanse itself and wildlife habitats were destroyed.

Widening the river was a problem, though. The families who owned the land that jutted into the river's path refused to have their riverfront acreage shaved away merely because it interfered with

---

[62] Today's Highway 37.

riparian traffic. Moreover, no one wanted the saline mud and sand from excavation to be deposited on their own property.

Effectively and permanently removing obstacles to transportation would be expensive. The Senate's River and Harbors Committee had funds for such projects. In 1912 a delegation from the War Department came to Mare Island at the mouth of the Napa River to inspect the facility in preparation for turning it into a maritime base.[63] Theodore Bell, Mayor Kyser and others with some pull had convinced the visiting VIP's that Mare Island and the War Department would benefit if the river route to Napa were improved.[64] Partly because of the War Department's recommendations, the small sum of $5,000 was portioned to Napa out of a total appropriation budget of about $33,000,000. It was also discovered that $4,000 remained available from a prior appropriation. This still wasn't nearly enough.

In January of 1914, while Mayor Kyser was trying to recuperate from the accident at Emigrant Gap, an Internal Waterways Congress convened in San Francisco to hammer out a meaningful restoration program for California's rivers. The ailing Kyser could not attend these crucial meetings. The only full-time Napa delegate was D.L. Beard, who served on the Ways and Means committee.[65] The cities with the greatest influence in the group would get the largest bundle when it came time to allocate funds. With minimal representation, Napa County did not get funds.[66]

To lack influence in the confusing and dangerous political spheres beyond the Napa Valley was to invite disaster. The Valley

---

[63] In January of 1914 some 1200 marines were stationed there, with more arriving later in the year. *NDJ*, 1-16-1914.

[64] *NDJ*, 6-8-1912.

[65] Assemblyman James Palmer, Napa City Attorney Wallace Rutherford, and Napa Granger F.L. Hunt also attended at least one of the meetings.

[66] And even if the money had been available, there would have been the problem of obtaining permission from the land holders to alter their property line; and if that had been wangled, there still would have been no place to deposit the salty sludge.

needed a strong representative, someone who could hold his own with power brokers at the state and even the national level. Theodore Bell was helpful, but he was preoccupied with other matters and a Democrat, to boot. (There was a progressive Democrat in the White House, but Republicans carried the day at the state level.) Napans turned to the Chairman of their Board of Supervisors. They convinced St. Helena's Bismarck Bruck to run for the Assembly in the 1914 elections.

Politics were now more important than ever, and folks followed them closely. On December 10, 1913, some 4,000 Drys had marched down Pennsylvania Avenue in Washington, DC to support the ever-growing drive for Prohibition.[67] Organized by the Anti-Saloon League, 1,000 of them demonstrated on the steps of the Capitol.[68] Around the same time, in a powerful speech in Columbus Ohio, J. Frank Healy, the former Governor of Indiana, proposed that Prohibition be made mandatory on a national level by constitutional amendment. He was the first to go on record with the idea.[69]

The people of the state of Illinois held an election in April of 1914 that caught the interest of many in the Napa Valley. Illinois had granted suffrage to women. It was one of the first in the United States to do so. Participating for the first time in the state's primaries, women were instrumental in causing Illinois to vote itself Dry, resulting in the closure of thousands of saloons and the apoplexy, no doubt, of tens of thousands of men.[70] Women's Suffrage was inextricably linked with the drive for Prohibition, and the two movements fueled each other. An immediate benefit of this to women was the opening of new, previously closed vistas. Margaret Woodrow Wilson, daughter of the President, for instance, became editor of a magazine; a group of women in San Francisco founded a newspaper, the *Daily Democrat*. California's Deputy

---

[67] Cashman, Op. Cit., p.10.

[68] Behr, Op. Cit., p. 59.

[69] Ibid., p. 58.

[70] Chicago refused to comply with its state alcohol laws, and it remained out of compliance for the next 18 years.

State Director of Public Education, Mrs. Edward Hyatt and her daughter Inez, became the first females to travel alone by car cross country (it took 3 weeks). In Napa, a "Miss Ogden" became, on April 28, 1914, the first woman to argue a case in Napa Superior Court. She won.

Napa Valley vintners redoubled their efforts to keep California a Wet state. In March of 1914, former Congressman Bell began a state-wide speaking tour touting the merits of wine and warning voters of the disaster that would befall California's grape and wine industries if Prohibition became law in California. He launched his campaign from St. Helena's G&G Theater.[71] Borrowing a tactic from the Anti-Saloon League, he urged Californians not to elect into office men who sympathized with the Drys. He named names. He spoke of the symbiotic union between the ASL and the national Prohibition Party, and he revealed to his audiences that a petition had already been signed by 80,000 people to put Prohibition on the November 1914 ballot. Anti-Saloon League orators, meanwhile, spoke to big audiences elsewhere in the state about the evils of drink. They were sharply critical of the wine industry.

Its numbers swelling with concerned viticulturists, the Grape Protective Association (GPA) issued frequent press releases regarding the wine and grape business. According to the GPA's Harry L. Johnston, Napa County's assessed valuation in 1913 was $15,791,655. Wineries and vineyards represented $6,000,000 of this. Thus almost half of the county's worth derived from the fruit of the vine, despite the many prune, walnut and other orchards that were now sharing the rocky soil.

Local "protective associations" also formed. The Napa County Viticultural Protective Association's original membership consisted of W.F. Bornhorst, Bismarck Bruck, J.H. Wheeler and Frank Pellet of St. Helena; E.W. Churchill, Joseph Migliavacca and Henry Brown of Napa, and Ephraim Light, C.N. Pickett and C.W. Armstrong of Calistoga. Others soon joined them.

---

[71] which became the Liberty in 1916 and the Cameo near the end of the century.

Napa Valley vintners had actually enjoyed a very good year in 1913, and they were feeling hopeful about the new season. F. Salmina & Company's business was expanding rapidly. A.J. Pirelli-Minetti took over as head winemaker at George De Latour's growing enterprise, Beaulieu. News of problems with the vintage in Germany cheered the vintners who competed with German producers in the East Coast markets.

The on-going and ill-advised war with Midwest wineries , however, suffered a setback. Reacting to the California-sponsored law to tax adulterated wine, eastern vintners wangled a tax on brandy. Winemakers, especially in the big wineries in the central part of the state, used brandy to fortify sweet wine. The new tax would hit not only the brandy makers, but many of the state's largest producers, as well. Midwestern wine lobbyists whispered that California wineries had been routinely evading taxes for years, an accusation that in some cases may not have been altogether false, although on behalf of the vintners Theordore Bell denied it adamantly.

California lobbyists rushed to Washington and negotiated a compromise that rescinded the tax on sugar in return for eliminating the tax on brandy. Vintners everywhere breathed a brief sigh of relief.

Chapter Six

Wars

N apa Valley vintners were arming themselves for a great battle in 1914. They still envisioned the battleground as being confined to the state of California, with the federal government and its taxation policies a variable that could be influenced and maneuvered by politicking. Other things of great moment, however, also captured the imagination of people in the wine country. One was the tremendous opportunity posed by the Pan-Pacific International Exposition, which would be debuting in San Francisco in 1915. After years of labor, diplomacy, disease and bloodshed, the Panama Canal opened in May of 1914, and with it came the hope of finally beating the Railroad's oppressive freight rates. California agriculturists could now send their products to lucrative eastern markets by ship without having to undergo the perilous voyage around the southern tip of South America. The Exposition would honor the Canal and all for which it stood.

Traveling through Latin America had perils all its own. Mexico in 1914 was undergoing a vicious revolution that made headlines in newspapers almost everywhere (except in St. Helena, where *Star* editor Mackinder avoided news from outside the region whenever possible). Napans could follow the unfolding drama through both of their city's newspapers, which had always covered national and international events. President Woodrow Wilson ordered American warships to be readied for engagement. The Assistant Secretary of the Navy, Franklin Delano Roosevelt, visited Mare Island in April of 1914 to oversee the Pacific fleet's preparations for intervention in Mexican waters.[1]

The California Viticultural Committee would have its own pavilion at the Exposition. As part of its anti-Prohibition public relations effort, the wine industry planned to assemble an eye-popping, jaw-dropping extravaganza that would show the world that California wines were on a par with the great vintages of Europe. The French, Germans and Italians would also come, they hoped, and fair-goers from all over the world would walk away impressed.

Some vintners made trial runs for their Exposition exhibits by participating in St. Helena's "Vintage Festival," an outgrowth of the annual local merchant's fair that celebrated the people and products of St. Helena. The 1912 Festival (the first) was a sparkling success, but the 1913 event was more elaborate. It lasted four days and included contests and artful exhibits, entertainment by anyone with any talent at all and the coronation of a Queen. The To-Kalon winery showed off its wine in a 12'-high pyramid of bottles. Bismarck Bruck promoted his grape juice by stacking bottles together to form one gigantic bottle, and the Charles Krug winery, where Bruck was still the superintendent, prepared an archway made of pillars of bottles filled with wines of different colors. Beaulieu's exhibit featured a pergola of redwood limbs supporting hanging baskets overfilled with grapes. Other wineries also participated.

Non-vintners were involved, as well: The Oddfellows and Rebekahs made a pergola. The Women's Improvement Club showed a wheelbarrow artfully overturned with grapes falling out. (The prior year they had exhausted themselves by constructing an elaborate bridge scene made entirely of walnuts.) Bell Brothers' general store on Main Street built bells out of prunes, Smith's Olive Oil Company on Railroad Avenue made a handsome booth with olive boughs, and local farmer T.G. Varner brought in a display of cactus, corn, beets, sunflowers, peas and peaches from his 47 acres three miles north of town. Many others also exhibited, and the

---

[1] *NDJ*, 4-17-1914.

festivities helped convince the celebrants that their world, blessed with plenty at last, was secure.

The Festival planners arranged for a motion picture to be made of the gala event. Old St. Helena, long synonymous with the wine industry itself, was thus one of the first little towns in America to be chronicled in celluloid. The Grape Growers Association completed its own movie about the wine industry, including in the film many scenes from the Napa Valley. When the Pan-Pacific International Exposition finally opened in San Francisco in April of 1915, hundreds of people each day for a year lined up to see a movie that combined the Grape Growers' film and footage from the St. Helena Vintage Festival. People left the viticultural exhibit at the California Food Products Palace believing, no doubt, that life in the Napa Valley was one big party.[2]

When the Pan-Pacific Exhibition opened, however, another story was hogging the headlines. On June 28, 1914, a Serbian terrorist named Gavrilo Principe fired two shots into the passenger compartment of an automobile that had taken a wrong turn in Sarajevo, Bosnia. Archduke Franz Ferdinand, nephew of Germany's Kaiser Wilhelm and heir to the throne of Austria-Hungary, bled to death, along with his wife, before their driver could reach a hospital. The result was World War I.

Austria declared war on Serbia at the end of July and immediately captured Belgrade. Germany followed suit by declaring war on France. On August 3 Kaiser Wilhelm ordered his troops into Belgium and also into Poland, which was part of the domain of his cousin, Tsar Nicholas II of Russia, with whom he therefore also went to war. For these trespasses, Wilhelm's English

---

[2] In contrast, the official exhibit of Napa County turned out to be a disappointment. Rather than touting the region's viticultural products and presenting them with the artistic panache that characterized the Vintage Festival, the county display was a jumbled mess, resembling, said one reviewer, the chaos of a general store (*SHS*, 4-9-1915).

cousin George V declared war on him and his country, as well as on Austria-Hungary.[3]

France prepared to fend off both the Austrians and the Germans. Switzerland declared martial law but managed to keep its neutrality. Italy severed the alliance it had held with Germany and Austria since 1882,[4] and in a few months it, too, would be in the war as part of the "Allies."[5] Bulgaria and finally Turkey jumped in on the side of the Teutonic "Central Powers."

Transatlantic service between the United States and continental Europe was suspended, because German U-boats prowled the coastal waters and tried to sink whatever ships came their way. Many British firms were forced to withdraw their money from the American stock market to finance their war effort, and the New York Stock Exchange closed from July, 1914 through the end of that year.

War ravaged Europe throughout the rest of 1914 and into 1915. Most Americans wanted nothing to do it. The War, however, began to involve itself with Americans. A German airplane attacked an American ship, the *Cushing*, and soon afterward a German U-boat torpedoed the *Gulflight*. Americans were killed in both instances. More Americans died when an Austrian ship sank an Italian passenger liner. Austria-Hungary disavowed the act and agreed to pay an indemnity to the Americans' survivors.

When Captain Walther Schweiger of the *U-20* fired a single torpedo at the British liner *Lusitania* on May 7, 1915, the huge cruise ship went down in 18 minutes, drowning 1,198 civilians.[6] One hundred twenty-eight Americans were on board, among them multimillionaire Alfred G. Vanderbilt. President Wilson went into the Rose Garden and wept when he heard the news of the

---

[3] See Martin Gilbert, *The First World War: A Complete History*, Henry Holt and Company, New York, 1994.

[4] Italy had been linked with the other two powers via a secret treaty that established the "Triple Alliance."

[5] England, France and Russia.

[6] Gilbert, Op. Cit., p. 157.

Lusitania's fate.[7] William Jennings Bryan, now Secretary of State, wrote a respectful yet forceful letter of protest to Germany, warning that America would safeguard the right of its citizens to travel wherever they wished on the high seas.

The sinking of the *Lusitania* brought forth an outpouring of anti-German sentiment. All things German—including German wealth and German fondness for wine and beer—seemed suddenly somehow tainted.[8] *The New York Times* editorialized that the United States should seize German ships in retaliation. In an oft-quoted expression of horror, *The Nation* called it "a deed for which a Hun would blush, a Turk be ashamed, and a barbary pirate apologize."[9] The United States Ambassador to England urged Wilson to declare war, as did former President Teddy Roosevelt. "We owe it to humanity, to our own self-respect," Roosevelt exclaimed.[10] Roosevelt published a book in which he warned all Americans of German descent to remember they were now Americans and "in honour bound" to view the war from the American viewpoint.[11] The ominous inference was that because they were German in origin, they might not.

The wine industry's dream of luring the great vintners of Europe to the Pan-Pacific Exposition never materialized. By the time the Exposition opened, Western Europe was engulfed in flames, and the few Europeans who might have wanted to make the long journey to San Francisco feared perishing in the Atlantic under the torpedoes of German U-boats. Not even France's Prosper Gervais, Secretary of the Permanent Viticultural Commission, could make

---

[7] Douglas Botting, *The U-Boats*, Time-Life Books, Alexandria, Virginia, 1979, p. 32.

[8] Maddock, Op. Cit., p. 67.

[9] As quoted in Maddock, Op. Cit., p. 137.

[10] Botting, Loc. Cit.

[11] Theodore Roosevelt, *America and the World War*, John Murray, London, 1915.

the trip. "My son, my only son, is dead on the field of Flanders," he wrote. "I cannot come."[12]

With so many Napa Valley readers from Germany, Austria and the German-influenced cantons of Switzerland, the *Journal* published whatever positive material it could about their suddenly very unpopular homeland. It reprinted an article of praise from the *American Review of Reviews*: "Germany's sea power cannot be broken," the story said. "Germany's amazing power of organization and unified action, together with her advantages to date to operating from an inner position, renders her practically invincible—at least from a defensive standpoint—in a war on land."[13]

The German-American Alliance, rather than taking a low profile, engaged in pro-Kaiser propaganda in various parts of the country. This further eroded the public's tolerance for things Teutonic, especially the alcoholic products of beer and wine.

Germany responded to America's disfavor with anti-US propaganda. German newspapers accused the supposedly neutral US of betraying its long-time ally by sending war supplies to the Kaiser's enemy, Great Britain. The charges were true. The United States did what it could get away with to aid the Allies, and when England blockaded vessels[14] headed for German ports or ports contiguous to Germany, the American government did not protest. The Ambassador to Germany wrote the State Department that he believed the Kaiser would probably intensify the U-boat activity against American ships by the end of the year or early in 1917.

Allusions to the castled estates of Europe—a fantasy that had been at the heart of the wine country's appeal to visitors from the beginning—lost its timeliness completely. To be Beringer, to be Krug, to be Pabst or Busch or "Bismarck" Bruck or to possess any other German-sounding name, was to be vulnerable to a measure of the same kind of xenophobia that beleaguered Mexicans, native Americans, African Americans and Orientals. Bruck tried to

---

[12] Pinney, *Op. Cit.*, p. 369.

[13] *NDJ*, 1-6-1916.

[14] All vessels, including US ships.

cement relationships with fellow members of the State Assembly. One morning each Assemblyman arrived at work to find a bottle of Bruck's grape juice awaiting him.

On the national level, there was little to cheer Bruck or any other Wet. The Anti-Saloon League was profiting from the nation's rising anti-German sentiment.[15] Reinforcing in the public consciousness the link between Germans and the alcoholic beverage industry, the League was able to persuade an increasing number of legislators to come out for Prohibition. The threatened tax on brandy reappeared and this time became law, as part of the "Revenue Emergency Act." Fifty-five cents were now tagged on to every bottle of brandy sold. Wine was also taxed outright. As a direct result, the production of wine in California in 1915 was $1/6^{th}$ of normal, most of this affecting the manufacturers of sweet wines in the Central Valley. The California Wine Association was unable to buy all of the grapes for which it had contracted, and Napa Valley growers had to wait months to receive cash settlements.

A delegation from the Viticultural Commission went to Washington in January of 1916 to try to get the emergency tax removed, but they were rebuffed. The Revenue Emergency Act soon gave way to the Kent Act, which levied a permanent, costly tax on wines. Significantly, it was modeled after the wine tax protocols used in Germany. It was promoted in such a way that again linked alcohol with Germany in the public mind.

Clearly in denial about the otherwise unmistakable public trend against alcoholic products, the Secretary of the California Board of Viticultural Commissioners, Edgar Sheehan, effused that "the outlook for vineyardists of California who produce wine grapes is exceptionally bright."[16] Sheehan's effulgent comment would be the last positive remarks the wine industry would hear for many years.

---

[15] It also both profited from and forwarded anti-Irish feelings. The Irish, overwhelmingly Catholic, were world-class beer drinkers and initially resisted entering the war against Germany.

[16] *SHS*, 1-7-1916.

Even Nature herself seemed to be siding with the Prohibitionists. Early on a Sunday morning in May, 1916, a disastrous frost crept into the Napa Valley, turning nearly half the vineyards black. It was the worst Spring frost since 1873. The price of grapes might be reasonably good, but only because the supply of grapes would be disastrously low.

Prohibition continued to ooze its way across the nation until it was practically seeping under the doors of the wineries. Cars of the SF, N & C interurban carried advertising put out by the Anti-Saloon League. When confronted about this, the train's owners confessed that they had contracted out their advertising spaces to a firm in San Francisco and could not remove the displays.[17]

The City of Napa voted into law new, stiffer ordinances regulating saloons. Everyone selling liquor would have to pay a monthly licensing fee, and bars had to shut down at midnight. They had to stay closed from midnight Saturday until 6 AM Monday mornings.

Families sold their vineyards, and for a while real estate brokers were busy, because there were those who believed that Napa Valley land would soon regain its value. When the heirs of Jacob Schram sold their old estate to a San Franciscan, the agent who closed the deal gloated. The *Star* published his comments:

> The properties here being so accessible to San Francisco and Oakland are especially sought after in exchange and whenever we get hold of a good property it is no trouble at all to find parties with good income properties who are willing to exchange for them. [18]

One who took advantage of the falling price of Napa Valley acreage was D.P. Doak, a San Francisco steel magnate, who had been quietly buying up acreage in Oakville. His biggest purchase was *Far Niente*, the Benson ranch. There, on a knoll with a

---

[17] The line was turning over a nice profit now that it had changed its upper management.

[18] *SHS*, 5-19-1916.

dramatic view, Doak started work on a mansion.[19] John McLaren, the San Francisco landscape architect who laid out Golden Gate Park, designed the grounds, using shrubs and trees left over from the Pan-Pacific Exposition.[20] An orchard of about 80 cherry trees graced the property to the east and north, and there were marble fountains imported from Italy.

Local gossips could take dark pleasure in the unhappy fate of Doak's neighbors, the Churchill family. They were principals in both the To-Kalon winery of Oakville and the Goodman Bank in Napa. Mary Churchill, mother of E.W. Churchill (To-Kalon's president and treasurer of Goodman's bank) brought suit against her son and daughter-in-law, saying that they had defrauded her after she had turned power of attorney over to them back in 1903. The younger Churchills had charge of Mary's shares in the Napa City Water Company, the California Cable Company, the winery and the bank, and although all those concerns made significant amounts of money, she only received $27,000 during that time.[21] Her son and daughter-in-law, however, were able to enjoy an extravagant lifestyle. The case was finally settled out of court, but the Goodman Bank—which did not need another scandal—shut its doors forever.

As the Napa Valley, with her many Germans and her increasingly unpopular principal product continued to lose ground, she encountered problems in other areas. The State of California, despite strenuous local objections, opened an honors work farm in Yountville for convicted prisoners. Assemblyman Bruck finally had to author a bill in order to have the thing removed. Even more ominous for the county's future growth, Rear Admiral H.T. Stanford of the US Navy complained that the channel at Mare Island would prove inadequate for the big battleships the Navy planned to build. The place should be closed down, he advised.[22]

---

[19] *SHS*, 6-29-1917.

[20] Gordon Eby, *Napa Valley*, Eby Press, Napa Valley, 1972.

[21] *SHS*, 8-25-1916.

[22] *NDJ*, 1-16-1916.

To prove its loyalty to the United States and thus lobby for its naval facility, the City of Vallejo held, for the first time ever, a huge July 4th celebration. The cities of the Napa Valley did not hold their customary Independence Day parades so that an impressive attendance would be assured.

As people in the Up-Valley sold out and moved away, the City of St. Helena lost revenue. It could no longer afford to employ a full complement of fire fighters. Oddly, the firemen who remained demanded that the City buy them a brand new fire engine. When Mayor Swortfiguer refused because the city treasury could not support such a purchase, the remaining firemen walked off the job. The community pressured Swortfiguer, and he capitulated. Soon after, the local electric power company refused to light the town's street lamps at night, because St. Helena couldn't pay its electricity bill.

The California Grape Protective Association joined the campaign against saloons and officially resolved that it was strongly in favor of "drastic steps" to "clean up" the places where spirits, wine and beer were sold.

> The Association is not wedded to the American saloon. It never has been. It believes the evils of the present system would be practically exterminated if the people would awaken from their provincialism and follow the example of continental Europe. In the cafes and gardens of Germany, France, Italy, Spain, etc., where men and women, priest and rabbi and minister congregate...drunkenness is unknown...and even occasional intoxication is extremely uncommon.[23]

The Association's rhetoric could not have been more ill chosen. "Germany, France, Italy, Spain, etc." were by now mired in a hideous war of attrition that had reached astounding proportions. An entire generation of the young men who would have been in

---

[23] *SHS*, 1-19-1917.

those cafes not getting intoxicated were being blown to bits in trenches in the heart of France.

The Association then offended many of its own members. As a final appeasement, it supported a measure, the "Rominger Bill," that would outlaw saloons and the manufacture and importation of whiskey, gin and brandy as a beverage. It would also prohibit the manufacture of dry wine with more than 14% alcohol and sweet wine with more than 21%. Bismarck Bruck, J.H. Wheeler, Theodore Gier and a number of other vintners angrily withdrew from the Association. The fuming Gier denounced the GPA, charging that most of the members were Central Valley men who grew table grapes and raisins and had no concern for the plight of wine growers. The vintners' protest further fragmented the wine industry.

In October of 1916, just off Nantucket, the *U-53* sank five merchant ships belonging to Allied countries. This act of war so close to American shores shocked many, and when Wilson ran against Charles Evans Hughes for a second term in November, his tenacious neutrality nearly cost him the election. Wilson won, however, and would soon be called upon to make a number of momentous decisions.[24]

On January 19, 1917, Dr. Alfred von Zimmermann, the new German Foreign Minister, telegraphed a coded message to the German ambassador in Mexico City, to be delivered to the Mexican government. It stated that on February 1, Germany would begin unrestricted submarine warfare. The Kaiser's submarines would target all ships heading for British or Western European ports, American or otherwise, military or civilian. Zimmermann guessed that the US would remain neutral even under this escalated condition, but if it did not, the note said, Germany proposed

> that we shall make war together and together make peace. We shall give general financial support, and it is understood that Mexico is to reconquer the lost territory in New Mexico, Texas, and Arizona. The details are left to you for settlement.

---

[24] He won by 594,188 popular votes and 23 electoral votes.

> You are instructed to inform the President of Mexico of the above in the greatest confidence as soon as it is certain that there will be an outbreak of war in the United States and suggest that the President of Mexico, on his own initiative, should communicate with Japan suggesting adherence at once to his plan; at the same time, offer to mediate between Germany and Japan.

Germany, Mexico and Japan, each of whom the United States had insulted: these slighted powers should join against their common enemy, the United States, the message said. British agents intercepted the Zimmermann note. While they worked on breaking the cipher, they came across a second encoded message. Count Bernsdorff, the German Ambassador to the United States, had asked Berlin for $50,000 with which to bribe certain members of Congress into pushing for continued neutrality.

Proof of the Kaiser's intentions to escalate the sea war came quickly. The infamous *U-53* sunk an American cargo ship, the *Housatonic*, off the Scilly Islands. The bribery scheme as well as the proposed Mexican alliance came to light, and peace was no longer tenable. On April 6, 1917, the United States declared war on Germany.

America's participation in World War I was the result of a brilliant display of organizational planning. The week before Congress declared war, there were in the entire US Army only 5,791 officers and 121,797 enlisted men, and enough ammunition to last about a day and a half.[25] Wilson ordered the adoption of a selective service act, which named June 5, 1917 as the day that 10,000,000 men between the ages of 21 and 30 would be required to register for the draft. Each man was given a number. They would be called to train for action by lottery.

---

[25] Robert H. Ferrell, *Woodrow Wilson and World War I,* Harper & Row, New York, 1985, p. 14. There were also, however, about 200,000 men in the National Guard.

123

Some young men from the Napa Valley enlisted immediately, without waiting for their number to be chosen. Attorneys Frank Silva and Charles Trower drove through the county urging men between 18 and 40 to join in the great cause. Members of the Napa Ambulance Corps and the Napa Band climbed aboard the interurban and did the same. The Napa Ambulance Corps enlisted a dozen young men, most of them from well-known families. Richard Wilson, G. Amadeo, Alonzo Echfeldt, John Money, Charles Brocco, A.G. Griffith, Louis Cavalini, Stephen Jackse, Jr., Joseph Cheli, Edward Glos, H. Ericson and Bertrand Elgin were at the front by Christmas of 1917. Henry ("Boleta") Navone was able to join the Ambulance Corps as a chef.

Another stipulation of the selective service act—a coup pulled off by the Anti-Saloon League's masterful lobbyist, Wayne Wheeler—was that it would now be unlawful to sell alcohol of any kind to American servicemen. Supplying a sailor or soldier with alcohol was called "bootlegging." It would also be illegal to sell alcohol within five miles of an armed forces installation. The order specifically criticized the City of Vallejo, "a short business street with twenty-five saloons."[26] The saloons were said to be controlled by a German brewer.[27] With the War came a sharp increase in demand for workers at Mare Island and $1,200,000 for improvements to the base.

Civilians hankering for a glass of beer or wine or a shot of whiskey had to travel to Napa Junction, which was just outside the five-mile rim of fire and was home to a number of families of Italian and Greek descent. The four saloons there did a huge business, one of them selling as much as 250 cases of hard liquor a day.[28] The proprietress of one of Napa's whorehouses mentioned that she also procured most of her liquor in Napa Junction.[29]

Bootlegging to sailors immediately became a problem in Napa County. By February of 1918 there was so much action in the city

---

[26] *NDJ*, 3-7-1918.

[27] Idem.

[28] *NDJ*, 5-8-1918.

[29] Idem.

of Napa that the police planned a sting. They nabbed a waitress and a porter at the Hotel Cecille. As a result of the bust, Mrs. Hannah Flanagan, the owner, sold the place to Charles Baracco. Also swept up in the February dragnet were a bricklayer, a carpenter and a cabbie.[30]

Another immediate effect of the War was that seditious comments were now illegal. The St. Helena Police Department arrested a man named Karl Alberti when he made a derogatory comment about the American flag. They raided his home on Church Street and found "anarchistic literature" and pamphlets from the Industrial Workers of the World (IWW, sometimes called "Wobblies").[31] It turned out that Alberti, a German immigrant, was a socialist/anarchist: an offense egregious enough by St. Helenan standards to warrant driving him out of town.[32]

In Napa, Patrolman George Secord and Undersheriff Henry Mills arrested George Peterson, who was said to be pro-German and also a member of the IWW. A young woman who had grown up in St. Helena (her parents, the Heims, ran a business there briefly) made local news when her husband, Erwin Frederick Schneider, was arrested as a German spy in the Bay Area.

Harry Sawyer of Martinez hit the front page of the Napa papers when he declared in public that "America has no business in this war."[33] Sawyer, whose mother was German, was thrown in jail and escorted by guards to Angel Island. Perry Schriber, a German staying at the Connor Hotel in Napa, went to jail because of "treasonable utterances."[34] A.W. Porta of Calistoga suffered the same fate.[35]

---

[30] *SHS*, 2-1-1918.

[31] The IWW openly opposed America's participation in the war. One branch of "wobblies" advocated the takeover of American manufacturing companies by workers.

[32] *SHS*, 6-29-1917.

[33] *NDJ*, 4-14-1918.

[34] *NDJ*, 11-14-1918.

[35] *SHS*, 1-18-1918.

Teachers who had immigrated from Germany and Austria lost their positions. Cross-country motorist Mrs. Edward Hyatt, now the California Superintendent of Instruction, ruled that it was all right to tear from state textbooks any pro-German references, in story or even song.[36] The Napa Moose lodge discarded the bunting on their all-nations altar because it had on it the colors of Germany, Austria and Bulgaria. They substituted the Star and Stripes for it. Local attorneys John York, Clarence Riggins and Frank Coombs formed an "Alien Property Committee" to ensure that no one bequeathed property to citizens of countries with whom the US was at war.

These formalities were not sufficient for some. One night in March, 1918, under the illumination of a full moon, 16 cars with five to seven passengers each formed a caravan and quietly drove up the Valley. Their leader was the Sheriff, Ed Kelton. Their destination was a saloon in Calistoga, where they burst upon a party of five Calistogans of German descent who were said to be noisily celebrating the Kaiser's French offensive and von Hindenberg's claim that the Kaiser would take Paris by April 1. After bullying the terrified men, the posse made each of them kiss the American flag. One of the unfortunate Teutons was Felix Grauss, who had been chief clerk of the Calistoga post office for 16 years and was the brother of the town constable. A week after the raid, someone overheard him saying that the Liberty Loan drive[37] was worthless. Postmaster Owen Kenny dismissed him on the spot.[38] The next week, J.C. Lebner, Arnold Kosch and P. Siebreight were heard speaking German at night on a street in Calistoga. Their neighbors called the police, and they were arrested and carted off to jail for their own protection.[39]

The numerous instances of suspected sedition in Calistoga attracted the attention of the US Secret Service, which sent an investigator there. The spy found that Felix Grauss was, indeed, pro-German, and he arrested him. Anyone who still held affection

---

[36] *NDJ*, 4-21-1918.

[37] a program of fund-raising to help pay for the war effort

[38] *NDJ*, 4-4-1918.

[39] *NDJ*, 4-21-1918. They were soon released.

for the Kaiser had best keep his mouth shut.[40] The penalty for "disloyalty" was 20 years in prison and a $10,000 fine—a punishment that was rarely carried out.

Somebody telephoned Theodore Brauer, bartender at the St. Helena Brewery Exchange, who had in fact registered with St. Helena's Postmaster Galewsky as an "alien enemy," a new requirement for German immigrants. The caller told Brauer that he'd better leave town, or he'd be tar-and-feathered. Brauer fled for his life, although later it was revealed that the call had been a prank.[41] Martin Skala, a 26-year old Austrian living in Pope Valley, may also have received a crank call. He was found dead of a bullet wound from his 30-caliber Winchester rifle, said to be self-inflicted.[42]

There actually was a threat from unhappy, seditious Germans in Northern California, although not a grave one. Someone set off a small bomb in the Capitol building in Sacramento. There were unexplained cattle poisonings. In February of 1918, Fritz Hagerman, alias Charles Aisenbach, was arrested in Susanville for accepting German money for influencing the IWW "to incendiarism and destruction on the Pacific Coast." Among Hagerman's services to the *Vaterland* was arson at the Red River Lumber Company in Lassen County.

The Farm Labor Committee of the State Council of Defense recommended to California's Governor Stephens that if the law failed to protect people from "the IWW and their idleness and seditious teachings," citizens should personally "take them by the neck and drown them in the rivers."[43] Napa's lead judge, Henry Gesford, applauded the Committee's position and elaborated on it at a well-attended war rally. Seditious people shouldn't have to kiss the flag, he said. They should be shot.[44]

---

[40] *SHS*, 7-24-1917.

[41] *NDJ*, 4-5-1918.

[42] *NDJ*, 4-6-1918.

[43] *NDJ*, 3-17-1918.

[44] *NDJ*, 4-27-1918.

The Council of Defense warned the public that German spies were everywhere, stirring up trouble. On the Pacific Coast, they said, German activists were responsible for "bad feeling" between Americans and those of Japanese descent. Increased ill will between Mexicans and Americans in the border states and between races in the South was also, they said, due to German interference. "An attempt is being made," they said, "to show that Catholics are obtaining control of the government in Protestant territory, while in sections where Catholics predominate stories are going out to the effect that the Catholics are being discriminated against."[45] Prejudice, discrimination and bigotry, which had long been features of the dark side of the public mentality, became potential tools of enemy manipulation.

Wilhelm Peterick, identified as a "German spy," was arrested in Vineburg. He had in his possession carefully hand-drawn maps of the Spreckels ranch, the Jack London estate, the railroad tracks in Glen Ellen, and, clenched in his fist, a German iron cross.[46]

A 29 year-old German immigrant, a Napan named Max Jasnau who had a tailor shop on North Main Street, was arrested for seditious comments and then accused of molesting two little girls.[47]

Somewhere on the Pacific Coast, American forces captured a boat, the *Alexander Agassiz*, which German sympathizers were outfitting as part of small fleet. The pirates hoped to prepare several such craft and with them overtake a larger vessel. With a suitably armed big ship, they intended to harass US shipping.

Nearly the entire staff at the German consulate in San Francisco was charged with espionage and sabotage. It was a violent, bloody case. During the trial one of the defendants was shot and killed by another man in the courtroom. A US Marshall then shot and killed the assassin. The consul himself, Franz Bopp, came to St. Helena's St. Gothard Inn for one last outing before he was to be arrested. He telephoned from the Inn to assure the authorities in San Francisco

---

[45] *NDJ*, 3-20-1918.

[46] *NDJ*, 4-13-1918.

[47] *NDJ*, 5-4-1918.

that he would turn himself in.[48] He did as promised and was sentenced to a fine and two years in prison.

Long-time St. Helena vintner Frederick Hess of La Jota winery was a friend of Franz Bopp's. He was the editor of the German *California Demokrat*, a venerable German-language newspaper in San Francisco. Hess decided to shut down his press,[49] ending a career in journalism that spanned more than 60 years. It was a wise move. M. Duval, editor of a Germanophile paper in Paris called the *Bonnet Rogue* was executed for his point of view, and Hess could have suffered the same fate.

Another St. Helena vintner found himself in deep trouble around the same time (spring of 1918). Millionaire Theodore Gier, the influential wine man who had recently led the protest at the Grape Protective Association, was charged in Oakland with singing German songs, toasting the Kaiser and wishing the enemy success in their western offensive. Three of the nine men arrested in the raid were employees of Gier's. Gier made bail for all of them and denied the charges.

One of the most disturbing acts that spring involved none other than the Napa Valley's favorite son, Theodore Bell. Bell was counsel to a small Berkeley religious group, the Church of the Living God, whose members sought exemption from military service as conscientious objectors. An angry mob burned their church to the ground on April 19, 1918. Mysteriously, a letter survived the blaze and was plucked intact from the smoldering ashes. It was from Theodore Bell to Reverend Joshua Sykes, agreeing to represent the church for a fee of $1,000. He would need another $1,000, the letter said, if he had to take the case to the Supreme Court—something he felt justified in doing in the name of religious freedom. The Bar Association of California began an investigation of Bell for "unethical and unpatriotic conduct." Bell's strong advocacy of the wine industry had already won him enemies among the ever-growing ranks of Prohibitionists. Now he was in jeopardy of being disbarred. Nothing came of it, however.

---

[48] *NDJ*, 4-13-1917.
[49] *NDJ*, 5-8-1918.

While the war in Europe had degenerated into a hideous, protracted bloodbath, the American war of the Wets vs. the Drys was nearly over. By the summer of 1917 the Drys had all but won. The Senate voted to ban the manufacture of whiskey from grain, because grain was needed for the war effort. It also outlawed the importation of whiskey. The vote was 65 to 20. Brandy, a grape product, could still be made to fortify sweet wines. The law left to President Wilson the power to cancel beer and wine production when and if he felt the need.

A state law later in August put a cap on the number of bars permissible in a given locality. Napa had to reduce from 23 to 12 the number of saloons that could hold licenses. The 12 bars that remained in town were required to raise money to pay a closing subsidy to the 11 others.[50]

St. Helena hosted a 1917 Vintage Festival in September (its Fifth Annual), but participation by wineries was minimal and lackluster. The few wineries that did display anything said they were trying to keep as much "vintage" in the festival as they could.[51] Nevertheless, thousands came to see it. They celebrated a world that was about to vanish.

President Fontana of the California Wine Association was well aware of the danger facing the wine industry and was among the first to verbalize the grim reality. Seeing little hope for the CWA's future, he urged growers to liquidate as soon as possible to cut their losses. The CWA itself did not stop operations but started

---

[50] The survivors were: Jules Thebaut, "Buffet," Brown Street; C.L. & J. Carbone, "The Gem" Pearl St.; Franco & Delucca, "The Gilt Edge," Main St.; Nussberger & Mayfield, "The Assembly," Main St; Roney & Vieusseux, Brown St.; E. H. Manchester, "Oberon," Main St.; Green & Gstrein, "Russ House," Brown St.; Charles F. Hargrave, Main St.; A. Zeller, Palace Hotel; S. L. Martinelli, Owl Hotel, D. Cavagnaro, Brooklyn Hotel and A. Dollman, Napa Hotel.

[51] *SHS*, 9-7-1917.

downsizing. Over the many years of its existence it had spent more than a million dollars experimenting with wine grapes. It owned 8,000 planted acres. At its height in 1916, its inventory exceeded $6,700,000. But, faced with never-ending opposition that was powered by an unfailing supply of money, it knew it was fighting on the losing side. Many had trouble computing the CWA's pessimism. The price of grapes was promising to be excellent, and many believed that the battle could still be won.

Some of the gloom in the Napa Valley about the war of the Wets vs. the Drys was allayed by the tremendous emphasis being placed on the clash of Good vs. Evil in Europe. The buttons of patriotic fervor were being tweaked to an extreme. Preparedness Day parades, Liberty Loan rallies, banquets for boys going off to boot camp and the fear of being suspected of sedition by not participating in the spirit of the times combined to produce intense emotions.

Now that it was worse than politically incorrect to display any fondness for things German (or Austrian), or to criticize participation in the war, many went out of their way to show their loyalty. There was a sharp rise in the sale of American flags. Citizens were urged to buy War Savings Stamps. They cost $4.12 but would yield $5.00 when they came due in 1923. They were purchased at the post office, were made out in the name of the buyer and were non-transferable. Lower income folks could buy a single US Thrift Stamp for 25¢, and when they filled a stamp book with 20 they could redeem the book for a single War Savings Stamp. Government guidelines asked that everyone purchase at least $1.66 worth. Citizens were also urged to plant war gardens, an endeavor vigorously pursued by the Boy Scouts.

The trend toward legislating public morality, which began with the Progressives and resulted in the snowballing drive for Prohibition, seemed now to avalanche, with lack of patriotic verve now a sin. The newspapers listed the names of everyone who contributed to the Liberty Loan and other war fund drives. Those whose names were omitted were shamed into participating.

131

In March of 1918 the city of Napa launched a big "War Community Campaign" that began with a rally at the Opera House. All the school children in town got to see a propaganda movie at the Empire Theater about the war, and when it was over there was a round table conference entitled "Pinning Old Glory on the School Child's Heart." The women's Economy Club had a "Hoover luncheon"—a small meal intended to emphasize the importance of not being wasteful. To "Hoover" something meant to follow the dicta of Herbert Hoover, chief of the Federal Food Administration, who encouraged Americans to waste nothing so that more food could go to the soldiers in training and abroad and to the citizens of countries ravaged by war. Children who did not finish what was served them were urged to consider the starving children elsewhere and eat "for" them, a practice that probably resulted in guilt-induced obesity for some.

Cities all across America were called upon to raise money for the war effort. Napa had from the first week in April to the first week in May, 1918, to come up with a minimum of $370,000. They met their quota the first day. Throngs gathered in the open air outside the Courthouse to demonstrate their enthusiasm for buying Liberty Bonds. They heard speeches, honored 11 local Boy Scouts for their success in growing liberty gardens, cheered, sang songs and breathed on each other.

President Wilson declared April 26 to be "National Liberty Day." Since the date corresponded with the day the Al G. Barnes circus was coming to town, Napa's officials combined the two events by having a big circus parade, with local Red Cross volunteers in chariots and the town's "Liberty Loan Ladies" riding elephants. The parade went from the Fairgrounds on Third Street to Main Street, up to Pearl, over to Brown, to First, to Coombs, to Second, to Brown, to Third and back to the Fairgrounds. It was spectacular. Practically the whole town showed up. The only people who stayed home were the ones who were sick, and many of them showed up, too, infecting others.

An unusually large number of names started appearing as obituaries in the local press. Some of them were elderly people who had been in ill health for some time, but others were young, some

*Superior Court Judge Henry Gesford
(immediately above) was fiercely patriotic
and wanted Axis sympathizers shot.
Colonel Nelson Holderman (above, right)
was a hero in the Great War and became
Commandant of the Veterans' Home.
Calistogan Felix Grauss (right) uttered
pro-German sentiments and was arrested.*

Men, women and Napans of all ages dropped everything when the circus came to town. Dave Cavagnaro arranged a parade each time the big top arrived. He joined a circus troupe as a roustabout during Prohibition, probably to avoid arrest as a bootlegger.

in the prime of their lives. Some were children. Three-year-old Amelia Hernandez got sick and died. Nita Toccrelini, age 15 months, breathed her last in May, 1918. Frank Massa, age 13, caught an illness, lingered for two weeks, and succumbed, leaving five brothers and sisters. Mrs. A.B. Fletcher came down with it and died, leaving behind a grief-stricken husband and four children. Henry Wolf, proprietor of the Napa Hotel, also got it and succumbed. Asa Willis of Calistoga got sick on a Sunday afternoon and died on Tuesday. He was 35. A. Krause of Calistoga, Albert Dowdell of St. Helena, vintner Christian Adamson of Rutherford, Virgilio Molteni of Napa and the Reverend E.H. King of the Napa Methodist church[52] all fell victim to a mysterious disease and perished. The official cause of their deaths was listed as pneumonia.

Some people caught it and died while away from home. Angelo Sculatti got sick in the state of Washington and died in a hospital there. William Frisby passed away in British Columbia. Robert Feliz, age 28, was dead within days after entering a hospital in Sacramento.

The local press did not comment directly on the sudden sharp increase in illness and death, but Walden of the *Journal* did note that James B. Newman was doing a very brisk business at his marble works on Third and Brown Streets.[53] Nobody else thought much about it either. Five hundred inmates at San Quentin contracted the illness, and three died.[54] Authorities chalked it up as unusual, but not especially alarming. Life went on (for most).

Several men from the Napa Valley signed up to serve in the War, and many more were drafted.

Albert Carpy, Donald de Veuve, Tony Oreil, Oliver Warren, Jesse Campion and Andrew Wake were among the sons of the Napa Valley who were fighting in France before the end of 1917.

---

[52] father of young lawyer Percy King

[53] *NDJ,* 4-2-1918.

[54] Lynette Iezzoni, *Influenza 1918*, TV Books, L.L.C., New York, NY, 1999, p. 25.

Ready to join them as soon as their bootcamp ended were George Lobinger, Earl Johanssen, Tonie Ezettie, Trumpler Mast, Willie List, Walter Poncetta (the acting Corporal), Joseph Hall, John Vienop, Henry LeClair, John Smith, Henry Pestoni, Frank Monahan, James Ghirardi, Elvo Poncetta, Paul Parker, Arthur Lobinger, Oliver Clark, Alfred Domingos, Milton Ransford, Ferdinand Beard, Felix Navoni, John Peper, Elmer Leffingwell, Anton Ghirardelli, Michael Parnell, Joseph Abate, Ralph Stallings, John Hippely, Alonzo Roberts, John Ek, Paul Bohen, Dayton Gardner, Verne Pyle, Albert Litz, Charles Haus, Gekindo Boraschi, Steve Regalia, William Pedroni, Charles Harry, A.F. Kennedy, William Bayless, Armand Malandrino and William Schmidt. Another wave of was right behind them: E.T. Williams, Stanley Long, A.G. Haskell, Henry DuFour, Frank Maloney, Charles Greenfield, Edwin Bruck, Edward Cavalini, Everett Risley, Joseph Pedroni, James Newell, Phillips Lovering, Stanley Persons, Howard Decker, L.J. Snow, Richard Forsyth, Marvin Canetti, Cleo Fightmaster and Charles Schultz.

Chris Busch also marched off with this first batch of soldiers. He was killed in action, the first Napan to die abroad in World War I. Russell Murr was also among the first casualties. His mother, Louise, was very active in the local VFW auxiliary. To honor these two fallen Napa County men, the post named itself the Busch-Murr chapter of the VFW.

The son of Mr. and Mrs. Robert Corlett, Benjamin, was commissioned as a Lieutenant and was one of eight officers selected for special training in the use of a new device, a machine gun.

One of the first to enlist never made it to the front. Theodore B. Lyman, son of vintner W.W. Lyman, had signed on as a cadet aviator: a pioneer among those who took to the air in the name of their country. While hundreds of fellow cadets watched helplessly from the ground, his plane and another met head-on in mid-air. Both pilots were killed instantly.[55]

---

[55] *NDJ*, 9-14-1917.

Most Napa Valley soldiers received their basic training at Fort Lewis, Washington. They left according to their lottery number, often feted at businessmen's luncheons before they boarded for the long train ride to camp. A train leaving at the end of October, 1917, was loaded with soldiers-to-be from the Napa Valley, most of them probably underestimating the horrors that were waiting for them when they finally crossed the seas.[56]

Louis Guisto was among the draftees. He had been a sports hero on the Napa playing fields. His best sport was baseball, which he was playing at St. Mary's when he joined the army. Later, Guisto was drafted by another irresistible force: the Cleveland Indians. The *Napa Journal* reported on Guisto's experiences in the war. Hometown papers printed the letters of several young men who wrote family and friends from "Somewhere in France." Louis Gasser wrote to his friend Nathan Coombs, the DA, and the *Journal* followed some of his adventures.

Louis "Bonnie" Rossi, who was born in Switzerland, was among those who received a free ticket back to Europe courtesy of Uncle Sam. He served in France as a member of the "Grizzlies," a California artillery outfit.[57] Despite a heavy barrage of enemy firepower, he spent two days atop telephone poles, coolly repairing the lines to enable Allied communication. For this he received, ten years later, the *Croix de Guerre*.

While Louis was on the telephone poles, a future resident of Yountville was surrounded by Germans in the dim recesses of the Argonne Forest. Captain Nelson Holderman was in charge of Company K, a battalion of 554 men who had been cut off from the

---

[56] Embarking together that day were B. Ghiringhelli, Herbert Wichterman, Robert Bell, Harry Winfrey, I.W. Christianson, G.J. Catachules, Francis Collins, Julius Buck, B.F. Chapman, Ernest Ericson, Jesse Ransford, Soteros Kokolios, L.E. Merriam, Henry Ferguson, Leslie McLean, Albert Volper, William Lutge, Louis Gasser, Edward Vienop, Frank Stetson, Louis Guisto, Jack Caskey, Hudson Monroe, N.A. Frank, Attilio Rossi and Attilio Aratta.

[57] *SHS*, 9-25-1936.

rest of the Allied forces in a ravine that ran along the Hindenburg Line.[58] They crouched among their dead and dying without food, water or medical supplies, subject to fierce machine gun fire, some of it from their fellow Allies. Wounded and exhausted, Holderman encouraged his men not to give up. His efforts to send out patrols all failed—none made it past the wall of German bullets that hemmed them in. Finally he resorted to carrier pigeons, which he released, one by one, with messages about the Company's plight. At least one bird survived the hail of lead, and soon afterward the Americans arranged an airdrop of food and surgical supplies. But the payload missed its target, and it fell behind enemy lines.

German flamethrowers attacked the ravine, and Holderman's men climbed out and killed them. Holderman continued to lift the morale of his charges, manning a shovel to bury the dead, despite his own grave injuries. One of his men was captured while trying to bring water to the battalion. The German commander sent him back to Holderman, with instructions to surrender. Holderman refused, and later that night the Germans withdrew. Company K, the "lost battalion," clambered from the ravine and down the hillside the next afternoon to rejoin their comrades. Three-hundred-sixty American men perished. Captain Holderman recovered and became the commandant of the Veterans' Home in Yountville, a post he held with dignity for many years.

At first, not everyone who went to Fort Lewis was able to continue. It was common for men to be refused because of physical limitations. Some were probably relieved, but others were gravely disappointed. Sergeant Jesse Treadway of Napa failed officer candidate's school because he became sick and lost his voice. To make matters worse, his dog Pep, who went with him to camp, was hit by a car and killed. Jesse sent the animal's carcass home to his undertaker father to have it stuffed and preserved.[59]   Guilio Brovelli, an Italian who had emigrated to St. Helena, was refused for duty because he was not native born. He pled with his recruiting

---

[58] See Martin Gilbert, *Op. Cit.*

[59] *NDJ*, 3-31-1918.

officers to let him go, saying that he had chosen to be an American and wanted to be counted among its heroes. They finally relented. Brovelli was killed in action.[60]

---

[60] *SHS*, 11-15-1918.

Chapter Seven

Influenza

Once America's involvement in the war was in full swing, bodies that were somewhat less able were included with the physically fit. On April 30, 1918, for example, 2,480 men from the western states arrived at Fort Lewis, almost all of them by train. In one hour and 15 minutes, 480 men passed through the camp's receiving office and were inspected by the physicians. A cold here, a sore throat there, a cough and some sneezes were not worth notice, and as the men filed into the military, so did a "Spanish Lady"—the name given to the influenza virus that probably originated in America's Midwest early in 1918.

The first version of the deadly disease may have begun by a chance cross-contamination between a sick duck flying south for the winter and a pig that somehow became infected by it, perhaps by ingesting the bird's droppings. A human being then came in contact with the stricken pig and caught the illness.[1] The epidemic that struck Napa around the time the Al G. Barnes circus came to town was probably part of this first phase.

---

[1] Iezzoni, Op. Cit., p. 19. Or, a duck could have caught it from a sick pig and given it to a human being.

The genetic accident that yielded the new virus came at a time of migratory activity that was unprecedented in the history of mankind. Because of the war, more people than ever before traveled from the Western Hemisphere to the Eastern, and from the Southern Hemisphere to the Northern. The demand for soldiers overran barriers of ocean and mountain that usually provided natural quarantines to plague and pestilence. Men and women from 20 different countries intermingled: Germany, Russia, France, Belgium, Austria-Hungary, Britain, Italy, Romania, Turkey, Bulgaria, Canada, Australia, India, the United States, Serbia, New Zealand, South Africa, Portugal, Greece and Montenegro.[2]

Perhaps because of this unique and sudden mixing of gene pools, the virus that had begun with the bird and the pig then underwent a second transformation. Deadly enough before, in August of 1918, in France, it mutated into an acutely infectious, savage super-virus, known today as H1N1.[3] When servicemen and Red Cross nurses returned to their native lands, they brought home the new, improved version of the virus. By autumn it was pandemic. In America, an estimated 25,000,000 contracted influenza; 670,000 died.[4] In contrast, only 48,000 Americans perished in the Great War itself.

It infested army camps all across the country, and eventually the army was forced to quarantine the camps, thus ending the supply of American reinforcements. Several of the young men from Napa County who had ridden off so proudly in trains to Camp Lewis and points beyond fell victim not to Germans but to germs. Nevertheless, their families and communities celebrated them as heroes.

"Spanish influenza" typically began with a nosebleed followed quickly by a high fever, wrenching cough and pain. When the fever broke, patients sometimes lapsed into coma. After the initial phase of flu symptoms, sufferers risked developing sudden, severe pneumonia. When that occurred they experienced copious amounts

---

[2] Gilbert, Op. Cit., p. 541.

[3] Iezzoni, Op. Cit., p. 43.

[4] Ibid, Op. Cit., p. 17.

of fluid in their lungs, and death was often the result of something akin to drowning. Waterlogged, their lungs were unable to supply blood cells with fresh oxygen. The skin of oxygen-deprived influenza patients turned purple, and their feet turned black. Death could be agonizingly slow or amazingly quick. Influenza could attack isolated areas of the body, as well, and thus was often initially misdiagnosed as scarlet fever, appendicitis, tuberculosis, heart attack, even stroke. It was just as contagious in its disguised form as it was in its more common presentation. Not everyone who contracted influenza died of it, but many did, especially when it lodged in a vital organ or became pneumonia.

The Spanish Lady came to the Napa Valley in her deadliest guise in October, 1918. She came early to the Amstutz family, who had a jewelry business on Main Street in Napa. Little Louise Amstutz, age 9, developed the flu around October 3. About a week later, her aunt, Elvina Amstutz Otter, suffered an unexpected stroke, followed by paralysis of the throat. She died in her sleep. Louise's flu developed into a similar throat paralysis, and she, too, died, casting suspicion on the true nature of the "stroke" that her aunt had suffered. The Pickle family on the corner of Lincoln and what is now Jefferson Street was also an early host to the illness. Hollis Pickle, age 20, died around October 19. His mother followed a week later.

Suddenly there were outbreaks of the flu everywhere. Frank Priest, a Chiles Valley man who had been driven from his home by the big fire in 1913, contracted the disease in Oakland and died. Pioneer vintner Charles Brockhoff also died in Oakland. Alfred St. Supery, formerly of Oakville, died in San Francisco, as did Lolita Wilson, the only sister of Bismarck Bruck. John H. Paap, farm manager and science teacher at Angwin's Pacific Union College, died in Lodi. Rodney Hudson, lawyer and son of pioneer David Hudson, died of it in Bakersfield.

The virus would have permeated the towns of the Napa Valley anyway, because the disease was so easily transmitted. But it received extra momentum on October 18, when the long-awaited "Trophy Train" rolled into Napa. The Trophy Train carried a special exhibit of war materiel, much of it captured from the

Germans in France. On display were Colt's machine guns, Lewis machine guns, artillery guns, automatic rifles and shells of all kinds. There were helmets and gas masks, including some worn by the enemy. There was an Austrian rifle with a hand grenade attached to the muzzle. Especially fascinating to many was a knife with a death's head on the haft, said to have been used by a German soldier to slit the throats of American prisoners. Captain George C. Gardner was in charge of the event and present to impose order on the 3,457 people who passed through the train during its three-hour stay that Friday morning. He was accompanied by Mayor E.J. Drussel and the rest of the City Council (of which Gardner was also a member). The very next day, Gardner, Drussel and most of the rest of the council came down with the flu, as did hundreds of others.[5]

It came to the other communities of the Napa Valley in full force about a week later. Oscar Abram Clark, 37-year-old member of the biggest landowning family in Berryessa, died of the virus around October 23. Seventy-six year-old Mrs. Mary Clark may have caught it at the funeral; she died in Oakville in November.

Old Edwin Angwin, patriarch of Howell Mountain, died of a heart attack the last week of October, followed immediately by his daughter, Mrs. Ethel Sylvia Johnson, who died of the flu. The minister who conducted their funeral, Rev. H.C. Shropshire, lost his six-year-old son to the epidemic that same week. Angwin's heart attack might well have been the flu, because it was not at all uncommon for that vital organ to be a target of the disease. Autopsies of flu victims often revealed swollen, bloated hearts. Edwin Laurence Angwin, Ethel's brother and Edwin's oldest son, died of the disease in January, 1919.

A St. Helena doctor, F.C. Newton, went to San Francisco to help at an emergency clinic that had been set up to receive the massive influx of flu cases there. Dr. Newton did not get sick. One of his colleagues at the clinic took to smoking big black cigars in the wards. "The juice from the cigar butt has considerable

---

[5]The councilmen all recovered, but Gardner resigned to become the Napa County Recorder, a post he held until 1926.

antiseptic power," explained the *Journal*, "while the smoke, though slightly irritating to the throat membranes of some people, has a deterrent action on any bacteria."[6] Hospitals, however, soon proved to be inadequate for treating the illness and were in many instances instrumental in helping its spread. Napa State Hospital suffered the most intense outbreak of the virus in the county. Dozens of patients died there during the epidemic's three-and-a-half month life in the area, and hundreds were sickened. Numerous attendants also perished. The epidemic was so severe at Napa State that when an Austrian immigrant named August Groff went berserk in Chiles Valley, he had to be detained in Oakville until the virus at the mental institution ran its course.

Carol Wyckoff died of it at Camp Colt near Gettysburg, Pennsylvania. His remains were shipped back to Napa for a well-attended funeral where a quartet featuring Miss Jessie Corlett, Mrs. Charles Trower, A.V. Oliffe and Ernest Mayer entertained the bereaved. Many of the guests at the funeral caught it, and three weeks later it was quartetist Jessie Corlett whose short life was being remembered.

Because so many guests at funerals seemed to be catching what the deceased had died of, the Napa City Council asked citizens to restrict the attendance of indoor services to the deceased's immediate family. Outdoor funerals were still permitted. Theaters, saloons, schools and even churches throughout the county were ordered to close while the epidemic was at its worst. The popular Brooklyn Hotel in East Napa stopped offering its special Sunday night dinners. Lodge meetings and other regularly scheduled events were canceled. Husbands were forced to stay at home, where they could defy tradition and help out with routine household chores or, where illness had struck, assist in family crises. Some men, of course, resisted this. J. Ryan was arrested and jailed for public drunkenness while his wife and children, all sick with the flu, had

---

[6] *NDJ*, 10-17-1918. At the time the disease was thought to be bacterial, not viral, and frantic attempts were made to find a serum to counter it.

no one to care for them. "The family is in wretchedly destitute circumstances," said a horrified observer.[7]

City Fathers throughout the Valley ordained on October 23 that citizens could not go outdoors without wearing gauze masks, a precaution that municipalities across the world mandated as vital to prevention. "Mask slackers"—people who refused to wear a mask or wore it improperly—were arrested and fined $15. While the masks themselves might not have actually stopped the transmission of the submicroscopic viruses (millions could rest on the head of a pin), wearing them may have been such a bother that the healthy preferred to just stay home. Anyway, with so many things closed there wasn't much to do. The gauze mask requirement was removed on November 26, and happy Napans threw them into a bonfire someone started in front of the police station on Third Street. But like a monster in a B movie, the virus sprang back to life immediately. The day after the bonfire, Napa State Hospital reported six new cases of flu. Scores more contracted it throughout the Valley, and on December 14 the mask ordinance was revived in Napa. St. Helena re-adopted it a week later.

Quite often it was the caretakers who succumbed, while those who were in their charge fought their way back to health. The daughter of Mrs. B. Maggetti, Mary Varozza, contracted the flu while nursing her own sick child. Mary died. Effa May Walters was the first in her little family to contract the disease. Her husband, Laurel, nursed her as best he could. As his wife lay near death in their top floor apartment at the Kibble Building in downtown St. Helena, their toddler, Curtis, fell ill too. Then Laurel caught it and quickly perished. Three days later, Curtis died. Father and son were buried together in the same casket, Curtis resting as if asleep in the arms of his father. Effa May survived.

Madeline Bassett, a nurse who had been assisting the ill, came down with it herself and made it home to St. Helena by the electric railroad in time to die. A young woman who answered the newspapers' pleas for nursing volunteers, Katherine Fairbanks, left her home in Napa to attend the sick in Grass Valley. She joined

---

[7] *NDJ*, 10-31-1918.

them in their illness and became a casualty, too. St. Helena physician Dr. Lawrence Welti did not seem to come down with the flu, but his 4-year-old daughter did. His wife then caught it, and in her the disease accelerated so quickly that Dr. Welti panicked. He rushed her to San Francisco, where he hoped she could get the best care available. She died en route, on the ferry. One of her sisters, Mrs. Roscoe Griffin, came down with it the day Mrs. Welti died. Already afflicted with asthma, she, too, perished.

Two men rooming together in Pope Valley, George Rhode and James Samuels, both fell ill with influenza. They hired a nurse, George Washington Mann, to tend to them. Mann had been a doctor but had turned to nursing, perhaps because it more fully expressed his personal mission to care for others. Mann arose at 3 AM on the morning of January 13, 1919 to administer medicine to his charges, then went back to his cot, which was placed in front of the woodburning stove for warmth. An hour later the sick men heard a clatter, as if someone had fallen. After a silence of several minutes, Samuels, whose condition was less critical than Rhode's, got out of bed to investigate. He found Mann's body slowly roasting on the side of the stove. He moved it, covered it with a sheet and waited until morning, when Sam Haus, a neighbor, would come by to tend to the morning chores. The official cause of death was heart failure: Mann's heart was strangely bloated. Mann's father had died of the same condition a month earlier.[8]

Alexander Hull, Health Officer for the City of Napa, worked day and night throughout the epidemic until it captured him as well. He struggled with the disease for a week but was defeated. He was 33.

People were astonished at how many of those felled by the virus were in the prime of their lives. Irwin Wilson of Calistoga was sick less than five days before he died, and an hour before he was stricken appeared to be in perfect health. David Scribner of Napa, the city clerk, was in line to advance to greater prominence when he fell ill. His case was among the many that deteriorated into pneumonia. He left a wife and a four-year-old daughter. Mrs.

---

[8] *SHS*, 1-10-1919. The older Mann dropped dead while crossing the street.

F.W. Mielenz, Secretary of the Women's Improvement Club in St. Helena, had just moved into a house formerly occupied by Mayor Swortfiguer on the corner of Madrona and Main Streets. She spent the day happily arranging things in her new nest, went to bed and never got up again. The elderly and the infirm succumbed to its ravages as well. Two of the most tragic cases involved women who were near term in their pregnancies. Lena Nichelini of Calistoga, wife of William A. Nichelini, was already the mother of an 18-month-old baby. Lena came down with the flu the day after Christmas. Two days later, terribly ill, she gave birth to twins, a boy and a girl. She died within a week. Rosalie Dellapietra of Napa was also nine months pregnant when the Spanish Lady visited her. She, too, gave birth while in the throws of the illness, and she, too, died. Her husband died of it a few weeks later, orphaning the couple's four children.

Napa Valley people were dying in trenches in France and in their bedrooms in Yountville; grim reapings were everywhere, and no one knew where the sickle would swing next. In the midst of the plague, patriotism developed a paranoid intensity. War rallies seemed to take place weekly. The papers listed how much each family contributed to each Liberty Loan drive, causing people to empty out their coffers to ward off public rebuke and, for the superstitiously paranoid, influenza. When naturalized citizen August Lutge and his wife refused to donate, the Liberty Loan Committee declared them "undesirable citizens," passing a resolution that Walden of the *Journal* spread across his font page:

> We...censure such actions and refusals and declare them un-American and unpatriotic...and we...do not desire any business dealings with such citizens, native or naturalized, and [resolve] that people of this frame of mind should be completely ostracized.[9]

---

[9] *NDJ*, 10-15-1918.

Local realtor, would-be oilman and former State Assemblyman Walter B. Griffiths authored the resolution, and 26 prominent men signed it.[10]

Lack of patriotism had become a social sin. The Valley's worthies continued their efforts to extirpate the original sins, as well. Napa's Mayor Drussel denounced "rowdy dancing" at the Opera House, which was now being used as an Armory. Mary Selowsky's pleasure establishment, the Stone Bridge Saloon in St. Helena, was raided often. Mary went to jail a few times, and every time she was released she set up shop again.

Infuriated at the persistence of the oldest profession in the City of Napa, authorities raided their local brothels in the wee hours one morning in December 1918. They netted two of the women, but also captured in their dragnet 40 male customers. Some of them must have been esteemed citizens, because their names were never listed in the newspapers.

World War I ended in the middle of the influenza epidemic. Church bells rang, and there was celebration, but in Napa County there may not have been the untrammeled joy that would be expected. Too many people were mourning their losses to rejoice over their victory, and parties may have been less spontaneous when everyone had to wear gauze masks. In Rutherford, Armistice Day festivities resulted in a big fire that burned down the village hotel and several other buildings: just one more misery in a chain of untoward events that seemed to be taking Biblical proportions.

Even after the war ended the draft continued, and America's communities still held Liberty Loan drives. Napa County bootleggers continued to be arrested for selling liquor to sailors and soldiers slipping away from Mare Island. Other things continued as

---

[10] They were A.L. Voorhees. Chairman; A.H. Smith, Henry Brown, H.H. Sawyer, F.H. Daly, E.L. Bickford, Joseph Migliavacca, J.C. Sweet, A.G. Prouty, J.E. Beard, E.J. Drussel, C.E. Trower, Dr. T.H. Stice, W.R. Walling, F.G. Noyes, E.G. Manasse, Robert Lamdin, William Schwarz, S.G. Fisher, William Bamburg, Robert Corlett, F.G. Easterby, E.M. Gifford, Joseph Schuppert, Father John Cantillon and Harry Morris.

before, too. Theodore Bell ran again for Governor of California, this time as an Independent with the endorsement of the Democratic Party. He contracted a mild case of the flu and had to curtail his campaign stump for several days. He recovered, but the voter turnout was light, and he lost again. He was beaten by a wider margin than before, although for the first time all the papers in Napa County supported him. His defense of the wine industry against the storm surge of Prohibition was stalwart, and California voters defeated the Drys statewide. The battle was won, but Wet forces were losing the war.

Chapter Eight

Prohibited

On November 29, 1918, President Wilson signed into effect a law upholding the emergency anti-alcohol measures he had approved back in the spring. This apparent endorsement of Prohibition paved the way for further, ever more restrictive legislation. On January 16, 1919, Congress passed Texas Senator Sheppard's "bone dry" constitutional amendment to outlaw liquor in America. The amendment's terms were explicit:

> After one year from the ratification of this article, the manufacture, sale or transportation of intoxicating liquor within, the importation thereof into, or the exportation thereof, from the United States and all territory subject to the jurisdiction thereof, for beverage purposes are hereby prohibited.

The alcoholic beverage industry would thus go belly up at 12:01 AM, January 17, 1920. Its authors called it "the greatest piece of moral legislation in the history of the world."[1]

Just before the 18th Amendment went into effect, Congress provided the machinery for implementing it. Its author was a dour Norwegian with a big mustache, Andrew J. Volstead, a Republican from Minnesota, but the real brains behind Volstead's act belonged to trim and tidy Wayne Wheeler of the Anti-Saloon League. The

---

[1] *NDJ*, 1-17-1919.

passage of the Volstead Act marked the pinnacle of Wheeler's success as a behind-the-scenes political manipulator.

The Volstead Act offered some large loopholes. Exempted from it were industrial alcohol, sacramental wine, some patent medicines and toilet preparations, flavoring extracts, syrups, vinegar and cider. It was permissible for doctors to prescribe one pint of alcohol per patient per 10-day period and for heads of households to make up to 200 gallons of wine for their family's use. The Volstead Act gave agents of the Treasury Department the right to investigate suspected violators and specified the penalties for conviction. President Wilson vetoed it, because he saw that it meant a gross infringement on the basic liberties of US citizens, but his epiphany came too late. Swept up in the bone-dry current, Congress overrode his objection

Winery people reacted to the passage of the 18th Amendment in various ways, according to their personal styles. Realistic about the need to cope with a force he could not control, Bismarck Bruck introduced a bill to have a committee of five appointed, with instructions to determine how much money the state's winemakers would lose because of Prohibition. He wanted them to be reimbursed for their losses.

The ever-litigious Theodore Bell immediately challenged the amendment. Representing Calistoga vintner Ephraim Light, he obtained an injunction to freeze California's ratification of the amendment, on the grounds that the people themselves had only months earlier voted it down. If Bell won his case, other states would do the same, and the Wets could at least win a stay of execution. Bell and Light lost.

At Greystone, Superintendent Anker Miller prepared labels describing the California Wine Association's wine as sacramental.[2] He signed an affidavit assuring that it was made for purposes other than as a beverage. In addition, he got ready to go into the grape juice business, as did J.H. Wheeler on Zinfandel Lane.

Georges De Latour of Beaulieu readied to make altar wine, utilizing his many contacts in the Catholic Diocese of San

---

[2] Sacramental wine could not be above 18% alcohol.

Francisco. Having worked as a representative for a cream of tartar company before starting his winery, de Latour was one of the few vintners who envisioned a market for his product in other industries. He was able to sell wine legally as an additive in curing tobacco.

The Beringer family built a dehydrating plant to dry their grapes, and they put together a few contacts for a small sacramental wine business. They tightened their belts and hoped for a better day.

The Charles Krug winery scrambled to find a way to de-alcoholize wine so it would maintain its taste, thus staying within the law. They failed and eventually gave up, and where once cellar workers had been dragging hoses, soon spiders were spinning webs.

Joseph Migliavacca planned to make wine that he could sell before January 17 and arranged to turn over the winery to Napa's German *braumeister*, George Blaufuss. Previously Blaufuss had been the owner of the Napa Brewery, making beer in huge vats at his plant on Soscol Avenue and Eighth Street; now he would make cider—at least for a while.

Lafayette Stice at Sutter Home Winery met with Theodore Bell, who optimistically encouraged him to plan on leasing the winery as before and going through with the crush. Bell still believed that wine would be exempted from the amendment. Stice promised to "take care of" the growers from whom he agreed to buy grapes, as did Gaetano Rossi and John Poggi, who had a winery on Spring Street in St. Helena.[3] Felix Salmina said he would crush. So did W.F. Bornhorst.

The Doak family at *Far Niente* elected to dispose of their inventory. Barrel after barrel of pungent wine ran into the ground, most of it not very good anymore. Doak had not put much effort into rehabilitating the winery when he bought it from John Benson's heirs in 1917.

In August, Bell once again represented Light, in a last-ditch effort to dodge the law. Bell and Light argued that wine should

---

[3] *SHS*, 8-27-1919.

never have been included in Wilson's emergency war measures, because it is not made from a basic staple, like beer and whiskey, which derive from grains. Despite affidavits from numerous sources attesting to wine's non-food nature, Prohibition lawyers Annette Adams and Justus Wardell convinced Judge van Fleet to rule against the wine industry.

Soon after, the Treasury Department ordered all producers of alcoholic beverages to inventory the unsold product still on hand so it could be disposed of. Anyone wishing to make wine before January 17, 1920 needed a special permit.

The season, meanwhile, was maturing, and the grapes were ripening. It would have been a big year. Left with far fewer places to sell their crop, growers hustled to ship fresh grapes cross country, where there was a demand for juice grapes for home winemaking. Growers needed crates and railroad space. Neither was easy to find.

Just as the 1919 crush began, part of the city of St. Helena caught fire. A strong south wind whipped up the flames, which easily overmatched the town's shiny new fire engine and few firefighters. Reinforcements came up from Napa to help put it out, but not before four buildings were destroyed, two of them hotels, the Grand and the Colombo. The latter had once been the Swiss Union Hotel and before that Elgin's livery stable.[4] The charred remains stood for months, looking grim and symbolic of what was about to happen to the town's major industry.[5]

Thousands of people came to the Napa Valley to collect as much wine as they could before the January deadline. Prices were rock bottom. The Ghisolfos, who ran the Mount View Hotel in Calistoga as well as a winery, laid out their inventory on the floor

---

[4] The destruction of the Colombo was especially hard for its proprietors, Maurizio Mori and his wife. Maurizio had labored many years for Antone Sardelli at the old Lemme ranch on Spring Mountain.

[5] Finally, in March, the Shell Oil Company bought the location and put in a service station.

of the bar and sold it for $1.00 a bottle.[6] Folks stocked up for a liquor drought, which many believed would last no more than four years at the most.

January 17, 1920 came and went quietly.

Federal agents soon arrived to padlock Napa Valley wineries and measure the amount of wine they stored. Well-known places with easy access and widely recognized names were the first they visited. The Neibaum family, owners of Inglenook, for example, found their large private collection encased in chicken wire and every entrance locked shut. They eventually found a way in.[7] The Ewer family experienced the same lockout at their winery in Oakville. They, too, had to sneak in to enjoy their own wares.[8]

The Ghisolfos' winery just south of Calistoga was another early visitation site. Treasury officials carefully counted every bottle, measured every barrel.

At first, most vintners made an effort to abide by the unpopular law. When a year had passed and it was still in effect, though, and when word of rumrunners on the West and East Coasts and bootlegging operations in the big cities reached Napa Valley ears, many had second thoughts about the virtues of obedience. Those who thought they could get away with it cleaned out their barrels and got back to work.

Small, out-of-the-way wineries had an easier time sidestepping the law. Besides the Ghisolfos', there were more than a dozen little wineries in the Calistoga area when Prohibition first arrived. After January 17th some closed, but others went into business for the first time. They sold wine on the sly to whoever happened to drop by with an empty jug. Bootlegging, once simply the crime of selling alcohol to servicemen and minors, now became a cottage industry. Joe Pelissa, for example, was doing a brisk business in 1922 at his Calistoga winery. Up in Pope Valley, Sam Haus and his father

---

[6] Joe Ghisolfo, in *History of Napa Valley: Interviews and Reminiscences of Long-Time Residents*, Napa Valley Wine Library, I, 1974, p. 61.

[7] Wallace W. Everett, Jr., *Interviews and Reminiscences*, III, p. 269.

[8] Idem.

obeyed the law and closed operations by day. During the night, however, they burned candles by the caseload.[9] It might have become easier by 1927, when they brought in electricity. Joe Yudnich had a winery in the northern part of Pope Valley, but he also had a small quicksilver mine. Mines were good places for storing contraband.

Gaetano Rossi knew the value of mines and other out-of-the-way places. "Captain" Rossi came to St. Helena in the 1880's from Chicago's Lakeside District, a mining area. Along with Louis Vasconi, Sr. he operated a small restaurant, the Europa, which was on Spring Street across from the more popular William Tell. He sold out and moved to a mining district in Idaho, where he also worked in hotels. He came back to St. Helena in 1898 after Vasconi died and went to live with Vasconi's widow. Rossi supervised the transformation of the former Tychson Winery (today's Freemark Abbey) into the Antonio Forni family's Lombarda Winery, using techniques he had learned about in Idaho. One of his helpers was a nephew of Antonio's, Charles Forni. Forni was destined to be a leader in the industry, although for now there was no industry to lead.

The Lombarda Winery did well at first, but it ran into debt, and Charles took over. Determined that his vineyards would outlive Prohibition, Charles went to Chicago and found buyers for his grapes, via Rossi's connections. Rossi, meanwhile, bought a secluded piece of property off the Silverado Trail at the end of a narrow country road (the site of today's Joseph Phelps Winery). He went into the wine business himself and bootlegged for fun and profit.

In 1921 the US Prohibition Commissioner announced a small but helpful change in the Volstead law. As of February, medical doctors would be permitted to prescribe wine not just in pints, but in as much quantity as they might deem necessary. Instantly, doctors gained more prestige than they had ever known before, and citizens who had heretofore enjoyed excellent health became ill.

---

[9] Sam Haus, *Interviews and Reminiscences*, I, p. 116.

When Theodore Bell hosted a big social event at his home in Bell canyon, a local dentist, Dr. Stern, and two MD's, Dr.'s Stice and Osbourne, were on the guest list. So were the president of Pacific-Portland Cement, a San Francisco Fire Commissioner, the San Francisco City Attorney, two officials from the American Import Company, a wealthy stockbroker, a famous chef/wine expert, Bismarck Bruck and several other VIP's. Selected locals were invited too, like St. Helena postmaster/general store operator Joe Galewsky and the proprietor of Smith's pharmacy, Walter Metzner, who was beginning to develop a keen interest in small-town politics. Coordinating a major bootlegging enterprise would take planning and the cooperation of many people.[10] If Bell did have such a scheme in mind, these were the kind of people he would need.

The California Wine Association now peddled their product for medicinal purposes, too, and continued to make as much sacramental wine as they could sell. Resourceful as they were, however, they netted nowhere near what they had in the past. In 1925, they sold Greystone Winery to the Bisceglia brothers of San Jose,[11] and the following year they closed their magnificent Winehaven.[12]

Down in East Napa, Dave Cavagnaro, whose Brooklyn Hotel was always a popular gathering place, saw in the medical exception an opportunity to put beer back on his menu. He approached George Blaufuss with a suggestion. "This county's drying up," he said. "Why don't you brew some beer? We could all use some medicine."

Startled but pleased, Blaufuss asked, "But what about the police?"

"We are the police," said Dave. "We'll fix everything. How much will it cost to start up?"

---

[10] Also on the guest list were Edward Bell and local businessmen Philo Grant, and Julius and Jake Goodman.

[11] *WC*, 4-24-1925. The Bisceglia brothers had a large sacramental wine trade.

[12] *NJ*, 1-31-1926.

"Well, I'll need hops and malt, and bottles, and labels…"

"No labels!"[13]

Dave was right: the local constabulary would be no problem. His brother Henry Cavagnaro (AKA "Punch" because of his fighting skills) was the city's leading traffic officer, and good old Charlie Otterson was now the Chief of Police as well as the Fire Chief. Blaufuss was back in business. Hundreds of Napans lined up at the brewery every day, and the scent of fermentation perfumed the air all over town.

It was no secret that wine, brandy, beer and other alcoholic wares were available in the Napa Valley. Practically every organization in the county hosted big barbecues and picnics open to the general public, to which Bay Area residents would flock on the weekends with empty containers in their cars. Alcoholic beverages were available by the jug or the glass. Well-known wineries produced a minimum of the beverages. Most of it came from small producers like the Ghirardelli family on Spring Mountain Road, who made not only wine, but apricot brandy and corn whiskey, as well.[14] During one of St. Helena's annual Vintage Festivals,[15] there were so many drunks in town that the liquor-friendly *Star* actually complained. Mackinder attributed the phenomenon to the great supply of jackass brandy on hand. Good Napa Valley products weren't cheap, but now that the War was over, people no longer needed to buy Liberty Bonds and had a little more money to spend.

Now there were "droves and swarms"[16] of autos coming to the Up-Valley on weekends. Highway 29 became one of the two most popular tourist routes in California. More than 2,000,000 motorists used the ferries to cross over to Napa County one year during Prohibition. They came, of course, for the wine and brandy. It was so well known that fermented products could still be obtained in the Napa Valley that the American Legion made a float about it for a big parade in San Francisco. It was of a boat called "The SS

---

[13] Anecdote courtesy of George Blaufuss, Jr.

[14] Anecdote courtesy of Stella Williams Raymond.

[15] The festivals continued for a while, despite Prohibition.

[16] *SHS*, 6-10-1921

Bootlegger," and it bore a sign describing it as "a rum-runner from St. Helena, where the good grapes grow."[17]

Despite this amazing influx of visitors, there were few places for people to spend the night. The City of St. Helena bought acreage behind the high school and turned it into a campground for motorists. They called it "Crane Park" for George Beldon Crane, the pioneer winemaker who first owned the land. There was also an auto park in Napa. Among other things, the auto parks may have made it easier for bootleggers and their customers to find each other.

The roads—now paved all the way to St. Helena—were jammed. People had been hoping for years for a bridge that would shorten the travel time between the ever-growing San Francisco/Oakland area and the thinly populated North Bay. The first span to be completed was the Carquinez Bridge, but because the routes through Solano and Napa counties were still primitively narrow, traffic remained terrible. Horrific traffic accidents were commonplace, especially in the southbound direction. Not only were the drivers often intoxicated from their Napa Valley sojourns, but many cars had inadequate headlights for night driving. A sharp bend near the County Infirmary on the road to Sonoma saw so many fatalities it was nicknamed "Death Curve." There was, therefore, a big crack-down—not on drunk driving, but on faulty headlights.

It was a car crash that ended the life of the Napa Valley's favorite son. Theodore Bell had spent the Labor Day, 1922 weekend at the Lagunitas Rod & Gun Club, one of the many organizations to which he belonged. He was on his way to his San Francisco residence late at night. The official story was that his chauffeur tried to pass a car on the Bolinas Grade, two miles from Fairfax in Marin County. There was another car coming in the other direction. Blinded by its headlights, the chauffeur swerved to avoid it and drove off a 40-foot embankment, while the other car continued on its way. Bell died instantly.

---

[17] Scharlach, *Op. Cit*, p. 127.

The news was a shock, and there were many who wondered if the tragedy was really an accident. Who was driving the other car? Why did it happen there, the perfect setting for an ambush? Three times a gubernatorial candidate and one of the wine industry's strongest advocates, he had followers everywhere, but he also had enemies.

Some 800 mourners attended his funeral, which was held at the Native Sons' hall in St. Helena—the largest space in town. It was the biggest funeral St. Helenans had seen so far, with people coming from all over the state to honor him. Bell was missed by many, but particularly by John Walden of the *Journal*.[18]

Bell left behind a wife, Annie, and a brilliant daughter, Maurine, who had just graduated from Berkeley with highest honors in philosophy. She was planning to get married later in the month. Maurine usually went by her middle name, given to her in honor of one of Shakespeare's great heroines, the female lawyer Portia. Later, as Portia Bell Hume, she, too, would gain fame; not as a lawyer but as an advocate for humane, effective mental health treatment. Portia Bell Hume has often been called the "Mother of Modern Mental Health."

The need for lawyers was definitely growing, because there was a pronounced rise in the crime rate in the Napa Valley. Bootlegging was only part of the problem. Because of a widespread rumor that Napa Valley citizens hoarded alcohol in their garages, there was a rash of garage burglaries, and people were warned to buy locks.

There were other problems. High rollers in big cars drove off with trunks full of "samples" from small winemaking enterprises

---

[18] In January of '22, Walden had sold half interest in his enterprise to a long-time employee, David Wilson of Napa, and a Vallejo man named Edward Longan. It is fascinating that there is no record of the paper being published for the next two days. Did Walden shut down the presses, or did he speculate in print about the crash, and were these two issues later removed from the *Journal's* archives?

like that of Stephen Jackse.[19] They promised to pay later but never did.

A gang working for the Southern Pacific diverted a railcar full of wine en route from Rutherford to points east. They broke the seal, emptied the car and placed its contents in a second freight car, then resealed the original one and sent it on its way. They re-routed the car with the wine in it to Napa Junction, where someone bought it for $8,000.[20]

Train robberies and the diversion of legal and illegal alcoholic products were a big problem nationally. The Christian Brothers had a winery in Martinez, where Brother Rayfield made sacramental wines and kept fastidious records so the government wouldn't bother the Order. Fearful that their wares would be stolen from the freight trains en route to the market, the Brothers packed the wine in barrels of flour, labeled "Mt. La Salle Products." They prayed earnestly for the safe arrival of their goods and for Repeal.[21]

Five tourists approached a French worker at Beaulieu and demanded to be let into the cellars where de Latour stored his inventory of sacramental, industrial and medicinal wines.[22] When the worker resisted, one of the men pulled out a gun. The worker ran around the building and yelled for the night watchman, who grabbed his own gun and fired birdshot at the would-be thieves. They jumped into their Ford touring car and drove off. A few days later, eight barrels of wine were discovered missing from the winery. St. Helena's Constable Johnson soon apprehended the five tourists, but the barrels of wine were never found.[23]

Two men knocked on Virgil Galleron's front door three miles south of St. Helena, asking to buy wine. Galleron said he didn't make it and had none on the premises. The men drew guns and pointed them at him, declaring themselves to be Federal agents.

---

[19] Steven Navone, *Interviews and Reminiscences*, II, p. 238. Jackse's winery was just east of the depot in St. Helena.

[20] *WC*, 9-11-1925.

[21] Brother Timothy, *Reminiscences* II, pp. 208-211.

[22] *SHS*, 12-29-1922.

[23] perhaps because de Latour himself bootlegged them.

They forced their way into his home over his protests, while Virgil's wife ran into the kitchen to telephone the police. Overhearing her make the call, the men fled.[24]

Other consumer violations were more benign. Skirting the regulations regarding sacramental wine was especially popular. Catholics, Episcopalians and Jews consumed most of the altar wine in America. In New York, which had large numbers of all three faiths, sacramental wine was rationed according to the number of members registered in each church and synagogue. Head counts in the pews were greatly exaggerated, and in some cases entirely fabricated. A 600-member New York City synagogue turned out to be a laundry. A delicatessen and an East Side tenement building tried to pass themselves off as places of worship, and the "Assembly of Hebrew Orthodox Rabbis of America" consisted of an Irishman named Sullivan.[25] Episcopalian parishes enjoyed phenomenal growth.[26] All of this activity did not go unnoticed by the Federal authorities, although the local constabulary—heavily Irish—looked the other way.

The first big Napa Valley producer to be caught bootlegging was Theodore Gier. In February of 1920, he and three others were arrested for violating the Volstead Act. Thirty witnesses testified before a Grand Jury presided over by regional Prohibition Director Samuel F. Rutter. Gier, his nephew Henry, his winery manager and another employee sold, transported, delivered, furnished and possessed large quantities of wine made in three facilities, St. Helena, Winehaven and Sequoia, a big ranch in Napa's western hills. Two hundred and twelve barrels came to his warehouse in Oakland for consolidation, along with 50 gallons of sherry and, sadly for Gier, several agents from the Treasury Department. Gier's lawyers were able to stall and delay the final pronouncement of his guilt, but in the end Rutter sentenced the affable German millionaire to three months in the Alameda County jail and fined

---

[24] *NJ*, 3-2-1928.

[25] Behr, Op. Cit., p. 157.

[26] The strictly Dry Methodist Church also grew. Almost 200,000 new converts swelled its ranks in 1919-1920. *NDJ*, 3-22-1921.

him $1500. "I did not anticipate any such fate as this," Gier told reporters, as the guards handed him a plate of stew and bread, "but I'm going to play the game like a sport."[27] The warden allowed his wife to bring him extra pillows and blankets for his rheumatism, but he was not afforded any other niceties.

Once they had Gier in their crosshairs, they were unwilling to stop targeting him, perhaps because of the bad reputation he had earned during the war. He lost his license to make any kind of wine at all, so after his release he tried to make grape juice, or so he said. The additive he put in his 100,000 gallons of freshly squeezed grape juice somehow failed to stop the fermentation process, and he found himself back in the wine business again. The government immediately swooped down on him, confiscated all the wine and compelled him to pay tax on it of 16¢ per gallon.[28] Over time, he had to sell off most of his land to meet his expenses and pay his fines. He was able to hold onto his large Napa property, Sequoia, for the rest of the decade, but not much else.

Federal authorities decided that Calistoga's Ghisolfo family was a major supplier of illegal wines, so they put them under surveillance for several months. While there was a discrepancy between the amount they were recorded to have and the amount actually on hand, they denied any wrongdoing. So certain was the US Marshall that the Ghisolfos somehow smuggled wine out of the plant, that he placed two agents on the premises. At first the family treated the two agents as honored guests, including them in family meals. As the months dragged by, however, their presence became annoying, and the family tried to have them recalled. The Marshall wouldn't budge. Despite the fact that no one had seen the Ghisolfos bootlegging, their wine was ordered destroyed. Nathan Ghisolfo, the patriarch, chose to fight the order in court and received an injunction that delayed the destruction. He waited anxiously.

The axe landed on George Blaufuss's beer operation August 1, 1922. Privy through his patrolman brother "Punch" to the plans of men with badges, Dave Cavagnaro warned the brewer on the night

---

[27] *SHS*, 5-11-1923.
[28] *SHS*, 12-24-1926.

George Blaufuss, Sr., brewed beer before and during Prohibition. Photos courtesy of George Blaufuss, Jr.

Superior Court Judge Percy King, Sr., above, protected many Napa Valley citizens from the consequences of behaviors that conflicted with the Volstead Act.

Dave Cavagnaro, below, was one who appreciated this. Dave owned a saloon and was considered the unofficial mayor of the wine-loving Italian section of the City of Napa.

Photo courtesy of John York

of July 31 that the authorities would be coming the following morning. Blaufuss and his wife were devastated, but City Attorney Wally Rutherford—also an insider—told them, "Don't worry. We'll fix everything."

The Blaufusses and their friends worked all night to bottle as much beer as they could (some of it was fermenting and could not be bottled) and hid it all over town. A lot of it went into a water tank behind the Brooklyn Hotel and into a barn at the State Hospital. When the T-men came the next afternoon, they arrested George for "having in his possession and unlawfully manufacturing liquor commonly known as beer, and containing more than one half of one percent of alcohol by volume."[29] It was a crime punishable by up to $10,000 and five years in prison. Blaufuss was sent before Commissioner James Palmer with bail set at $1,000, which was immediately posted by Knox Granatelli and Ernest Borreo. He was supposed to go to Sacramento to be tried, but Napa Judge Percy King quickly interceded. King heard the case, found him guilty, charged him a mere $200, closed the case and released him. Blaufuss had to drain the beer that was still fermenting into the Napa River, polluting the fish. Judge King also ordered him to donate 200 cases to the Veterans' Home at the Presidio in San Francisco and an additional 200 to the Veterans' Hospital in Palo Alto, for "medicinal" purposes. Wally Rutherford and Judge King's help in the matter endeared them to Napans, who loved their beer. Rutherford later became the DA, and King the lead judge of the Superior Court. Judge King's tendency to protect some but not others intensified as time went by, as shall be seen.

In October the Feds broke up a major bootlegging ring in Sonoma County that had participants in the Napa Valley. Included in the bust were Armand Regnier and his wife, who operated a small winery in Oakville. Winemakers from several spots in Northern California contributed their wares to the ring. Frank Silva was the Regniers' defending attorney. When Prohibition had first passed, Silva had gone to San Francisco to accept a post as a special prosecutor for Volstead cases. Fervently patriotic, he had

---

[29] *NDJ*, 8-2-1922.

been very active in the Liberty Loan drive and in recruiting young men for the war. He soon discovered, though, that he had chosen the unpopular side. Few in San Francisco favored the Dry laws. Matthew Brady, the DA in San Francisco, was Vice President of the California chapter of the Association Against the Prohibition Amendment.[30] San Francisco's sheriff, Tom Finn, also opposed the law. Silva returned to his practice in Napa and repented by defending violators. He wasn't able to get the Regniers off the hook, however.[31]

On December 21, 1922, the Wright Act went into effect, a California law that mandated sheriffs, constables, DA's and other peace officers to enforce the Volstead Act. Whether they wanted to or not, they now had to pursue an aggressive course against bootlegging. Napa Police Chief Otterson, who liked alcohol and disliked taking orders from anyone, quit.[32] It was weeks before the city was able to find a replacement.

The sheriff, Berryessa's tee-totalling Joe Harris, stayed on and, with a few deputies, got to work orchestrating raids of Napa County's thriving liquor industry. One of the first whom Harris targeted was Andy Bartolucci, who allegedly sold wine and jackass brandy to patrons at his little Oakville restaurant (formerly a saloon).[33] Only Mrs. Bartolucci was present when Sheriff Harris and his men entered the place with their warrants, and the family was able to get the case dismissed for insufficient evidence, although alcohol was found and confiscated. The Bartoluccis tore down the saloon, but they still owned a winery that had once belonged to August Jeanmonod, a pioneer vintner who had recently passed away. Whatever further plans they might have had for bootlegging went up in smoke when a fire burned down their home,

---

[30] Coffey, Op. Cit., p.168. Many of the liquor manufacturers contributed to this group.

[31] *NDJ*, 10-8, 10-19-1922.

[32] Otterson was both Chief of Police and Fire Chief, simultaneously. He left the force but stayed with the fire department.

[33] *SHS*, 1-19-1923.

winery, cooperage and almost new Dodge touring car on a hot summer day in 1924.[34]

Harris nabbed the proprietor of the Hotel St. Helena for selling liquor. The proprietor resisted, and a few things were broken, but no one got hurt. Maurizio Mori of the Depot Saloon in St. Helena was also arrested. He had been in court once before on Volstead charges. Mori was able to get several continuances, but in the end the judge fined him $800.[35] When Silvie Pastorino of the William Tell Hotel found himself confronted with Harris and his deputies, he tried to run out the back door. He lost a 50-yard chase down the street but was only fined $450.[36] G. Bertolini, the proprietor of the Colombo in Napa, had to serve six months in jail for bootlegging, and the hotel was ordered to close for a year.[37]

The Napa Valley was home to many small, illegal wineries during Prohibition, but there were also numerous stills that mass-produced brandy and booze. Mrs. M.F. Evits was "not a bit perturbed" when Harris came upon her little hooch factory at the Oat Hill mine. She ran two stills, a 25- gallon one and a 10-gallon.[38] One of the targets of an August 1923 bust was a major facility concealed in the bushes off Ink Grade Road in Angwin. D. Samuels of Pope Valley and Harold Stevens of Vallejo ran six stills there with equipment and inventory worth many thousands of dollars. They built the plant next to a stream, which not only gave them an excellent source of water to use in brewing, but also provided a thoroughfare for moving the booze. Following the creek bed, runners could travel up and down the mountain without making a telltale trail in the brush.[39]

---

[34] *SHS*, 7-18-1924.

[35] *SHS*, 12-29-1922.

[36] Idem.

[37] *NJ*, 9-13-1924.

[38] *SHS*, 10-19-1923.

[39] *SHS*, 4-11-1924. Twenty-one men and one woman were arrested in this bust. It took a week to round up all the suspects, who included well-

A big still on Hans Hansen's property on Soscol Avenue attracted the attention of Harris and his deputies in the summer of 1924. Hansen was an important man; he had been superintendent at the old Benson ranch since 1917, and his father had been there before him.[40] He was sentenced to five months in jail, but he may not have actually served it. Eleven people from Calistoga, St. Helena and Napa were rounded up in that raid.

Harris bagged a ring of five bootleggers who ran a still from a cabin in the heart of Yountville. One of the men, Andy Zandro, was proprietor of the Yountville Inn. Already arrested at least twice before for bootlegging, he had to stand trial, but it took a long time to find 12 impartial jurors who were willing to sit for the case.

Most of the people snagged in Sheriff Harris' dragnets were men, but there were female bootleggers, as well, like Mrs. Evits. Mrs. Gianna Brovelli had to pay $200 for selling liquor.[41] A 13-year-old girl was taken into custody in Calistoga along with A. Acquistapace and five other men, who were transporting a load of booze.[42] Over in Sonoma County, Emma Fetters of Fetters Hot Springs was among a dozen arrested in a bust at the US Bar on Fourth Street. There was a scuffle as one of the apprehended men tried to wrest the gun from a detective. The shock of the experience may have overwhelmed Mrs. Fetters, because she died less than two weeks later.[43]

Harris raided Calistoga restaurants frequently. He hauled in G. Musante of the Railroad Hotel, Pete Pizzutti of the Fior D'Italia Café at 302 Lincoln and Peter Molo of the Monte Carlo "resort" on Diamond Mountain Road. Molo's resort—aka speakeasy—was ordered to shut down permanently, because it was deemed a public nuisance. A. Brenta of the Swiss Chalet had to spend three months

---

known people like Charles Tucker, Joe Bianchi, Theodore Arighi, A. Nichelini and Joe Yudnich.

[40] *SHS*, 8-8-1924.

[41] *NDJ*, 10-31-1922.

[42] *SHS*, 12-21-1923.

[43] *NDJ*, 8-3-1922.

in the county jail and pay $500; the waiter who served the liquor there was also made to pay.

Calistoga's Joe Nolasco was one of 17 men arrested in August of 1923.[44] The August 1923 raid was a major one. It netted nine barrels of wine, several dozen bottles of liquor and a case of "real scotch whiskey," and it brought in $6,600 in fines. Besides Nolasco, A. Nichelini, Joe Baldocchi, A. Negri and Maurizio Mori were among the arrested: all well-known, well-liked Valley men.[45] Since Mori had been nabbed before, he had to pay the biggest fine.[46] Napans gathered around the truck and gawked as deputies unloaded the evidence in the Courthouse yard. No one had seen that much booze in a long time.

Napans could gape at an even bigger display of Wet goods the following year. When the authorities raided the Calistoga Hotel in the fall of 1924, they stored the evidence at Switzer's warehouse on Laurel Street, but its presence was a huge temptation for the neighbors. Shortly before Thanksgiving, when wine-lovers were getting ready to stock up for the holidays, Sheriff Harris helped his men pour 800 bottles of chianti and champagne and 700 barrels of red and white table wine on the ground behind the building.[47]

The raid of the Calistoga Hotel was the biggest seizure of alcohol so far in the Napa Valley. The manager, R.F. Hughes, was arrested on the spot. The owner, Calistoga city councilman and former Postmaster Owen Kenny, was in San Francisco for the evening. He received a phone call ordering him to report to Napa to be arraigned, which he did the following day, sweaty with fear. The

---

[44] *SHS*, 8-17-1923.

[45] Idem.

[46] He was ordered to pay $800.

[47] *NJ*, 11-19-1924. (The *Napa Daily Journal* dropped the "Daily" from its name around this time.) When the raid took place, authorities actually found 11 barrels and 1,000 bottles of wine, two barrels of vermouth, two barrels of crème de menthe and an assortment of other alcoholic beverages. Some of it belonged to other Calistogans, who had stored it in a shed behind the hotel. The rest may have been pilfered after the seizure.

Kennys were ordered to shut down their hotel, but it was still in operation four months later when the "Ropals"—wives and female friends of the local Rotarians—held a special dinner there for their men.[48] Outsiders were not invited. Editor Carroll wrote that "Mrs. Kenny went on with the preparations, notwithstanding her recent bereavement...Much heart-felt sympathy was felt for her, together with a feeling of admiration for her grit to go through with it."

The granddaddy of all Napa Valley raids occurred in September 1925 in Napa Junction, at a place known to locals as "Dago Mary's," a speakeasy run by the Negri family. It was a carefully planned drama. Several months earlier, Harris had nabbed a small-time bootlegger, Emil Pedrini, who had to serve time in jail. Pedrini was somehow talked into acting as an undercover agent for the Prohibition forces. With his help and the assistance of two other agents (Joe and A.W. Mastalatto), Harris, Calistoga Constable Carl Pierce and new Napa Police Chief A.F. Herritt were tipped off to a big rendezvous of sellers and buyers at the Negris' "joint." They put together an attack squad.

A cluster of police cars crept into Napa Junction in the dead of night, and the officers prepared their assault. They split into two teams. Simultaneously, one team burst into the place through the front door while the other came in through the back. The first team found a smoke-filled room packed with people, among them some of the Valley's leading citizens. The officers who came through the back, however, encountered Mary in the kitchen. Enraged at their invasion of her enterprise, Mary threw silverware, glassware, plates, pots and pans, small appliances and everything else she could get her hands on at the lawmen before she could be subdued. In the fray, Fortunato Martini, Joe Tamburelli, Eugene Venturino and Leslie Brisbin got away. Warrants were issued for their arrest.[49]

The raid captured 35 people, including three women. Dave Cavagnaro was among those arrested. He was fined $900 and may

---

[48] *WC*, 2-13-1925. All service and fraternal organizations were segregated according to gender, with the exception of some church groups.

[49] *WC*, 9-18-1925.

have paid the fines of several others, as well. Special police officer Uvoldi (a Prohibition agent) was also caught in the net and dismissed from his position. Immediately afterward, Harris went to Chiles Valley and arrested his own brother, Harry Harris, who also bootlegged.

When the Mastalatto brothers raided the Roma Hotel on First Street and the Depot Restaurant (formerly the Depot Saloon) on Third in February of 1926, their respective proprietors, Venturino and Tamburelli, were forewarned. A fight broke out in the kitchen of the Roma as the Venturinos defended their premises from the intruders, and one of the Mastalatto brothers dropped a revolver on the floor.[50] The Roma bust netted nothing more than a pint of liquor, for which Venturino was arrested and immediately released.

Sheriff Harris declared he would run for re-election, but a month later he withdrew from the race because of ill health. He would probably have been re-elected, because he was obviously doing an excellent job. Sheriff Harris was a highly principled Good Guy. But many people in the Napa Valley were not enthusiastic about Good Guys who enforced what most people felt were bad laws. Good people who were punished for defying bad laws did not like being criminalized. Nor did they appreciate the financial pain of their fines or the closure of their businesses. The community tended to rally around and support those who had been arrested.[51]

On October 20, 1926, the Napa Valley's beleaguered vintners suffered their greatest loss since the onset of Prohibition, greater even than that of Bell. Bismarck Bruck, the industry's most stalwart friend, died of heart failure. During his career he had been California Assemblyman three times, President of the County Board of Supervisors and the Board of Trustees of St. Helena, President of the Bruck Grape Juice Company and Superintendent of the Charles Krug Winery. He was Grand President of the Order of Native Sons of the Golden West and intensely active in all organizations benefiting growers and vintners. He was largely responsible for the original Black Point Cut-off, the institution of

---

[50] *NJ*, 2-20-1926.

[51] *WC*, 2-13-1925.

Admissions Day as a state holiday and promoting the process of bench grafting on St. George rootstock. Bruck was respected and dearly loved. The State Assembly passed a resolution honoring him and his life work. It said, in part:

> During his active career he was known as a man of
> sincerity, of courtesy, of truth, and of the highest
> courage. Whenever he thought a proposition was
> right, he became committed to it. Truth was his creed.
>
> In the pursuit of his aims he was fair and courteous, yet
> he never hesitated in his purpose because of the fact
> that it might, perchance, antagonize a friend or an interest.
> He never sought the even tenor, never avoided frictions,
> for purpose was his ideal. He was fond of his friends and
> they were legion. He had a foresight which fitted him for
> life's highest aims.[52]

The author of the resolution was Frank Coombs, who had re-entered politics after Bell's death and had easily won a seat in the Assembly. Bruck's funeral surpassed even Bell's in size. The rector of Grace Episcopal Church, Father Irving Baxter, was the officiating minister, and the funeral was held across the street from the church at the Native Sons' hall. A huge portion of the town turned out to honor the man who had devoted so much of his life to their well being.

Sheriff Harris' successor, Jack Steckter, conducted no busts at all for a long time. Not even a newspaper ad listing the menu at the Italian Catholic Federation's big dinner drew the squad cars:

Salame
Salad a la Milanese
Raviolas
Roast Chicken
Homemade Cake and Coffee

---

[52]Frank L. Coombs, *California Legislature, Forty-Sixth Session (Extraordinary)*, In Assembly, October 22, 1926.

Beer Extra[53]

The insiders' insider, Nellie Cavagnaro (Dave's wife), was in charge of catering the meal. More than 300 people attended, unmolested by the police.

Big raids continued elsewhere in California, but for almost a year it was as if Prohibition had never happened in the Napa Valley. Steckter and DA Rutherford were openly criticized by some for failing to uphold the law, and there was speculation that the Grand Jury would soon expose a bootlegging conspiracy. No such revelation took place. There was a sense, however, that things did not add up. There was a certain coziness among the well-known and the well-placed; liquor flowed, and everyone knew that Judge Percy King liked to drink.

When the axe fell, its recipient had nothing to do with Prohibition violations: William J. Blake, the Coroner/Public Administrator, was charged with malfeasance in office and misappropriation of funds. He was dismissed and replaced by local mortician Theodore Treadway, brother of Blake's felonious predecessor, C.C. Treadway. That same week, Johnny Walden sold his remaining half interest in the *Napa Journal* to a Vallejo newspaperman, Luther Gibson. (He had divested the first half in 1922.)

The Grand Jury was summoned to a special closed session, and the transitional editor—a son of Judge Percy King—wrote, "those in charge of the situation ask that nothing be said."[54] The Jury's audit revealed that Blake had been pilfering money regularly from the estates (and the bodies) of the deceased.[55] Walden may have been implicated in Blake's chicanery, because the *Journal* charged families a fee for running their loved-ones' obituaries, a practice that was illegal. John Walden's editorial voice was heard no more.

---

[53] *NJ*, 5-4-1927.

[54] *NJ*, 4-6-1927.

[55] See Jesse E. Godley, Foreman, "Napa County Grand Jury Report of 1927." On more than one occasion, Blake withdrew cash from the account of a corpse and deposited it in his own account.

Moody, perverse and hotly opinionated, he had been Napa City's great booster, a man who openly loved or hated local leaders and supported to the best of his ability the small businesses of his modest town.

Unable to find employment after the scandal (he actually ran for Sheriff but lost) ex-Coroner Blake could not keep up his mortgage payments. The bank called his loan. On New Year's day, 1928, he sat down by Sulphur Creek two miles west of St. Helena and shot himself. The note he left on his kitchen table said, "Take me to Noble's funeral home. Let Mr. Ward take care of me. I am tired and can go no further. Blake."[56]

The sacrifice of Blake and Walden may have diverted public attention from greater crimes. To still the critics, Steckter tried to take credit for putting an end to the bootlegging operation of a Mrs. McConnell, two miles north of Calistoga, but it was really Calistoga Constable Pierce who found her still after it blew up chicken coop. Mrs. McConnell's little business was apparently financed by other, wealthier Napa Valley citizens,[57] who remained anonymous and unprosecuted.

Steckter's failure to harry bootleggers protected popular Napa Valley locals, but as the criticism grew, he was forced to take action. Beginning in the summer of 1927, he and his men descended upon the residents of the tiny town of Yountville. Over the next few months, the sheriff and his deputies brought in dozens of Yountvillains for Volstead violations, while arrests in the Valley's other communities were few and far between.

The Feds themselves returned to the Napa Valley in 1929. They aroused indignation by arresting the local war hero, Louis "Bonnie" Rossi of Napa for possessing some 1300 gallons of wine, which the agents destroyed. Judge King fined him a mere $200. Three other persons were arrested at various Valley locations; less shielded by the halo of an admiring public and a sympathetic judge, they had to pay much more.

---

[56] *NJ*, 1-4-1928.

[57] *NJ*, 7-8-1927.

Meanwhile, across the nation, bathtubs filled with gin. Some beer makers in the Midwest converted their breweries into other things, like ice cream factories. The federal government denied the former German brewers permits to produce industrial, medicinal and sacramental alcohol. Instead, authorization to manufacture products of this nature went to small, upstart Italian and Irish companies. Names like "Pabst" and "Busch," long associated with the liquor industry, were now replaced by names like "O'Banion," "Moran," "Drucci," "Torrio" and eventually "Luciano" and "Capone."

Before the Volstead Act, approximately 90% of the nation's alcohol was consumed as beer. The new generation of licensees made illegal beer, but they also traded in equally illegal hard liquor, much of which was smuggled from Canada. In addition, they received licenses to manufacture industrial alcohol. The federal government forced industrial alcohol-makers to include in their product a poison, so that people wouldn't drink it. They drank it anyway and died or went blind, and even when there was an outcry against the needless misery this caused, Dry forces in Congress self-righteously refused to stop the practice.[58]

The Volstead Act ushered in a new age, a Jekyll-and-Hyde world where two oppposing lifestyles co-existed, one mostly by day and the other mostly by night. Saloons disappeared, to be replaced by coffee shops and ice cream parlors. Along with their demise went the cuspidor, the vessel into which men spat tobacco juice while hanging out and shooting the breeze. (The flu epidemic was also partly responsible for ending the practice of public spitting.) Cigar smoking declined. Men switched to cigarettes, the odor of which was generally less offensive to women, who could now join them for a Coca-Cola or an "ice cream fizz," as well as a cigarette.

The 19th Amendment—Women's Suffrage—passed shortly after the 18th. Awakening to the idea that they had rights, too, women left the dishes in the sink and sought entertainment. Couples did

---

[58] Poison American alcohol slipped into Canada, raising the death toll there.

things together more than they had in the past. One place they loved to go was to the movies. Stars and starlets became famous overnight. Napans went to the Hippodrome (the "Hip") and St. Helenans to the Liberty to see Rudolph Valentino, Theda Bara, the Marx Brothers and a host of other new faces. For many Californians, entertainers and film plots replaced politicans and public issues as objects of fascination.[59]

Coincident with the death of the male-only saloon was the birth of the nightclub, a place where, dressed in their finest, men and women could drink alcohol, watch entertainment and smoke cigarettes together.[60] The nightclub was a concept largely invented by a former New York City cabbie named Larry Fay, who parlayed money he made as a whiskey smuggler into a fleet of taxis and a series of high-class social establishments where patrons consumed champagne and booze by the carload and all the beer they wanted. The nightclub idea caught on quickly, and soon most big cities had them. Besides providing a place for men and women to socialize, they offered a forum where gifted people could display their talents. The biggest beneficiaries of this opportunity were those who had heretofore been excluded from the public consciousness. African Americans and Jews, two groups who suffered greatly under the exceedingly prejudiced dominant class, now had an opportunity to make a little money. Artists like Eddie Cantor, Louis Armstrong, Cab Calloway, Duke Ellington and Ella Fitzgerald brought their gifts to an appreciative and increasingly sophisticated audience.

By 1927, anti-Prohibition forces were gaining strength throughout the country. National organizations like the Association Against the Prohibition Amendment protested not only the

---

[59] With the arrival of the movie theaters, voter registration declined in the Napa Valley, as did voter turn-out in elections.

[60] They could also do cocaine together, an important ingredient in the original version of the aforementioned Coca-Cola. Both soon came to be called "coke." The proliferation of illegal narcotics was also spurred by Prohibition.

Volstead Act, but the methods many of the agents employed. In public testimony they reminded Congress that searching homes and businesses without warrants violated basic American law. Congress agreed.

Because lawyers could now successfully argue that improper methods had been used to obtain evidence, bootleggers started getting their cases thrown out of court. Moreover, the evidence could now revert to the hands of its owners.

Nathan Ghisolfo's situation became a test case. He was able to prove that when the Feds seized his wine, they did so without a warrant. He was cleared of wrongdoing on this technicality, and his wine was returned to him for his own use at the end of 1926. Two million gallons of wine that had been similarly impounded was also returned to its owners because of the Ghisolfo decision.

There was another ramification of this, as well. The process of obtaining a warrant made it possible for county personnel who were so inclined to warn intended targets that they were about to be raided, giving them time to dispose of incriminating evidence. There is no question but that this occurred in the Napa Valley. Wet forces rejoiced at this positive turn of events.

The Treasury Department brought the booze war to sea. It acquired from the Navy four destroyers to hunt down rumrunners.[61] A scary fire fight broke out on the Marin coast when smugglers armed with machine guns tried to make a landing and were met by armed federal agents. T-men were not worried about creating international incidents in the pursuit of their ideals. A US cutter shelled a British schooner, the *Eastwood*, because it was carrying booze, and agents seized beer from the first German boat to dock in San Pedro since the World War.[62]

But while the Coast Guard searched the high seas for liquor violators, Napa Valley vineyardists supplied bootleggers with the ingredients. The harvest's far-flung recipients squeezed grapes into juice, and the juice fermented. As a result, grape growers actually

---

[61] *NJ*, 3-18-1926.
[62] *NJ*, 5-29-1926.

profited from Prohibition. Since it was legal for heads of households to make wine for consumption by their own families, wine was the preferred beverage for many who wanted to enjoy an alcoholic drink while staying within the bounds of the law. The demand for juice grapes was strong, and prices rose sharply. Unfortunately, the best wine varietals were too thin-skinned to ship well. Growers had to graft on or replant with grapes that could go long distances in refrigerated freight cars. Georges de Latour introduced Californians to the Alicante grape, which stood up much better to traveling, although it made a very rough wine. Mission grapes also experienced a comeback, because they, too, shipped well, but the wine from the little black berries tasted no better than it had 50 years earlier. In 1923 Alicante and Petite Bouschet went for an astounding $85 a ton, because of the toughness of their skins. The more fragile Cabernet, Pinot Noir, Zinfandel, Grenache and Malvoisie sold for $55 per ton. The following year the prices of everything went up an additional $5.

A railroad strike and a shortage of railcars impeded the traffic in wine grapes for the first year, but when everything got ironed out it was possible for vineyardists to do very well for a few years. Nearly 1400 railroad cars left the Valley in 1923 loaded with grapes, a jump of about 40% over the previous year.[63] The 1927 crush was the largest the Napa Valley had ever experienced. That year, vineyardists filled 3,500 railroad cars with the fruit of their harvest. Prices were a little lower ($62.50 for the Alicante and $47.50 for Grenache and Zinfandel, for example), but the yield was enormous.

A few wineries converted their product into grape syrup or concentrate. The Montelena Orchard Company bought the Tubbs family's Hillcrest Winery in Calistoga and brewed more than 2,400 bottles of "California Sherry Wine Seasoning" a day. Other places concocted "Tokay Grape Syrup," "Riesling Syrup" and an assortment of other flavors. The syrup itself contained no alcohol,

---

[63] *SHS*, 12-7-1923.

but if the handy householder added water and sugar and let it sit for 60 days, it would have an alcohol content of about 12%.[64]

After a good deal of experimentation, Beringer Brothers developed yet another way to make wine. Using a dehydrator that they built on their property, they turned grapes into raisins and formed the raisins into bricks. The recipe for producing wine from bricks was quite simple: One brick plus one gallon of water plus one pound of sugar plus about one week would, under warm conditions, produce wine.

Not everyone in the Napa Valley opposed Prohibition. The increasingly successful Seventh-Day Adventist enclave in Angwin solidly supported the WCTU and its aims, and, when Elder John N. Loughborough died in April of 1924, he was lauded by many in both camps. Loughborough was instrumental in bringing Adventism to the Pacific Coast. Along with John H. Kellogg of Battle Creek, he established the Rural Health Retreat, which became the St. Helena Sanitarium. Thanks to his healthy habits, Loughborough lived to be 93.

Another, vastly different group that spoke out against the wine industry was the "Invisible Empire of the Ku Klux Klan," which opposed not only drinking, but also African Americans, Mexicans, Catholics, Jews and anyone else who wasn't white, Anglo-Saxon, Protestant and and least nominally Dry. Two hundred hooded Klansmen gathered in the moonlight one autumn night in 1923 in a field near Napa State Hospital. Two thousand spectators gathered to watch them ignite a 20' cross, which was held aloft by a man on a horse. The Klansmen formed a square, and the horseman led some 100 initiates to stations within it. About a quarter of the new members wore Navy uniforms.[65] The following year, the Napa branch of the KKK held a similar ceremony in St. Helena, only this time the spectators numbered between 8,000 and 10,000.[66] The KKK chartered a special electric train to the meeting, and someone

---

[64] Coffey, Op. Cit., p. 265.

[65] *SHS*, 10-26-1923.

[66] *SHS*, 8-8-1924.

counted 2,142 cars parked at the site, which was on a field just south of town. Sixty new members stood before a burning cross and swore to uphold the rules of the Klan. Near the end of the ceremony, the leader, Klansman J.R. Bronson, warned the audience that if there were any bootleggers in the crowd, the Klan would "get them."[67] Only 11 people joined the Klan when they came to Calistoga four months later. Klansmen blamed it on the weather, but if they had done their homework they would have realized that the heavily Catholic winemaking community had no use for the KKK. Nevertheless, Klansmen presented the new Calistoga Public Library with a Bible.[68]

Despite the mass of curious spectators who watched the KKK's proceedings, it is uncertain how many in the Valley joined, although Klansman Charles Brisbin claimed there were nearly 1,000 Napa County members. Brisbin ran for city council in Napa, and there was a last-minute rush of voters for him that people at first attributed to the Klan. "It ain't in the rules of the order to get involved in politics," Brisbin said, "and anyway I only campaigned for twenty minutes, and the vote I got came from neighbors. There ain't many men in Napa got the friends that I got," continued Brisbin. "Why just think of people following me down the street to vote for me. I'll tell you, that's something. Well, why shouldn't I have friends?" he asked. "I ain't never done nothing to have enemies."[69] Brisbin's affiliation was offensive to most, and he lost to Dr. T.H. Stice.

Sensing that their power was slipping, national Prohibition leaders fought back. They tried to revoke the permits that allowed heads of households to make 200 gallons of wine per year for their own use.[70] They campaigned to raise $50,000 as a war chest with

---

[67] Ibid.

[68] *WC*, 12-5-1924.

[69] Quoted in *NJ*, 5-9-1926.

[70] The revocation became tangled in technicalities, prompting the superintendent of the ASL to comment, "We are uncertain if the Volstead

which to combat Wets in the Senate. They stepped up their attacks on the powerful and intricate crime networks that had organized in places like Chicago and New York: an underworld that thrived in the shadow of their "greatest piece of moral legislation." Crime syndicates spawned by Prohibition fought among themselves for turf and contraband, including not only alcohol, but, increasingly, drugs, as well. There were bloody gang wars in New York, Chicago, San Francisco and elsewhere. The Treasury Department responded by hiring more agents.

Many of the people who enforced the Prohibition laws had trouble following them. It was common, for example, for proprietors of speakeasies to pay officers for turning the other way, a practice that led to spiraling graft. When Herman Peterman was charged with selling liquor at Napa's Russ House, one of the arresting officers failed to show up at court for the trial. The case was postponed twice with similar results. Peterman's lawyer, Frank Silva, finally learned that the officer had been caught accepting a $10,000 bribe in Santa Rosa and had fled the country. The case was dismissed.[71]

The watchman whom the government hired to guard Theodore Gier's outlaw wine conspired with an Oakland teamster to steal quantities of it and sell it, and he used Gier's wine-filled warehouse as a setting for what the newspapers called "woman parties."[72]

The Association Against the Prohibition Amendment gained ground as the 1920's went on. People across the country were growing tired of the gangsters, the speakeasies, the ever-escalating diatribes against Wets and Catholics. A Chicago-born socialite, Mrs. Pauline Morton Sabin, surprised her sister Republicans by going on record against Prohibition in 1926. A resident of New York, she had been president of the Women's National Republican Club, a delegate to the GOP national convention and a member of the Party's National Committee. Her objection was that the 18th

Act permits such manufacture, but if it does, we will suggest revision."
(*NJ*, 2-22-1931.)

[71] *NJ*, 10-21-1922.

[72] *SHS*, 7-21-1922.

Amendment was causing good Americans to disregard the law. Such widespread contempt for the law, she believed, was bad for the nation. She founded the Women's Organization for National Prohibition Reform. Joining her in this were some of her social peers: Mrs. August Belmont, Mrs. William Draper, Mrs. Pierre du Pont, Mrs. Caspar Whitney, Mrs. Archibald Roosevelt and others of equal wealth and status. Attractive, articulate and assertive, Pauline Sabin was Someone who could not be ignored.

Setbacks like these ate away at Wayne Wheeler of the Anti-Saloon League, but he maintained his monomania to the end. He suffered a horrible personal tragedy in August, 1927 when his wife was burned to death before his eyes by an exploding gas stove.[73] He remained calm and seemingly unshaken by the catastrophe, but he deteriorated physically, and a week later, suddenly shrunken and sallow, he died. A maverick, highly political Methodist-Episcopal bishop named James Cannon took over leadership of the Dry forces. That Cannon was racist and rabidly anti-Catholic did not seem to bother many of his followers. He did lose a lot of his credibility, however, when it came out that he was having an affair. He lost even more when he was discovered to have invested large sums in a shady stock brokerage. It was revealed that the firm, Kable & Company, often told clients that it had invested their money at one level, but actually held their funds until the selected stocks dropped to a lower level, then kept the difference for itself. All was well if the stocks dropped as anticipated. But when the market rose, clients demanded their winnings. Preferred clients like the Bishop did not get this shoddy treatment. Needing the spuriously gained profit to stay afloat, the company could not pay its clients, and it failed. Most investors with Kable lost money, but Cannon made $9,000 in eight months on an initial investment of $2,500.[74]

The Methodist church frowned on love affairs and did not approve of stock speculation. A further blot on Cannon's 'scutcheon occurred in 1930. Monies contributed to defeat the Wet

---

[73] Coffey, Op.Cit., p. 212.

[74] Ibid, p. 252-3.

candidate, Al Smith, in the 1928 presidential election did not make their way past the Bishop's hands, it was charged. What became of it? The Senate subpoenaed Cannon. He testified that the accusations were a plot cooked up by Catholics to discredit him and walked out of the hearing. Frightened of Cannon's great political power, no one dared stop him.

People in the know were seeing weak spots in what had once been the impenetrable Dry wall. Wealthy Americans in England began to buy up good European wine. They stored it in the wine cellars of their friends in London. Surely they intended to drink it some day.

Chapter Nine

Reversals of Fortune

The bottom fell out of the grape industry in 1928. It was sudden, unexpected. The season was late and the quality was down, but those were not the primary causes of the disaster. When Congress tried to tighten the laws on home winemaking, many law-abiding citizens turned their wine barrels into planters; at the same time there was so much hard liquor around that the less conscientious could slake their thirst without having to trouble with crushing lugs of fruit and waiting for the juice to ferment. Wine was a beverage for slowing down, for sipping while savoring a good meal, but America was manic in 1928: everything was speeding up. Perhaps it was the revolution in transportation that brought about this rapid acceleration of life pace. The newest cars could go an incredible 65 miles per hour. Airplanes and dirigibles could cross continents, span the oceans.

This was the age of the "flapper," dressed in feathers and beads; a prolonged episode of indiscretion. Popular music reflected the tempo of the times—it was hot, frenetic. People danced all night and drank. Many drank themselves to death. Twelve thousand died of alcohol poisoning in 1928, more than 1,000 of them in New

York, where there were estimated to be 32,000 speakeasies.[1] The death rate from alcohol was 40 times what it had been in 1920. There were many deaths in the Napa Valley due to alcohol, several of them occurring in Yountville, which by now was viewed by many as the booze capital of the Northbay. Many of the hard-drinking old soldiers at the Home there had no use at all for Prohibition, and their thirst sometimes led to violence. Veterans John Daley and John O'Keefe were drinking together heavily one day late September, 1928. Somehow O'Keefe got hold of Daley's false teeth, and when he refused to return them Daley stabbed him to death.[2] Three months later, the son of a San Francisco police officer brought five gallons of liquor to a clandestine party at the Veterans' Home. It was poisonous and killed three people, including the Home's chief dietician.[3] Both stories made national news and further eroded the little village's reputation.

Edwin Wilson, the old postmaster at the Veterans' Home, fell hard to the illness of the times.[4] The route to his downfall was another intoxicant: love. He met a much younger woman from Southern California who claimed to have psychic powers. Swept away in an ecstacy of infatuation, Wilson bought her gifts. She claimed to see images of things she desired—clothing, jewelry—in a crystal ball, and whatever she reported seeing, Wilson acquired for her. Pretty soon he ran through his savings. In order to keep her satisfied, he dipped into the funds of the post office. By the time he was caught, he had embezzled $2,201.64 to make his paramour happy. He was sentenced to 15 months in federal prison.

Even more alluring to many than fantasies of love were dreams of unlimited wealth. The speediest way to Easy Street was through the stock market. Prices rose throughout the '20's, and by 1928 the market was soaring. Those who had bought in early had made a fortune. The *Journal* wrote of a rumrunner named "Teddy" in

---

[1] William A. Klingaman, *1929: The Year of the Great Crash*, Harper & Row, New York, 1989, pp. 51-3.

[2] *SHS*, 12-28-1928.

[3] *NJ*, 2-21-1931.

[4] *NJ*, 9-28-1928.

Butte, Montana, who had been managing a decent but difficult living "importing" fine liquors from Canada. Teddy was a good man. He charged 50¢ less for beer than his competitors and never raised the price of whiskey in winter months, when snowstorms restricted his access to the supply. His customers loved him, and in gratitude some of the wealthier ones offered him stock tips. Thanks to their good advice, he quickly made a million dollars on the market, enough to retire from the liquor business. His many friends would miss him, the article said.

The publication of Teddy's story may have tempted some Napa Valley bootleggers to speculate with stocks, but on the whole, most of the resident farmers and honest crooks were more interested in borrowing money to get through the coming year. The bad 1928 harvest inspired many to yank out more of their vines and replant with prunes, which for the first time brought in more money than grapes. They weren't alone; farms throughout the nation faced rough times in the midst of what seemed like plenty. Dry Herbert Hoover, elected President in 1928 by a landslide, promised to look into some form of financial relief for the tillers of the soil, who were growing dirt poor.

Five percent of the nation's population had a third of all the money.[5] Among the five percent was Napa's Alma de Bretteville Spreckels, who was now a widow. She made fashion news when she appeared at a function in New York wearing bright red lacquer on her fingernails and toenails: Alma was one of the first socialites to use nail polish. Liquor and fine wines flowed as writers, artists and other persons of note gathered at "Alma Villa" south of Napa on the weekends she was there. She had torn down Patrick Lennon's old ranch house and erected a 57-room mansion, filling it with treasures from around the world. Each of her children had his or her own private wing. A dozen employees lived in a separate bungalow on the ranch, tending to the horses and dairy and running the place. On October 17, 1928, fire broke out in two locations of the mansion. No one was injured, but the villa burned to the ground, taking with it a fortune in *objets d'art*. Two employees

---

[5] Ibid, p. 177.

were eventually charged and convicted of arson. Having money to burn, Alma would soon buy the Sonoma home of her brother-in-law, Rudolph, whose own wealth would go up in smoke in 1929 when the stock market crashed and burned.

Only a handful of Americans were truly experiencing the boundless prosperity that so many believed typified their times. Many middle-class Americans who looked prosperous because of their new cars, homes and fashionable clothes were actually very deeply in debt. The money to pay for these elegances would come, they believed, any day now.

The same mentality affected American industry. Driven by envy of the few who had made killings on Wall Street, the directors of major companies used their capital not to build new plants or develop new products, but to speculate on the stock market. The lure of ever greater riches made some lucky speculators millionaires practically overnight, but it also led to increased instances of fraud and defalcation and a thinning job market, as industries failed to expand.

Stock speculation put the banking industry in a precarious position, although few could understand this at the time. Over-extended because of their own investments in the inflated market, financial institutions would topple if too many of their depositors demanded their money at once. In a time of such heightened emotion, people were prone to panic. There were bank closures like the Bank of Calistoga disaster throughout the 1920's, often due to embezzlement on the part of officers followed by runs on the banks. The Central Commercial and Savings bank of Vallejo, for example, folded in 1925; its assets still hadn't been redistributed two years later, so its former investors sued.[6]

In April, 1927—the same week that the Blake scandal erupted—Charles Kather, an executive with the First National Bank of Napa, stepped into a phonebooth at the bank and shot himself.[7] He had

---

[6] While there was occasional malfeasance in large banks, 80% of the embezzling took place in small, local ones.

[7] *SHS*, 4-8-1927. There may have been a connection between Kather's death and Blake's apprehension.

been with First National since 1904 and was a member of a powerful local family. Financial impropriety was suspected but never brought to light: another result, perhaps, of John Walden's abrupt departure.

Later that year, the French-America Corporation absorbed the principal competitor of First National Bank, the Bank of Napa. St. Helena's Charles Carpy had left the wine industry just after the turn of the century to become French-America's first president. He kept most of the Napa bank's personnel in place. Carpy bought a St. Helena bank, as well, an institution that began life in 1887 as the Carver National Bank.[8] Very soon after Carpy closed the deal, he unified the purchases by making them all part of something called the United Security Bank and Trust Company.

Like a big fish in a pond of fingerlings, A.P. Giannini devoured Carpy's United Security. It was one of hundreds of little trout Giannini gobbled up. He grouped the former Carver Bank bank into his Bank of America of California and bought land on the northwest corner of Main and Adams Streets to erect a big new building for it. Giannini also bought the Bank of St. Helena. This one he tucked under his Bank of Italy aegis, where it joined B of I branches in Napa and Calistoga. Thus both of the banks in St. Helena were Giannini's.

The Bank of Italy worked hard to bring the local citizenry and their assets into its midst. An officer in its public relations department actually came to Rutherford and explained to a packed audience how they could borrow from the bank. There were new criteria for lending in these modern times, the man said. "Formerly," he told them, "it was by mortgage on land or by endorsers on notes, while now the merit of the borrower and his success as a businessman are taken into consideration."[9] He also gave them an elementary lesson in agricultural economics: don't plant when the market is at its peak, because it will soon be glutted,

---

[8] D.H. Carver was an influential St. Helenan who lent money to his vineyardist friends beginning in 1868.

[9] *SHS*, 2-3-1928.

and prices will fall. You might not be able to keep up your payments.

Since his expeditious action during the 1906 earthquake and fire, A.P. Giannini had been expanding his business at a rapid clip. By the end of 1928 he owned nearly 300 financial institutions and had set up a series of branch banks to better serve his growing clientele. Giannini hated the investment craze. He warned investors not to buy his Bankitaly stock, because it was grossly overvalued, and he knew that prices would eventually fall, taking the investors down with it. Particularly disruptive, Giannini believed, was the practice of buying on margin. Speculators could put down as little as 10-20% to buy a block of securities. Their banker or broker would front the rest. As collateral, they used their savings or, often, other stocks in their portfolios. All would be well if their stock made money. They could repay the broker for the loan with the profits from the rising stock. If the stock fell, however, they would have to pay the broker "more margin"—that is, more money up to the full amount of the original investment for stocks whose value was now worth much less.

The very rich might weather fluctuations in the stock market, but the average investor could not. Charles Stewart of Los Banos ended his financial distress by jumping off the steamer *Monticello* on the way to Napa. He left a note for his family that said, "I owe the bank so much money I can never get out of debt."[10]

President Hoover bought into the illusion that the sky was the limit and promoted it to the American people. Brokers' loans totaled nearly $5 billion when Hoover was elected to office, but this did not alarm the man who was known as "The Great Engineer" for his background as a geologist. Wall Street loved him. Hoover for President was "the soundest business proposition for those with a stake in the country,"[11] cooed the *Wall Street Journal*.

One of the stock market's biggest drawbacks was that it could be rigged. Pools of insiders could assert undue influence on the price of securities, driving them up, where they would sell them

---

[10] *NJ*, 3-17-1929. He owed money to the Bank of Italy.

[11] Klingaman, Op. Cit., p.23.

and then down, where they could buy anew. Only a select few (all of them white, Anglo-Saxon Protestants) were allowed into the inner circle. A.P. Giannini was not. To protect his enterprise from manipulation by the other financiers and from being stampeded by a panicking public, he gathered his many businesses under one umbrella, the Transamerica Corporation. Investors could buy into Transamerica, but they could no longer get their hands on individual institutions like the Bank of Italy and Bank of America, which it sheltered. Transamerica had a combined capital investment worth more than a billion dollars by the beginning of 1929.

On October 17, 1929, the directors, employees and friends of St. Helena's Bank of Italy branch met at the St. Helena Hotel to celebrate the institution's 25th anniversary. Giannini and the B of I's new president, Arnold Mount, sent the partiers a telegram congratulating them on the branch's success, as did the out-going president, James Bacigalupi. One big happy family, the St. Helenans responded with a telegram of their own to Giannini and the top brass at their celebration at the rebuilt Pacific Union Club in San Francisco. It was just this kind of personal contact that Giannini encouraged.[12]

Exactly one week after the party, the stock market crashed. It rallied slightly, then went down even deeper the following Tuesday. Respected authorities like A. James Simpson of Marshall Field & Company in Chicago tried to tell the public that business conditions were fundamentally sound, but they were wrong—conditions were rotten to the core. Convinced that government should not interfere with the operations of big business, President Hoover did little to intervene in the rapid downward slide. In December, long after things had spun out of control, he proposed a 1% across-the-board tax cut, thinking this would leave the wealthiest with more money to spend, and that this

---

[12] *SHS*, 10-18-1929. The "big happy family" suffered a divorce in 1931-32, when Mount and Bacigalupi tried to oust Giannini from the presidency. Giannini masterminded a dramatic win in the proxy drive that ensued, and his enemies were forced to resign.

would trickle down to everyone else, causing the situation to right itself. This, too, was mistaken.[13]

Sales of grapes were modest in the Napa Valley in 1929, and prices continued to drop. Other fruit growers suffered similar setbacks. Unable to make a profit on apples, Napa Valley ranchers were forced to let their Gravensteins fall to the earth and rot. Walnut and prune growers might have seen prosperity in 1929—after all, their products were less perishable and could wait for more favorable prices—but a wicked April frost had wiped out 80% of the walnut crop and 70% of the prunes.

Napa Valley farmers were not alone in their loss. The price of other commodities was also plunging. Wheat, corn, cotton, soybeans, indeed, practically everything that came out of the ground or grew on trees sold at lower-than-expected prices in 1929 and into 1930. To make ends meet, farmers planted more crops, hoping to make up in volume what they could not achieve in price. This solution actually exacerbated the problem. Now there were even more grapes on an already grape-glutted market.

Farmers in America's southeast and midwest tried the same thing, wringing their overworked land to squeeze out more production. Just as they were doing so, Nature itself went Dry. A great drought began in the heart of the nation that would continue for several more years.

The bad economy forced vineyardists to borrow from their banks, which themselves were destabilizing. More than 85% of the vineyards in California were mortgaged by the end of the decade for amounts equal to or exceeding their sale value. The cost of food at the store, however, rose. A woman visiting the Napa Valley from Pittsburgh, PA, commented that she had to pay 45¢ for a bag of prunes back East—an outrageously high price for the times and more than most people could afford. Yet for farmers the profit on

---

[13] The Crash of '29 did not in itself cause the Great Depression, although it helped along a process that was already underway. Rather, it popped the bubble of denial in which so many Americans had been living for so long.

prunes was so low that it was hardly worth growing them. The woman said she couldn't get Bartlett pears at all; yet Bartletts had been shipped there from the Napa Valley, and growers had to pay ridiculously high prices for freight.

> Something is very wrong when people in some parts of the country cannot get California fruit at any price, or cannot buy it because it is so high, while growers cannot make a profit from what they have to sell...[O]ur smart Senators [should] investigate where the difference goes between 5 or 10 cents a pound received by growers of prunes and 45 cents paid by the ultimate consumer; and the investigation might...be extended to include pears, grapes and other products of the farm.[14]

Napa County's elected officials did not suspect the depth of the problem now facing farmers and the small businessmen who supported them. Up in St. Helena, Mayor Walter Metzner instituted a number of improvements intended to spruce up the town. Resenting the use of funds for cosmetic purposes, the locals there voted out the three city councilmen most responsible for the beautification effort, electing instead a slate of officers who pledged to "spend only the money absolutely necessary to carry on the affairs of government."[15] Regarding the election as a negative plebescite on his use of city funds, Metzner resigned and returned to his drugstore.

The town of Yountville, still home to prodigies of bootleggers,[16] asked that it might be given, at long last, coverage in case of fire. It received a rural fire engine in February, 1930. The even smaller hamlet of Rutherford was offered the same opportunity, but its citizens declined, saying they could not afford to be taxed for such luxuries.

Charles Trower, who had been Mayor of Napa since 1920, ended his long tenure with a major campaign to clean up the Napa

---

[14] *SHS*, 9-26-1930.

[15] *NJ*, 4-8-1930.

[16] who may have been among the few people in the Valley making any money

River in the winter of 1930. Of particular concern was a spot called "Jack's Point," which had been used for decades as a refuse dump. One of the Mayor's biggest objections to the thoroughly objectionable river was that tourists found it repulsive, an opprobrium that spoke ill of the Valley to which it was still, for some, a gateway. For Napans it was the municipal sewer. Everything that could possibly float in it, unfortunately, did, including dead bodies. Drowning in the river was a popular mode of suicide. Fishing in it also bordered on the suicidal, although people did so every Sunday. [17]A "Napa River Club" formed, wherein 24 local businessmen created a pool of $5,000 for Trower's cleanup drive. Dr. Charles Bulson chaired the Club. Their first project was to move the seven Chinese families who still populated Napa's Chinatown to another location.[18] Unfortunately, many of the small businesses abutting the river could not afford to tidy up their waterfront. Their contemporaries may have regarded them as slackers, but money was tight and getting tighter. Nevertheless, Dr. Bulson's committee planted $5,000 worth of flowers, shrubs and trees and started a park on the site that had been Chinatown.

President Hoover asked his friends in business to voluntarily lower their profits to make life more bearable for average folk. The Southern Pacific responded by ending its passenger line in the Napa Valley and cutting river service from South Vallejo to Napa Junction. It turned the delivery of mail over to the interurban, which was having financial problems of its own and had to terminate its runs within the city of Napa. Grossing an average of $10.50 per month in Napa, the line could not come close to meeting the $63,000 the city assessed it as its share in turning Calistoga Avenue into the northern extension of Jefferson Street, one of Trower's big improvement projects.

An Oakland aviator who wanted to put in a private landing strip bought a hayfield northwest of town from the Beringer family, who

---

[17] *NJ,* 2-25-1930.

[18] What was left of Chinatown hugged the riverbank between First and Second Street.

needed to sell land to make ends meet.[19] Excited by the possibility of luring more tourists, Napa's service clubs leased 80 acres from an adjoining dairy. A landing strip and a hangar were soon in place, and within a month the Napa Municipal Airfield was ready for business.[20] Despite this promising addition, however, the Valley was transitioning along with the rest of the world from a time of modest well-being into a period of scarcity. Napa city officials were shocked to learn that the census showed a population drop of 1,000. Farming was not profitable. People were selling out, moving away.

Before the stock market crash, Herbert Hoover's deepest worry had not been about the nation's finances, but about the escalating violence associated with bootlegging.[21] He cited some grave concerns about abuses in the system, which was now nine years old. Huge amounts of liquor continued to enter the country, and it was very easy to get. Elected officials at all levels, including Senators and Congressmen, drank. Some were accused of protecting bootlegging and narcotics rings. Hoover established a blue-ribbon committee, the Wickersham Commission, to study Prohibition and come up with recommendations for its improvement.

It did not take a panel of experts to conclude that the "noble experiment" was failing in its purpose. Both houses of Congress sizzled with oratory. A retiring Senator from Missouri took the Senate floor to blast his peers for voting Dry but living Wet. "The United States," he roared, "is in a reign of hypocrisy and cant, of violence, chicanery, false pretense and fraud!" He predicted that Americans would soon awaken to the fact that "the Prohibiton law is the worst crime that has ever taken place."[22]

Freshman Congressman Fiorello LaGuardia of New York tried to have the House proclaim that Prohibition was dead. This failed,

---

[19] *NJ*, 4-1-1930.

[20] *NJ*, 4-6-1929.

[21] Ibid, p. 179.

[22] *NJ*, 2-17-1929. The Senator's name was Reed.

and when a fellow Representative from Illinois protested the government's penchant for protecting agents who shot people, the Drys insisted his remarks be purged from the record. A Representative from Maryland urged Congress to stop the practice of poisoning industrial alcohol. His motion failed, but Senator Tydings of Maryland was able to read into the record a summary showing that 1360 people had been killed during Prohibition enforcement. Sometimes members of Congress were themselves discovered breaking the Volstead Act.

The illegal sale of narcotics rose dramatically in the late 1920's. Sheriff Steckter confiscated 160 cubes of morphine and some hypodermic needles from the cabin of a Yountville man named Merle Meyers, who was thought to be the major drug supplier of the area.[23] The bootlegging business tended to be a local industry with occasional large networks like Capone's; the narcotics trade required a greater degree of organization, partly because its basic ingredients usually had to be imported. A woman from a prominent Napa family, Miss Mabelle Bush, became entangled in a high-level scandal involving the State Narcotics Division, where she worked as a secretary.[24] Miss Bush claimed that she was forced to resign because she had uncovered a widespread ring of corruption. If she spoke to anyone about it, she said, certain parties would reveal a personal relationship that she preferred to keep secret. She went public, and so did her affair with a small-time criminal. The chief of the Narcotics Division[25] refused to comment on Miss Bush's charges. At first Governor Young promised to investigate the charges fully, but a few days later he changed his mind. The work of the Division, he claimed, was to cure and rehabilitate addicts; they could not possibly be involved in anything as unsavory as Miss Bush had charged...[26]

The increase in crime associated with the narcotics trade made people increasingly uncomfortable: Evil things were growing in the

---

[23] *SHS*, 8-17-1928.

[24] *NJ*, 1-31-1929.

[25] ex-Senator Frank Benson

[26] *NJ*, 2-3-1929.

191

shade cast by the 18th Amendment. Congress was developing an oddly two-minded view about what it had wrought. When a Dry Senator from Georgia proposed adding $25,000,000 to Volstead enforcement, Treasury Secretary Andrew Mellon opposed it. His Assistant Secretary explained that Prohibition was more effective than ever and needed no buttressing. Obligingly, F. Scott McBride, general superintendent of the Anti-Saloon League, backed Mellon's dismissal of the money. Methodist Bishop Nicholson, James Cannon's successor as head of the ASL, immediately shot Mellon a scalding telegram and saw to it that McBride was relieved of some of his legislative duties. McBride whimpered that he had actually favored increased appropriations, but that he also agreed with Mellon that the funds should not be "handed out haphazardly."[27] The House eventually voted $15,000,000 more to aid in Prohibition enforcement. Everyone waited for the Wickersham Report to resolve matters. They waited and waited.

While they were waiting, Dry forces resolved to investigate the grape industry. To whom, they wondered, did vineyardists ship all those wine grapes? Once the recipients were identified, they could be tracked to make sure none of them made illegal wine from their grape juice. They would begin by gathering data via a questionnaire for people to fill out and mail back.

The Chicago racketeer Al Capone immediately bent this plan to his own profit. Posing as federal agents, his men descended on the railroad yards with questions and forms, as if to take careful records. Consignees of grape shipments, fearful of being investigated, would deny that they had ordered the grapes and leave without them. Capone and his friends were free to haul away whole carloads, at no expense to themselves.

Murders like the St. Valentine's Day Massacre, where eight mobsters were eradicated by a competing gang, made lurid headlines in the Napa papers and on the radio—a new appliance that became a gathering point in every household that had electricity. Handsome four-foot-high consoles with stations like

---

[27] *NJ*, 1-25-1929.

KGO, KYA and KFRC brought otherwise sheltered Napa Valley folk ear-to-ear with an increasingly frightening world. Violence reached the Napa Valley by 1930. Just before the first of the year, an undercover federal agent named Jones bought alcohol from a Yountville couple, the Souths. He obtained a warrant from local Prohibition commissioner James Palmer and went with another officer, Robert Freeman, to arrest the Souths. They found alcohol in the kitchen and set the bottles on the counter, then went out to investigate the shed in the backyard for more booze. Officer Freeman returned to find South pouring the evidence down the sink. He "remonstrated with the alleged bootlegger," and they came to blows. As Freeman and South fell to the floor, South grabbed a gun from the shelf and fired it, but the bullet went wild. Hearing the shot, Jones ran into the house, drawing his riot club. South fired again, this time aiming at Jones, but Freeman forced South's arm upward so the bullet whizzed past Jones' head. Just as he was about to bash South with the club, Jones felt the muzzle of a double-barreled shotgun jab his spine: It was South's wife. "If you hit him," she seethed, "I'll kill you!" South started to rise to his feet. He shot a third time, but as he did, Jones wheeled and knocked the gun from Mrs. South. It went off, sending shot into the woodburning stove. Freeman grabbed his chest. "I'm hit," he said. "Let's get out of here."

Jones dragged the bleeding Freeman to the hospital at the Veterans' Home. He was quickly rushed to Napa's new Victory Hospital on Jefferson Street for surgery, but the 25-calibre bullet that had ricocheted from the stove to his lung did its work, and Freeman was dead in a few days. South was charged with murder.

Calling themselves Fruit Industries, Inc., a cooperative of grape products manufacturers—mainly Central Valley raisin growers—merged in order to heal their ailing treasuries. The co-op applied to major banks for loans and was rewarded, especially by the Bank of Italy.[28] The B of I ran ads in Napa Valley newspapers

---

[28] *NJ*, 5-13-1930.

promoting the idea. "In Unity," they said, "There is Strength." The Unity ad ran in the *Napa Journal* June 12, 1930.

One month later, it came out that Transamerica's valuation had dropped by a billion dollars over the past fiscal year, and the giant's stock plunged. The next day it reached an all-time low, 20 3/8, because investors learned that the dividend would be 15¢ lower than anticipated. Giannini urged investors not to withdraw their money. Many did anyway, and the Bank of Italy was temporarily in no position to help the grape industry or anyone else.

With the B of I thus hamstrung, Fruit Industries worked out an alternative arrangement with the federal government, as part of the newly founded Federal Farm Board's effort to stabilize prices. Grape ranchers who signed up with the co-op would receive subsidies, provided that 85% of all vineyardists joined in. The pressure to sign up as part of the co-op was great, even violent in some parts of the state. If even a fraction fewer than 85% signed on, there would be no Farm Board money.

Never friendly with or trusting of raisin growers, and certainly not happy with the federal government, many key Napa Valley vineyardists resisted. Fruit Industries finally made its quota in time for the 1930 harvest, but only after pleading for an extension. As soon as the sign-ups were complete, Fruit Industries, Inc. began to operate from its other identity, that of a governmental agency called the California Grape Control Board. The Control Board quickly determined that grape tonnage exceeded the market's needs by 125%. It divided the growers into districts and allocated to each a portion of the money pool. Nobody was paid in full, but everyone got something. In Napa County, for example, 100% of co-op members' white grapes were accepted, but only 40% of the black grapes were. Napa Valley growers who signed on were awarded $17.50 per ton for black grapes and $15 for whites, and had to pay a "stabilization fee" of $1.50 per ton. Not a single ton of co-op grapes was allowed to go directly to the consumer. The Board controlled it all. These were the worst returns so far for wine grape growers.

The Fruit Industries scheme infuriated Al Capone, because it meant the end of his premium wine business. In November, 1930 he sent word to his aides in Chicago to "wage war" with anyone who dealt with Fruit Industries. "A few deaths," he threatened, would be the reprisal for any attempt to market wine elsewhere.[29] There were stories of cars being driven off the road by thugs, but not in Napa County; most of the important Napa Valley growers refused to sign up with Fruit Industries. Their primary allegiance was not with the federal government.

Fruit Industries, Inc., bought all its members' surplus grapes at minimal prices for its private use and profit. It produced a grape concentrate it called Vine-Glo, which sold at $10 to $30 per keg and was in direct competition with products like Beringer's grape bricks. Vine-Glo, like the bricks, could be used to make wine. When a Chicago-based company tried to do the same thing (probably using grapes from California) its directors were charged with violating the Volstead Act.[30] Fruit Industries' attorney, Thomas T.C. Gregory, laughed when a US Senator suggested that his company benefited from Hoover's "discriminatory and friendly administrative attitude" toward it. Gregory scoffed at charges that the government harried independent grape growers while it smiled on Fruit Industries' contractees.

On September 12, the St. Helena *Star* reported that the Bank of Italy would be subsumed into the Bank of America, with officers of both institutions combined. Giannini himself came to the Napa Valley that week as the guest of Dave Cavagnaro, to reassure investors that all would be well. Dave drove him around the Valley and later met with citizens throughout the former wine country to reassure them that their money was still safe. Cavagnaro himself bought as much stock as he could.

One person he could not persuade was his friend Theresa Tamburelli, who ran the Depot Restaurant with her husband, who was still reeling from the fines he had incurred from bootlegging. Theresa rescued her money from the B of I and hid it in her house. In a tiny way, she went into competition with Giannini, making

---

[29] *NJ*, 11-14-1930.
[30] *NJ*, 9-1-1931.

loans to friends and neighbors who had become equally suspicious of big business. For the next three decades, she was to be the unofficial banker to East Napa. The Depot was a favorite hangout not only for East Napans, but for the whole city. One evening around this time, after she had cooked up her special veal and cheese stuffing for the raviolis, Theresa was startled to find that she had run out of flour for the pasta. Diners were beginning to arrive. Unperturbed, she boiled small dollops of the stuffing without their cases and served it up as *malfatti*,[31] an original culinary invention that quickly became a favorite. The Depot prospered.

Theresa's sister, Rosie Martini, also had a way with money. Her husband ran the Genoa hotel/restaurant. At Rosie's insistence, the Martinis used whatever cash came their way to purchase land in the northern part of town. A big piece at the corner of Trancas and the newly paved and upgraded Jefferson Street, for example, was among her holdings, and on that location she and her husband eventually started the Napa Valley Inn, which also became a favorite local gathering place and a rival to her sister's.

The wine industry was dead, but there would be an afterlife. Of this no one was more certain than the Christian Brothers, whose prayers for Repeal were apparently not falling on deaf ears. They were so certain the odious ban would go away, that when Theodore Gier put Sequoia up for sale in 1930 the Brothers snatched it.[32] They had been operating their Mt. La Salle winery in Martinez throughout Prohibition, but their new location in the woods on Mt. Veeder, eight miles northwest of Napa, would be much nicer. They demolished Gier's old buildings[33] and put in new ones of their own.

County Clerk James Daly oversaw the incorporation of a new business up valley: the Calistoga Vineyard Company.[34] Its

---

[31] "poorly made"

[32] The Christian Brothers were a teaching order founded in the 17th Century by St. Jean Baptiste de La Salle.

[33] Gier had run Sequoia as a resort, a kind of dude ranch for wine buffs.

[34] *NJ*, 2-22-1931.

directors, Charles Forni, Adam Bianchi and J.C. Flannery, sensed there would be a future for the industry after all.

The same week that Theresa Tamburelli was entering the banking business, Franklin Delano Roosevelt, Governor of wringing Wet New York State, went on record against Prohibition. In a letter to fellow New Yorker Robert Wagner, he stated:

> It is not a matter of the Volstead Act or the Jones Act or any other piece of mere legislation, federal or state. It is the Amendment itself...The sale of intoxicants through state agencies should be made lawful in any state of the Union where the people of the state desire it, and conversely, the people of any state should have the right to prohibit the sale of intoxicants, if they so wish, within its borders.[35]

Roosevelt thus introduced the concept of "home rule," a states' rights theory that denied the federal government's jurisdiction in matters of personal choice. The Democratic Party, a composite of Dry southern conservatives and Wet northeast urban liberals, imploded, the two factions threatening to tear each other apart. In the November Congressional elections, though, Democrats gained control of the House, and the stock market fainted, losing a billion dollars. The Great Depression now had the country by the throat.

The long-awaited Wickersham Report finally came out in January, 1931. In introducing the report to Congress, President Hoover came down squarely and unequivocally for Prohibition, much to the disgust of New York Republican Pauline Sabin and her growing cadre of influential female followers. Hoover thus forced his party into maintaining the Dry point of view and kept Prohibition a major issue for the 1932 presidential election.

Hoover characterized the Report as being solidly Prohibitionist. Close reading, however, revealed that two members of the commission were actually for Repeal, four advocated some kind of revision in the Volstead Act and five wanted further trial of the

---

[35] Quoted in *NJ*, 9-11-1930.

"noble experiment," with strict enforcement.[36] The blue-ribbon panel concluded with what everyone but the most benighted Drys already knew: "there is yet no adequate observance or enforcement."[37]

After the Wickersham Report, prominent Republicans abandoned the Party. Probably the most damaging defection was that of John D. Rockefeller, oil magnate and financier. His family had been among the most generous supporters of the Anti-Saloon League,[38] but it was clear to him that "many of our best citizens, piqued at what they regarded as an infringement of their private rights, have openly and unabashedly disregarded the Eighteenth Amendment."[39] Like Pauline Sabin, Rockefeller feared the ultimate consequences of this widespread snubbing of the law.

Refusing to admit defeat, the Prohibition faction came down even harder, adding wire-tapping to their arsenal and stepping up raids. The Napa Valley was a prime target. Frank Saviez, Stephen Jackse, Jacob Buhman and Ed Haus were arrested for making wine. Eight federal officers nabbed 10 men who operated an elaborate electric-powered still on the Brandlin Ranch off Redwood Road, adjacent to the Christian Brothers' new facility.[40]

A raid in Loveall Valley, a wild and lonely section near the Sonoma County boundary, yielded $35,000 of equipment, 40,000 gallons of mash and 40,000 pounds of sugar. Officers went back to the same area a few months later and found signs of more bootlegging. Agents Buckley and Morgue were prowling the brush for the still they suspected was there, and Buckley tried to ward off

---

[36] The report was cumbersome and labyrinthine enough to allow for misinterpretation. James Reed, a Missouri legislator, called it "a conglomeration of contradictions obscured in a wilderness of words."

[37] NJ, 1-22-1931.

[38] Coffey, Op. Cit., p. 296.

[39] Ibid, pp. 296-97.

[40] Brandlin's place had been the winery of a family named Fischer before Prohibition. Brandlin sold his ranch to Jack and Mary Taylor in 1941, who eventually transformed it into Mayacamas Vineyards.

the chill of the night by sipping from a flask. Two bootleggers—surnamed Prassa and Providently—were in a truck that rumbled up the dirt road leading to a chain gate, the former on the flatbed with a load of sugar for the still, and the latter in the cab, driving. They ran into the agents. Providently had a rifle and shot at the T-men. Buckley returned fire and dropped Prassa, who fell from the truck. He then picked up the wounded bootlegger, and, using him as a shield, continued firing on Providently until he grazed him on the head. Providently surrendered. Prassa died from gunshot wounds to the stomach, inflicted by Buckley.

The agents did find a still; they seized 100,000 gallons of mash and a huge copper boiler. But Morgue testified to the coroner's jury that Buckley had been drinking from a flask and was himself a Volstead violator. Shaken by the incident, Buckley quit working as a Prohibition officer.

Perhaps because the agents of the law were breathing heavily down the necks of Napans, Dave Cavagnaro, "Mayor of East Napa," did an unexpected thing. At the age of 58, he joined the circus, leaving Nellie in charge of the hotel and the children. Fascinated with the sights, sounds, smells and personalities of the Big Top since Al Barnes and the elephants paraded past his front door in 1918, Cavagnaro skipped town.

> He pitched hay, ran errands, helped in the front office, sold tickets, collected tickets, unloaded animals, set up and tore down tents, carried water to the animals…acted as a booking agent, functioned as an advance man, and a roustabout.[41]

While his flight from town may have been merely expedient, his love of the circus was actually quite genuine. For the rest of his long life, Cavagnaro took annual sabbaticals with circus troupes, traveling with the Tom Mix Circus, the Buffalo Bill Wild West

---

[41] Carolyn and Martin C. Mini, *Two Families: Cavagnaro and Guisto*, self-published, Napa, 1998, p. 44.

199

Show, Ringling Brothers-Barnum and Bailey, the Clyde Beatty Circus and several others.[42]

The raids continued. A squad of federal officers busted a huge still operation in the wilderness above Calistoga in the winter of 1931. Five San Franciscans had bought the property from a local man and set up $40,000 worth of equipment, including a new Nash touring car and a Pierce-Arrow.

As 1931 closed, federal raiders driving through Rutherford detected the aroma of mash emanating from a location in the brush near the R.E. Wood ranch. No one was there, but everything was ready for operation. They called it one of the most up-to-date, sophisticated "alcohol plants" ever seized.[43]

The next year they broke up an enterprise at the O'Hara ranch in Conn Valley. It was part of a major booze racket apparently headquartered at a drugstore in Emeryville. Twelve men, seven cars, two trucks and 50,000 gallons of mash were confiscated. Nine liquor depots and joints were broken up in connection with the Conn Valley distillery. Further details began to emerge regarding this particular bootlegging ring. The drugstore, it turned out, was across the street from the Emeryville Police Department, and the officers found a truck full of booze parked in the police lot, between a squad car and the ambulance. The ranch itself did not belong to O'Hara, it turned out, but to former Napa attorney Edward Bell, brother of the late Theodore Bell. Edward's practice was now in Oakland, and it so happened that he was O'Hara's lawyer. O'Hara said that he had sublet the barn where the still was found to someone whose last name was Silva, and he claimed that he had no knowledge of the activity that was going on in there, although the place was in full view of his house. Commissioner James Palmer said he believed O'Hara and returned to him the $2,000 bond he had posted. He dismissed the case.[44]

---

[42] Idem.

[43] *NJ*, 12-30-1931.

[44] *NJ*, 9-10-1932.

To be an adult in the Napa Valley during these years was to play a strange and hypocritical game of cat and mouse. Little children often enjoyed their own variation of the same game, having adventures by pushing fate, skirting the law. Edna and Rita Guisti grew up on Levee Street, now Riverside Avenue along the Napa River near the Sawyer Tannery, shoeless all summer and dressed in ragged cotton frocks bleached by the sun, with bloomers underneath to protect their modesty. They often climbed the big oak of Oak Street, which was by the water. It had a rope swing, on which they swung as high as possible before jumping off into the water. Fire Chief Otterson threatened to send any children he found swimming in the River to the Children's Detention Home: a threat on which he never made good.

Surprisingly, the river was still clear enough to see the fish. On warm evenings carp would come to the surface, and boys tried to spear them with sharpened willow branches, to sell to Napa's seven Chinese families. Otterson strolled along the riverbank at night trying to chase the children away.

Another favorite but forbidden playground was the abandoned crushing facility for the big, empty, bat-ridden Migliavacca Winery on Division Street. Before Prohibiton shut it down, Migliavacca's dumped its pomace into the Napa River via an aerial gondola. Now the most daring among the sisters' friends hauled themselves up into the creaky, unused gondola and rocked it until it would move, risking life and limb.

Grownups also had a favorite, forbidden play spot near the spooky old winery. A German named Bill Manson had a small grocery store across the street. There was a "card room" in the back into which customers would disappear for a while and emerge tipsy. Bill was popular with the kids, too, because he brought back free pocket knives for them from his frequent trips to the *Vaterland*. He was not a favorite with the Treasury Department, however—they shut him down.

Another dispenser of gifts was the Bank of Italy/Bank of America. They gave the Guisti sisters small metal coin banks, from which it was impossible to extract the money that had been dropped in. They had to take the tiny banks to the real bank where a teller had a special device with which to open them.

The big whistle on top of the water tower at the Sawyer Tannery was one of life's regulators for children like Edna and Rita, and for their parents, as well. It blew every day of every year at 6 AM, 12 Noon, and 4 PM. Sometimes the overly loud fire siren blew, too, startling everyone and drawing onlookers. The siren had a special code that advertised the part of town the fire was in, so anyone who wanted could go and watch. A common cause of fires during Prohibition was the explosion of home-made stills. Another was the unexpected spread of the rubber tire fires that people burned to disguise the smell of fermenting mash.

Chapter Ten

Relief

By 1932 most of the country had no use for Prohibitionists or their cause. President Hoover realized that if his party were to have any chance at all in the upcoming election, he had to broaden his position. Former Napa DA and Bank of Calistoga attorney Raymond Benjamin, whose career had taken him all the way to Washington, DC, was now a close friend of Hoover's. He helped the "Great Engineer" construct the Republican platform, which contained wording that echoed Roosevelt's "home rule" option. But it was too late. The American public associated Hoover with Prohibition and with the fact that 6,000,000 people were now unemployed.[1] "We might as well face the fact," said a resigned F. Scott McBride of the ASL. "There will be no landslide in 1932."

Contributing to Hoover's crisis was a widely publicized miscalculation concerning World War I soldiers and a promise they had received. A group of out-of-work veterans in Portland, Oregon, decided it would be helpful if they could cash in early on a federally sponsored bonus that was scheduled to come due in 1945.[2] If the money were theirs, they reasoned, it should be distributed now rather than later. They headed for the nation's capital with their request, and as they did so, hundreds of other unemployed veterans and their destitute families joined them. Soon

---

[1] Coffey, Op. Cit., p. 299.

[2] Arthur M. Schlesinger, Jr., *The Crisis of the Old Order, 1919-1933*, Houghton Mifflin Company, Boston, 1956, pp. 256-265.

their request became a demand, and their journey became a march. "Bonus Marchers"[3] numbering in the tens of thousands took up residence at the nation's capital, living in the crudest of makeshift shelters. Their drama lasted several weeks. Unable to dissuade the marchers from their stubbornly held position, Hoover finally summoned General Douglas MacArthur and his aide, Major Dwight D. Eisenhower, to forcibly uproot the movement. The 3rd Cavalry mounted their steeds and brandished their swords at the vets, who thought at first that the troops had come to honor them. But behind the horsemen came a machine gun detachment, the infantry, the 13th Engineers and six tanks. Some Bonus Marchers resisted and were attacked. The rest ran across the Anacostia River to a huge encampment they had set up there. Contrary to orders, MacArthur pursued them, launching tear gas and setting their wood and paper shanties ablaze. A hundred people died, including two infants. "Thank God we still have a government in Washington that still knows how to handle mobs," said Hoover,[4] who was puzzled why his comments often drew boos.

Bands of dejected Bonus Marchers roamed the country for months afterward and at first received little sympathy from their fellow Americans, because the press published misinformation identifying the group as a gang of communist-led criminals. Napa Valley papers were typical in their non-support of the Bonus Marchers.

Joining the veterans in the militance of their discontent were farmers of the Midwest. Milo Reno, a 65-year-old Iowan who wore a Stetson and seemed more hayseed than economist, evolved as the leader of a brief, grass-roots agricultural revolt. If farmers couldn't profit from the produce they grew, said Reno and his followers, they should withhold their goods from the market and force prices up. They would have a Farm Holiday. "Stay at home—sell nothing" was their slogan. The Farm Holiday failed to make a dent in the problem and resulted in several instances of

---

[3] AKA the "Bonus Expeditionary Force."

[4] William Manchester, *The Glory and the Dream: A Narrative History of America, 1932-1972*, I, Little, Brown & Company, Boston, p. 61.

violence, but its central idea of inducing scarcity would eventually impact Napa Valley grape growers.

Opportunistically, the Communist Party staged a hunger march in front of the Capitol in Washington, chanting "Feed the hungry, tax the rich." They sent agitators to rural settings to inspire what some hoped would be a nationwide proletariat revolution. Red sympathizers were active in several places in Northern California, among them Winters, Vacaville, Fairfield and Sacramento. They did not demonstrate in Napa County, perhaps because the party was actually banned here and a vigilance committee organized to eradicate it if it appeared.[5]

Jobs were hard to come by for younger men. Throngs of shabby drifters blew into towns across America like dust, seeking work. Some 2,000,000 Americans were thought to be on the road in the summer of 1932.[6] Some bundled their belongings into a handkerchief or cotton sack and became hoboes. They rode the rails and set up "jungles," informal communes around warm campfires, where pots of beans and coffee simmered. Some hobo encampments were benign, but many were nasty places.

Only slightly less objectionable to the good people of middle-class towns like Napa were traveling salesmen, itinerant merchants who breezed in with a suitcase full of cheap merchandise to sell door-to-door. Napa merchants grew wary of these gentlemen, because they often wrote bad checks and boarded the next train out of town before they could be caught. A particularly cheeky traveling salesman actually dropped by the Napa Police Department and tried to interest Captain Dick Kermode in purchasing a pair of socks. "You're not going to sell any socks in this city after dark," snarled Kermode, "and if you don't have a license you aren't going to sell any at all." Officer Ed Glos overheard this interaction, and when he saw the man trying to sell socks to Harold McCormick, who ran a service station at Second and Coombs, Glos arrested him for soliciting without a license.[7]

---

[5] *NJ*, 8-18-1935.

[6] Manchester, Op. Cit., p. 20.

[7] *NJ*, 11-2-1932.

Agriculturally depressed and tainted with the stain of much that was rotten about the Prohibition problem, the Napa Valley was spared from the worst depredations of 1932 by some very good luck: its proximity to Mare Island. The shipyard there had become one of the Navy's most favored scrapping and building locations. At the time of Repeal it was the largest single industrial plant in Northern California. Working 24 hours a day, men and women from all over took apart old vessels and built new ones. Mare Island crews received national recognition for constructing a top-of-the-line cruiser, the *USS Chicago*. It was one of the lightest, fastest ships afloat and perfect in every detail, including the fact that it was produced in only three months and only cost $7,780,000, well within budget.[8] More than 300 Mare Island workers made their home in Napa in 1932. They deposited their paychecks in Napa banks and patronized Napa establishments. They were let go each time they completed a project and rehired as soon as new ones came along.

The Basalt Corporation grew up around the massive quarry south of Napa. It benefited from the military presence that Mare Island represented. When the Navy built a practice bombing site in the estuary off nearby Marin, much of the contract work went to Basalt. Barges of rip-rap poked their way down the Napa River and along the winding coastline to fortify banks, make sidewalks and fulfill many of the building needs of the facility. After showing skill on that project, Basalt was invited to help build the Bay Bridge.

A few other Napa enterprises thrived during the Depression. One was the Sawyer Tannery, which was located in Napa's main residential district and employed both men and women. Among other things, Sawyer processed the wooly linings that had become popular in coats. Fleece-lined cloth coats were standard wear for a generation of little boys, who also wore corduroy knickers, knitted

---

[8] *NJ*, 3-22-1931. Less than two years later, Mare Island crews were on hand to repair the vessel when it was accidentally rammed in the open seas and nearly sank. Its life ended in 1943, when Japanese torpedo planes sank it.

caps and high, laced boots. Ten of America's largest sporting goods manufacturers bought leather from Sawyer to produce baseballs and baseball gloves. America's love affair with its national pastime was at a peak: Babe Ruth had his best World Series ever, and Lou Gehrig was on a roll. Calistogans closed up shop and went to cheer for the Oakland Oaks, who chose their small Up-Valley town to practice in.

The Napa Paper Box Company at the end of Pine and Ornduff Streets profited from a fad that brought families together in ways that had not been experienced back when Dad had plenty of cash to spend. Napa Paper Box made jigsaw puzzles, 20,000 of them a week. The huge demand for these fractured paper pictures kept its staff working overtime. The wine industry had gone underground, and agriculture was dying, but at least for some there was still employment.

For others, there was an unemployment relief committee, run in Napa County by service clubs and private individuals to help able-bodied local men (but not necessarily women) find work. The committee sponsored four relief camps in the summer of 1932 that provided work for 84 people. The men cut down trees, hauled the logs to Migliavacca's vacant winery and sold them as firewood to markets outside the Valley, so as not to compete with local enterprises. The largest camp was off Monticello Road between Wooden and Wildhorse Valleys.[9]

As the year matured, the numbers of needy Napans grew. Maud Chaffee of Napa coordinated a mass effort by the Salvation Army, the Elks Club and many churches and fraternal organizations to bring Christmas baskets to nearly 900 destitute local families. The next year a federally sponsored "re-employment" office opened in Napa to help the still-swelling numbers of jobless men find sources of income.

Newspapers urged shoppers to avoid chain stores and "buy local." "Chain stores are undermining our local economic structure," complained the *Journal*.[10]

---

[9] *NJ*, 7-29-1932.
[10] *NJ*, 9-30-1932.

Another local relief measure dovetailed with Mayor Trower's civic improvement theme. The narrow bridge over the river at Third Street was unsuited for automobile traffic. The city determined to erect a new, modern Third Street bridge. They hired a contractor from Oakland, J.P. Brennan, to make it so and acquired financing through a combination of bond issues and arrangements with the county and the state. The city passed a law that Napa men would receive first consideration as laborers on the bridge. They then expanded the ruling to say that men from Napa County in general would be the first hired. Disappointed outsiders hoping for a chance to make a few dollars pushing wheelbarrows walked away glumly.

The bridge took much longer than expected to complete, which kept Brennan and the laborers employed well beyond the anticipated termination date. A winter storm knocked down one of its primary cement pillars, and Brennan said it would take weeks to remove the remains from the riverbank. A state engineer sent to supervise the project disagreed, and another man was hired to work under Brennan, an expert who had overseen the construction of the Richardson Bay Bridge. The expert removed the fallen pillar in two days. Fearing, perhaps, a timely end to a project that was putting gravy on his own bisquits as well as that of his Napa laborers, Brennan fired the expert, and the work resumed its plodding pace. When it was finally done, they dubbed it the George M. Francis Bridge in honor of the editor of the *Napa Register*, and they had a big parade to celebrate its long-awaited opening.

Brennan then went on to supervise the construction of Christian Brothers' La Salle novitiate in the western hills above Napa. Six subcontractors involved in the project sued the Order for non-payment, but the Brothers' attorney said they had paid Brennan in full and that he should pay the subcontractors. Judge Percy King found the Order guilty and refused them a new trial, despite charges of irregularities on the part of the plaintiffs, irregularities in the proceedings of the jury and jury misconduct.[11] Brennan had

---

[11] *NJ*, 3-21-1934.

become an "insider;" the Christian Brothers, newly arrived from Martinez, were not.

By November of 1932, the number of jobless Americans reached 13,000,000.[12] The number of people on relief via the local unemployment program in Napa rose to 1665. Mrs. Chaffee's committee hit a snag; of the $15,000 it needed, only $5,000 had been collected. Soon there would be nothing left to give. In most big cities, people were standing in line for handouts of bread, soup, milk and other staples. Banks across the nation were closing their doors, as frightened customers queued up to withdraw their money, sucking out more cash than the institutions had on hand. America's infrastructure was collapsing.

Closings and breadlines were occurring all over the world. In Germany, where reparations payments and the worldwide Depression had bled the economy white, a veteran of the Great War named Adolph Hitler slithered up the ranks and into the hearts of his countrymen. Many cheered when, as Chancellor, he dissolved the Reichstag and became dictator in order, he said, "to save the German farmer for the maintenance of the nation's food basis; and...to rescue German labor by a gigantic attack on unemployment."[13] It soon became clear that a key element in his strategy would be the vicious persecution of a large segment of his own population, the Jews.

Franklin Delano Roosevelt defeated Herbert Hoover in a resounding victory in the Presidential election, and there were many who believed that he, like Hitler, should assume dictatorial powers. The _Journal_ printed an editorial that sounded warm to the idea.

When Roosevelt took office on March 4, 1933, the national economy was spinning out of control. On March 1, 17 states had declared "bank holidays"—a euphemism meaning the doors were shut, the lights were out, and no one could make deposits or

---

[12] Schlesinger, Op. Cit., p. 440.

[13] _NJ_, 2-2-1933.

withdrawals. California Governor "Sunny Jim" Rolph closed the state's banks on March 2, and the rest of the nation's monetary centers[14] collapsed the morning Roosevelt came to office. Roosevelt kept them all closed so that America's financial machinery could be retooled. California's banks stayed closed until March 16th, while the books of each institution were inspected for solvency.

All of Napa County's banks (the vast majority of them belonging to the Bank of America/Bank of Italy) survived the crisis, but many elsewhere did not. When a Napan named John Franco learned that both of the Sacramento banks that held his life's savings had folded, he threw himself into the Napa River and drowned. Three other Napa County men did themselves in that same week because of financial despair.

Roosevelt had been so vocal in his advocacy of Repeal that many expected the 18th Amendment to vanish before he took office. The Drys, however, refused to submit; a clumsy, confusing *pas de deux* ensued. While Chicago's new Mayor, Anton Cermak, invited brewers to fire up their boilers, for example, the Federal Prohibition office in Illinois hired more agents. Forty federal agents raided a congress of 50 New York bootlegger-businessmen who were in the process of merging their retail liquor outlets and forming a trade association. In St. Helena, Bertha Beringer reported that her winery would double its production and revealed that it already had 300,000 gallons on hand; meanwhile, federal raiders staged 35 busts in Vallejo and nabbed four more bootleggers in Yountville.

Prohibition went away in stages. The first step was a measure that worked its way slowly through Congress to permit the manufacture and sale of "light" beer containing no more than 3.2% alcohol. FDR signed the beer bill in March, 1932. It would go into effect April 7, after individual states had a chance to determine if they would become Wet or stay Dry. At one minute past midnight, the first truckload of legal light beer left a San Francisco warehouse

---

[14] including the stock exchanges

for a Napa destination. Ray Cavagnaro, Dave's oldest son, supervised its loading, and it went directly to the Brooklyn Hotel, where it was greeted by happy Napans who lined up on the street with their mugs and pitchers. Ray dispensed as much as he could right from the truck. It was the only supply of legal brew to come to the Napa Valley for several days.

Three Up-Valley men[15] organized something called the Northbay Rainier Company, which would distribute Rainier beer throughout Napa, Lake and Solano counties. The St. Helena Bottling Company would serve as its headquarters. Wine with an alcoholic content of 3.2% was theoretically permissable, too, so Beringer winemaker Fred Abruzzini sent Rainier a batch of wine to de-alcoholize and then bring back to 3.2%.[16] Abruzzini and the Beringers found the results so without character that producing it would be a waste of time. The wine industry would have to remain in its coma until 3/4 of the 48 states—36 in all—ratified the 21st Amendment, which repealed the 18th.

In the meantime, St. Helenans tried to find other things to cheer them up. In an attempt to bolster civic pride, Frank Mackinder of the *Star* ran, for two weeks, a front-page feature about a pretty senior at St. Helena High who had been chosen to assist the daughter of the president of the W.R. Grace cruise ship company in christening a new liner, the *Santa Elena*, in Kearney, NJ.[17] An honors student, 17 year-old Arlene Bassford was feted by the Chamber of Commerce and seen off to the Overland Limited for her trip back east with a huge bouquet and a bottle of Beringer's

---

[15] Walter Sink, Alwyn Ewer and Eric Lawson.

[16] Fred Abruzzini, *Interviews and Reminiscences*, III, p. 82.

[17] The *Santa Elena* was the last Grace Line ship to provide cargo and passenger service from the Pacific Coast to the East. The $5,000,000 vessel was pressed into service during World War II. A torpedo attack by German planes nailed it while it was transporting 1700 Canadian troops in the Mediterranean in the summer of 1944. It sank, but almost all of the soldiers were rescued.

211

Sparkler for the launching, specially authorized by the Treasury Department through the aid of Bertha Beringer. Chaperoning Arlene were the wife of the high school principal, the wife of a local businessman and Arlene's mother. "Miss Bassford will have something to remember all her life long," glowed Mackinder, "and St. Helena will receive world-wide advertising through the press, by radio and in pictures."[18] Royally entertained at dinners, luncheons, theater parties and sightseeing tours, Miss Bassford performed admirably at the launching but caught a cold there. It developed quickly into double pneumonia, and she died within a couple of days in a hotel room at the Waldorf-Astoria. It was a tragic denouement that further discouraged an already depressed community.

Calistogans polished up civic pride in their little city with a strong "buy local" campaign. Merchants ran "Saturday specials" featuring prices low enough to lure in outsiders. "Last Saturday," wrote editor Carroll, "many new faces were noticed in town, and several merchants remarked an immediate response to the Saturday special plan."

The name of one of the shoppers was quite familiar to shopkeepers, a man in his 50's calling himself Charles Forni. He was a ne'er-do-well nephew of the well-known vineyardist. This Charles Forni went shopping. He wrote 39 phony checks in Calistoga and various other places in Northern California before he was stopped and arrested. He pled guilty and was sentenced to four years at San Quentin.[19]

The other Charles Forni had money troubles now, too. His association with Captain Rossi had helped him get started as an independent supplier in the dangerous, Capone-dominated market in Chicago, and his vineyard business with Adam Bianchi had done well. Bianchi and Forni often accompanied their juice grapes to the railyards in Chicago and profited from the hot grape market until the 1932 harvest, when the price of grapes suddenly plunged to a

---

[18] *SHS*, 11-25-1932.

[19] *NJ*, 2-19-1933.

level even below that of 1928. Now nobody wanted their grapes, or anyone else's, either.

Many of the hardy souls who had survived the alcoholic beverage industry's Ice Age met together in San Francisco in September to reacquaint themselves with each other and address the issues of reorganizing their profession. Forni was prominent among them. One hundred forty of California's 160 bonded wineries were cleaning off the presses for the 1933 vintage. It would cost an estimated $1,500,000 to get the industry up and running again.

Throughout 1933, in a grindingly slow process, state after state voted to repeal the 18th Amendment. The erstwhile bone-dry South responded positively to a plea from Roosevelt to go along with his pledge to bring back the Happy Days. It was tortuous, but by Fall there was no doubt at all that Prohibition, raids, speakeasies and bathtub gin would soon be history. Finally, on November 7, 1933, Utah became the 36th state to vote for Repeal and ratify the 21st Amendment. Celebrators broke out the good stuff and toasted the passing of a failed experiment in moral legislation. By law, Repeal actually came into being about month later, on December 5, after more than 14 years of adventure and heartbreak for the winemakers of the Napa Valley.

At a meeting of the newly organized Wine Producers' Association,[20] long-time vintner Felix Salmina mentioned that 15 large Napa County wineries and about two dozen small ones (some of them just bootleg operations) survived the legally imposed drought,[21] employing about 500 people in all. Salmina's own

---

[20] The original directors of the Wine Producers Association were a mix of familiar names from the industry's infancy and new ones from its reincarnation. Among them were Chapin Tubbs, John Ghisolfo, Fred Abruzzini, Stephen Jackse, Otto Jursch, Carl Bundschu, Georges De Latour, Dorothy Hess, J. Sehabiague and Jack Trainor.

[21] *NJ*, 2-9-1934. The value of the Valley's vineyards was only about $500,000—a fraction of the $3,000,000 they had been worth in 1923, their

winery, Larkmead, was among them, the larks in the meadow for which it was named having long since been eaten, along with healthy portions of polenta, by the Salminas and their Italian-Swiss friends during the lean years.[22]

Another Up-Valley survivor was Libero Pocai and Sons. Pocai also had at least one daughter; she married John Ballentine, who had been a manager at Greystone and had bought a small winery from a descendant of John Sutter. Ballentine aged his wine in barrels he acquired from Frederick Hess, whose La Jota winery did not survive World War I.

The Forni family, strapped for cash, sold their Lombarda winery to a Bay Area group who called themselves "Napa Cantina Winery, Inc." When the principals of Napa Cantina tricked and sued each other out of the business, the Fornis and some freinds took over and went back to calling it "Lombarda." Two of the new owners were Joseph Gagetta and Walter Martini, the latter having once run St. Helena's popular William Tell Hotel.

Charles Forni himself helped organize the Napa Valley Co-op Winery, a grower-owned association that bought Adam Bianchi's winery in Calistoga. Forni was feeling very positive about the prospects for the wine industry in the Napa Valley—so positive, in fact, that he persuaded a friend, Louis M. Martini (no relation to Walter Martini of the William Tell or Rosie Martini of the Napa Valley Inn) to relocate from Kingsburg in the Central Valley to St. Helena. Forni helped Martini select and purchase the site for a large, new winery just south of town. The Co-op did much better than expected, and the following year they bought the Petri winery,

---

peak year. Trying to replicate the great wines of Europe, the growers' favorite was Petite Sirah: about 40% of the vineyards were planted in these little grapes. There was little Cabernet and no Chardonnay. A quarter of the grapes were the Alicantes that shipped so well to the eastern markets, but these were hard to sell now. Zinfandel accounted for about 15%.

[22] Tony Quinn, "A History of the Salmina Family of Corcapolo and St. Helena," self-published, np, September, 1994, unnumbered.

Photo courtesy of Beaulieu Winery

*Through his connections with industry and the Catholic
Church, Beaulieu founder Georges de Latour kept his
winery going during Prohibition. His was one of the few
wineries to remain in business legally.*

Photo courtesy of the Raymond family

St. Helena's 1933 Vintage Festival hoped to recapture the lavish elegance of a bygone era.

which had gone into business in Theodore Gier's old St. Helena facilty just south of town. They crushed grapes in both places.

Forni also served as helper to a Chicago man, Louis Stralla, who for reasons of his own felt it wise to leave the Windy City, where he had been in the illegal beer business.[23] Stralla had probably met Forni and Bianchi when the latter brought their grapes to Chicago, and thus may have worked for Capone. He claimed to know nothing about winemaking, but he huddled often with Forni and Bianchi during his first months in the Napa Valley, living at the home of John Ghisolfo. The Ghisolfo family's impounded wine was now back on the market under a new label: the Calistoga Wine Company.

After sniffing out the Valley for bargains, Stralla rented the Charles Krug Winery from James Moffitt in the summer of 1933, before Prohibition had officially ended. He convinced the former winemaker of the defunct Ewer-Atkinson Winery[24] to oversee production of Krug's first vintage in 14 years. He renamed the place the "Napa Wine Company." By November Stralla had 400,000 gallons to sell. He packed it all in tanker cars and went back East with it, slightly ahead of Repeal. He found himself in competition with the Gallo family, who had tankloads to sell, too. Before the end of 1934 he had also started packaging wine in 12-ounce bottles that sold for 15¢ each and were returnable. They bore the "Betsy Ross" label.

Huge old Greystone Winery went back into operation, now in the hands of the Bisceglia family. They also ran a distillery, which burned down before the end of 1933. The California Wine Association, which had worn Greystone as a jewel in its tiara, also readied to go back into business again.

A man named Jack Riorda bought the "Sunny Hill" winery just south of St. Helena during Prohibition and renamed it "Sunny St. Helena" in 1934. It stood across the street from the site that had once been Chinatown. Before Prohibition, Riorda had been a winemaker for Italian Swiss Colony; during the dark years he

---

[23] *SHS*, 9-14-1934.

[24] Rufus Buttimer

shipped their grapes to New Jersey.[25] Riorda's wines were nothing special, and what little he sold of it went to markets Back East as bulk wine. He sold Sunny St. Helena to an Italian immigrant named Cesare Mondavi in 1937 and became a consultant to Julio Gallo, passing away in 1939.

Cesare Mondavi had been learning the wine trade in Lodi, where he had moved with his family. Before Prohibition Cesare ran a *pensione* in Iron Mountain, Minnesota, where he sold wine from barrels in the saloon downstairs. When the 18th Amendment closed him down, he traveled to California to procure grapes for home winemakers. Jack Riorda was one of his contacts. Cesare's boys Robert and Peter liked the idea of entering the wine business, and to give his sons something on which to cut their teeth, he bought Sunny St. Helena. He employed his son Robert as a "wine chemist,"[26] while his son Peter remained in Lodi for a while longer. The Mondavi family made wine and bought more. They quickly turned Sunny St. Helena into a money-maker.[27]

The Christian Brothers, reeling from financial setbacks caused by the contractor J.P. Brennan, lost their winemaker, a Frenchman who died in his sleep in January, 1934.[28] Rather than suffer the further expense of importing another trained enologist, they searched among their own and found a high school chemistry teacher, Brother Timothy, who was willing to learn the nearly lost art. He would become a major figure in the industry.

Another young man who would find his kismet in the Napa Valley was Roy Raymond. In 1932 Roy had been standing on a pier in San Francisco with a few thousand other guys looking for work. Two years later he was pulling in 40¢ an hour, 40 hours a week and dating Martha Jane Beringer, granddaughter of founder

---

[25] Ellen Hawkes, *Blood and Wine*, Simon & Schuster, New York, 1993, p. 70.

[26] Robert had studied chemistry in his senior year at Stanford. See Ina Wood and T.E. Wilde, "Robert Mondavi Tape," December 29, 1978, *Interviews and Reminiscences,* III, pp. 197 ff.

[27] *SHS*, 8-16-1939.

[28] Albert Duron, 55, had only been there since the previous September.

Jacob Beringer. Hard-working, straight-forward, fun-loving, honest and amiable, Roy seemed to be cut from the same cloth as Jacob. He began his labors in San Francisco under Jacob's son Otto, but quickly became indispensable to manager Fred Abruzzini, the first non-Beringer to direct the firm. To stay afloat, the winery had sold grape bricks, altar wine, dried fruit and land. It was Abruzzini who hit upon the idea of sending Beringer Sparkler to launch the *Santa Elena*. He was among the first to link wine with celebrity—a public relations notion that would carry the industry into the 21st Century. On December 6, 1933—the first day they could legally do so—Roy and Fred loaded carloads of Beringer's wine headed for the open market.[29]

A local celebrity in her own right, Mrs. Dorothy Churchill Hess had suffered painful legal and financial tangles with other members of her family and a divorce from her Germanophile husband. She continued to hold events at the former family home, Cedar Gables, which was now an inn. To-Kalon had been boarded up since before Prohibition, and there is no evidence that it even had enough life in it to bootleg. She tried to sell the place to a scoundrel named Oscar Kellstrom, who failed to make payments and defaulted. With nothing much else going on, Mrs. Hess brought To-Kalon back into the production of wine.

The Oakville facility that had once been Brun & Chaix and then part of the California Wine Association's vast holdings became the property of G.A.O. Covich during Prohibition. Covich lived in Ross. Louis Stralla saw oppportunity in Covich's facility and purchased it.

Lloyd Crellin bought pioneer winemaker Terrell Grigsby's old Occidental Winery from the Bank of Napa; he sold grapes and bootlegged.[30] Crellin loved the high life and was an intrepid socializer.[31] He sold Occidental to the Regusci family and retired to what was once the home of another *bon vivant*, William Scheffler, where he continued to party and spend gobs of money,

---

[29] See Lorin Sorensen, *Op. Cit.*

[30] Steven Navone, *Interviews and Reminiscences II*, p. 233.

[31] Attire was said to be optional at some of the Crellins' social events.

just as Scheffler had done. Like Scheffler, he came to a rather bad end, as will be shown below. Crellin's sister married a prominent Napa lawyer, Wallace Everett. Their son, Wally, Jr., inherited his father's profession and his uncle's love of the good life, as will also be shown.

Fruit Industries, Inc., kept a hand in the action. Their Colonial Grape Products plant crushed wine at the old Migliavacca Winery. Another Napa operation, the Carneros winery, also geared up for business under the leadership of Jack Trainor. [32]

Inglenook Winery sprang back to life again, hiring the son of San Francisco wine merchant Carl Bundschu as general manager. A good politician, Carl Bundschu, Jr. persuaded the Napa Chamber of Commerce to support the notion that wine was, after all, a food, so that the tax to which it was subject would be removed.[33] Despite the C of C's backing the plan failed. Had their scheme of removing the tax on wine been successful, they would have deprived Roosevelt's coffers of a considerable amount of revenue, for even after the ravages of Prohibition, grape and grape-related products were California's second largest agricultural industry.

The St. Helena community honored Bundschu's wealthy, good-looking secretary, Evelyn Doak, by electing her Queen of St. Helena's 1934 Vintage Festival, the first in more than a decade where people could drink legally. Martha Jane Beringer came in fourth. More than 40,000 people found their way to St. Helena that September, and the revelry lasted three days.

Beaulieu Winery had fared the best of any during the bad years, and it kept on with business as usual, although Madame De Latour took over more and more leadership in the business as Georges advanced in years and declined in health. Beaulieu was the first to land a substantial, up-scale contract to supply table wines in a significant market. Park & Tilford, commercial distributors in Manhattan, agreed to sell 25,000 cases of Beaulieu's fine, dry wine.

---

[32] Carneros Winery was in the path of a grass fire that whipped through the area in 1936 and burned down.

[33] *NJ*, 2-28-1935.

Much of it, unfortunately, never left the shelves and was returned unsold to the winery. Much of Beringer's wine also came back. Elation turned to concern as the Valley awoke to a hard fact—the market for fine California wine had dried up.

Gene Morisoli, a Larkmead employee stationed for the nonce in Manhattan, wrote a discouraged letter to the *Napa Register* dated April 8, 1934. The California wine industry faced "a very pitiful state of affairs," he said. Eastern wine manufacturers were concocting wine out of anything available and mislabeling it as Californian. But worse, he wrote, the market was flooded with inferior bulk and bottled wines, most of it from Central and Southern California. (He didn't mention Louis Stralla's tankloads of just-pressed, barely ripened wine.) Flooding had caused the prices to drop to as little as $7.00 a case. The better, more costly wines of the Napa Valley could not compete with these prices.

There were other problems, too, which Morisoli didn't mention:

- winemaking equipment and the art of winemaking had suffered over the decade to the point that even most of the good wines were not as appealing as they had been;
- the world was gripped by the Great Depression, and few could splurge on fine wine as an accompaniment to dinner;
- those who enjoyed wine had learned to make it themselves;
- lovers of fine wine had developed a taste for other beverages which were much easier to obtain.

Star editor Mackinder urged his readers not to sell immature wine:

> It would appear to us that the best way to again popularize wine and insure a strong trade from the start...is first to see that the quality is of the very best and that the price is as low as is consistent with the expense entailed in producing the beverage."[34]

Some tried to capitalize on the Napa Valley's identity as a source of alcoholic beverage by going into the distilling business. Sam Finkelstein, Philip Levin and Abraham Schorr, for example, took over the Engelberg Winery once run by W.F. Bornhorst and

---

[34] *SHS*, 4-27-1934.

turned it into the Metropolitan Fruit Distillery, producing "Mount Helena" brandy. Schorr was a Czechoslovakian rabbi whose family had been in the liquor business in the old country. He planned to run the winery under strict Kosher rules.[35] Carried away, perhaps, by delusions of wealth (or perhaps by his product), Schorr went on a spending spree.[36] Confronted about his excesses by Finkelstein's wife and niece, Schorr struck both of the women, who retaliated by snipping off his whiskers. Schorr was arraigned for assault. His lawyer, Wally Everett, won him a "not guilty" verdict, but the distillery folded.[37]

Pierre De La Montanya purchased the Hedgeside Winery, a huge, empty stone building on Atlas Way once owned by the Southern Pacific's unsuccessful gubernatorial candidate, Morris Estee, and announced that he would turn it into a distillery.[38] He would make it the largest of its kind west of Peoria, he claimed.

For the vintners of the Napa Valley, it was back to square one. They needed to pool their resources and, as much as possible, work as a unit to restore interest in their product. Many looked to the newly formed Wine Institute to represent them to the American people. Two thirds of the wineries in California and elsewhere signed up with this promotional organization.

Many Americans hoped that Franklin Roosevelt would be the Abraham Lincoln of the Democratic Party, freeing them from the captivity of their economic duress and ending the reign of lawlessness spawned by Prohibition. His popularity soared when he arranged for the WWI Bonus Marchers to receive their allotments. Napa veterans collected a total of $295,399.50.[39] On his birthday, Napa held a Roosevelt Ball in the East Pavilion to honor him, the proceeds going to research for a polio vaccine. Big loud speakers amplified his radio address to the hundreds who attended, as he

---

[35] *NJ*, 4-19-1934.

[36] *SHS*, 5-25-1934.

[37] *SHS*, 8-10-1934.

[38] *NJ*, 2-2-1934.

[39] *NJ*, 3-24-1935. The entire state would receive $123,833,011.

thanked them and others throughout America for their generosity. Most did not know that he himself had been stricken with the disease for which they were raising money, and he didn't tell them. He was a hero at a time when the nation truly needed one; and because the country needed someone to follow, most working people were prone, at least for a while, to practically deify him. To others, however, he was a traitor to his class and a menace. Frank Mackinder ran a full-page ad in the *Star*: "The Roosevelt New Deal Threatens to Ruin Your Business!"[40]

It was easy to think in black-and-white, good-versus-evil terms in America in the 1930's. Evil exemplars abounded, like the once powerful Samuel Insull, a midwest mogul who created a financial empire that fell like a house of cards when the market crashed, ruining thousands of small, innocent investors. Truly scary outlaws made names for themselves. The escapades of "Pretty Boy" Floyd and Bonnie and Clyde played a dark counterpoint to charming heroes like Wiley Post, Charles Lindbergh and scores of heart-throb movie actors.

Both good guys and bad were finding their way to the Napa Valley. Boxing hero Max Baer visited Beringer Winery just after he defeated Primo Carnera for the heavyweight boxing championship. John Dillinger's machine-gunner, "Baby Face" Nelson, hid out at the Connor Hotel on the northeast corner of Main and Third in Napa, while a nation-wide manhunt sought to bring him to justice.[41] A convicted swindler and big-time bootlegger named Mike Gallo tried to defraud the new owners of Cedar Knolls vineyard in Napa.[42] (Mike's nephews, Ernest and Julio, had already put a dent in the Valley's economy by engulfing the Eastern market with non-premium wine.[43])

---

[40] *SHS*, 11-4-1936.

[41] Joe "Fatso" Negri, a Barbary Coast bouncer with links to the Napa Valley, was indicted for harboring him. Negri ratted on 17 others who were also involved.

[42] *NJ*, 1-30-1934.

[43] NJ, 1-30-1934. See Ellen Hawkes, *Op. Cit.*

FDR's radio broadcasts were encouraging to many, but the statistics were not. In California alone, 595,185 people received unemployment relief between July and October, 1934. In the month of November, after most of the crops had been harvested, 659,239 people were on the dole: 11.6% of the state's population.[44] One way Roosevelt tried to resolve the unemployment problem was to create a Civil Works Army to do infrastructure repair like the upkeep and creation of dams and roads. More than 300 workers labored to repair and repave the highway between Napa and Vallejo, as well as other routes in the Valley.

The Civil Works Army had just begun to build a reservoir for the City of St. Helena when the program's directors announced they would soon stop their service for towns whose population was less than 5,000. Workers walked off the job, leaving a half-finished spillway, a half-filled lake and 800 sacks of cement. Local contractor Harry Thorsen completed the project, but it leaked. A similar reservoir for Calistoga was planned but never got started.

Vicissitudes of weather kept much of the nation in torment throughout the mid-thirties. The profound drought that had begun in 1932 in the middle part of the country had desiccated the once-fertile farmland by 1935. Billowing clouds of yellow dust darkened the sky from Central Missouri to New Mexico, creating a sweltering greenhouse effect and reducing visibility to zero. Dust fell like snow on Durango, Colorado and on Indio, California. There was no wind. Shifting silt blotted out the tracks of cars, trucks and wagons as ruined families in Oklahoma and Arkansas packed up their belongings and headed west. Many would find their way to the Napa Valley, especially to Napa, Napa Junction and American Canyon.

But while part of the country dried up and blew away, torrential rains battered the rest. Flood waters swept across two islands in the California Delta in April, 1935, and in May four people drowned at Colorado Springs. Five days of rain sent scores fleeing their lowland farms in Kansas. More than 200 died. By June the dust

---

[44] *SHS*, 3-1-1935.

cloud had given way to catastrophic downpours that isolated Austin, Texas and wreaked havoc in Mexico. Tornadoes swept through the Dakotas in July. The storm attacked Upstate New York and blew through Pennsylvania and New Jersey. It didn't let up. In August thousands in Ohio, Pennsylvania and West Virginia watched their lives wash away as the Ohio River reached its highest state since 1888. Three killer heatwaves singed the Mississippi River Valley.

The good folk of the Napa Valley, having survived their nadir during Prohibition, were spared from Mother Nature's Depression-era torment. They settled into a kind of weary peace. Only 151 people voted in Napa's city elections in May.[45] A mere 1/3 of the county's 10,568 registered voters bothered to cast a ballot in the 1935 state-wide elections in August. A Communist agitator left a pamphlet in a voting booth in Rutherford urging those making less than 40¢ a day to strike. Nothing came of it, but it held the potential for becoming a real problem. Some of the Valley's aristocrats made themselves vulnerable to ugly protest by their apparent oblivousness to social currents. Georges De Latour, for example, bragged that he only paid his workers 25¢ an hour, "and I will not pay them any more," he told winemaker George Deuer.[46] Sheriff Steckter set up a Vigilante Committee to keep Reds out of the county, and the confrontation he feared never materialized.[47]

Dave Cavagnaro brought the Tom Mix Wild West Show to town. It was a stupendous success. The VFW held a massive Fourth of July party in Napa—thousands attended—and St. Helena welcomed tens of thousands to its 1935 Vintage Festival, where Roy Raymond won a silver trophy for rolling a barrel down Adams Street, and yet another young woman became queen for a year.

The Bank of America announced it would raze the old "bank block" on Second Street in Napa and build a brand-new structure. The Carithers company put a department store in the old Behlow

---

[45] They elected Ralph Butler mayor—unanimously.

[46] George Deuer, *Interviews and Reminiscences*, II, p. 114.

[47] Two Red agitators were tarred-and-feathered in Sonoma County, however.

Building. Industrialist Nathan Rothman announced he would install a pants factory, "Rough Riders," on Soscol Avenue. It would employ 240-500 people. All of this seemed most encouraging. Things were looking up. People were more than ready to tear down the worn, leave the frightening bad old days behind and welcome in modern times. Decades later they would be criticised for demolishing their own architectural history, but Napans of 1935 felt like they were emerging from a dank pit and saw no value in old bricks.

Mare Island continued to receive work. Assistant Secretary of the Navy Henry LaTrobe Roosevelt, a cousin of the President, toured the facility and left impressed.[48] Congress agreed to allocate $100,000,000 to build 24 more warships, including 15 destroyers, two cruisers and six submarines, and some of the work would be coming to Mare Island. As long as there were ships to build, there would be money in Napa.

It was therefore with a good deal of self-interest that Napa's newspapers happily published details about the doings of the United States Navy's fleet in the Pacific. Of particular interest were the war games. Mare Island's former Commandant, Admiral Joseph Reeves, led a huge battle fleet of 177 ships and 55,000 men through maneuvers that covered more than 5,000,000 square miles of the Pacific Ocean. Vessels stole through the defense line of mock mines and showered pretend bombs on Oahu. Planes launched from carriers made make-believe night raids on Honolulu. Oahu was "rapidly being converted to a new Gibraltar," boasted one report; it was becoming "as impregnable as Britain's famous 'rock'" as a defense "against attack from the Pacific."[49]

A US commercial plane flew from California to Hawaii in 1935 and on to Midway Island, to prove it could be done. The Japanese newspaper *Nichi Nichi* claimed that this was proof that the United States was preparing to launch a military offensive against Japan and her interests in the Pacific:

---

[48] but died shortly afterward. His successor, however, also thought highly of the work being done at Mare Island.

[49] *NJ*, 1-30-1937.

The United States is undertaking a trans-Pacific air route under the pretext of civil aviation. The airway bears a great strategic significance, exposing to the whole world their aggressive naval plans against the Far East.

In appropriating $300,000 for Pearl Harbor repairs, America seeks to strengthen her post as an important base for an advance across the Pacific. America's planned construction of 555 naval planes and increasing officers to 8176 are all part of her preparation for a Far Eastern campaign.[50]

It was, of course, Japan that was doing the aggressing. After its brief post-war prosperity, the land of the rising sun suffered from the stock market crash and subsequent depression along with the rest of the world. Hemmed in by ocean and sea, its expanding population faced the double crisis of too little money and not enough room. Its leaders looked west for a solution, and they saw mainland China, a country rich in resources and wide-open spaces, too poorly managed to defend itself very well. Japanese forces conquered and occupied Manchuria in 1931 and overran Shanghai in 1932, killing thousands of civilians. Japan continued to torment the Chinese throught the 1930's.

Predators were also rising up in Europe. Benito Mussolini took control of Italy with the goal of churning through Europe and North Africa and creating a new Roman Empire. His "Black Shirts" attacked Abyssinia in 1935 and continued to assault North Africa in 1936. Perhaps confused over where to place their loyalties, a group of Napa Italians took up a collection to aid wounded Italian soldiers, the same week that Italian fliers were bombing an American Red Cross hospital. Mussolini ousted Haile Selassie, had himself declared Emperor of Ethiopia and withdrew from the League of Nations. In Germany Adolph Hitler had begun an attack on the Jewish population that would eventually reach a hideous crescendo.

---

[50] Quoted in *NJ*, 4-26-1935.

A deadly civil war gripped Spain. St. Helenan Doris Pellet was on the last boat of foreigners evacuated from Mallorca. Rebels took the British-owned island early in the war, and for many months Pellet, along with several other well-bred women, refused at first to leave.[51] She returned as soon as she could.

Encroachment was also taking place in California. The great prize which the state's powerful counties sought to take from weaker ones was water. Thousands upon thousands of Americans were leaving their drought- and/or flood-stricken farms to seek work in cities like Oakland, San Jose and Los Angeles, urban centers that did not have plentiful supplies of fresh water. In 1935, the California Supreme Court ruled that the owners of lands through which streams flow cannot prevent others from using the water. Moreover, "a riparian owner holds rights only to such water as he can put to beneficial use."[52] In other words, if a rancher couldn't use all the water that ran through his property, other people could have some. This cleared the way for urban communities downstream to demand water from upstream rural areas. It was a decision that would wreak havoc on the Napa Valley one day.

Napa County was not growing at the same rate as its Bay Area neighbors. In five years its population had only increased 6.4%. But despite its slow growth, it, too, was low on water. A dam in Rector Canyon had been proposed years ago to provide water not only for Napa, but for the Veterans' Home, State Game Farm and State Hospital, as well. Sleepy Napa voters did manage to pass a bond measure for it, but since the project required state funding, it appeared on ballots throughout California and lost big.

Few in the Napa Valley realized that they would one day become the victims of outside conquest in the war over water. Indeed, in the '30's the only troublesome incursion into their territory was the sudden appearance of a strange, six-legged insect with pincers on its tail: the earwig, which first made its appearance

---

[51] *SHS*, 10-9-1936.

[52] Quoted in *NJ*, 2-2-1935.

in the Napa Valley in 1934 in the western part of the City of Napa.[53] Farm Advisor Herman Baade promised that an earwig-eating parasite would be imported to check their spread. It was an early experiment in pest control that clearly failed.

The people of the Napa Valley could hear about these predations on the radio and read about them in the paper. They watched newsreels of national and world events at the movies before the main feature. Having outlasted the moralists who destroyed their wine-based economy, they took comfort from the belief that they were safe from right-wing dictators and left-wing labor agitators, if not from garden bugs; Napans were more interested in matters that seemed immediate to them, especially things that felt positive. It would be hard to budge them from their new-found tranquility.

There was, therefore, no heated outcry in 1935 when the US Bureau of Prisons condemned the Napa County jail on the top floor of the Courthouse as "highly unsanitary" and ordered that prisoners not be lodged there except in emergencies.[54] Its decay rendered it less than secure. A well-known cat burglar named Phil Strahan escaped fom it one March by jimmying a hole in the ceiling of his cell, climbing through it and down into the shower next door, prying loose a steel vent there and slipping out onto the roof of the building. From there he let himself into an open window on the corridor outside the superior court room and sauntered down the stairway into freedom.[55]

The disturbing conditions at Napa State Hospital—property of the State and not technically part of Napa County—did not excite champions of reform, either. The total patient population was about the size of Calistoga and St. Helena combined—3,200 people. Some people had been warehoused there for as long as 25 years.[56] More than 400 were housed in wretched little shacks that had been built as temporary shelters after the 1906 earthquake. In the main

---

[53] *NJ*, 5-15-1936.

[54] *NJ*, 9-18-1935.

[55] *NJ*, 3-19-1938.

[56] *NJ*, 1-20-1935.

wards, patients sat on the floors of the long, dark corridors and slept on mattresses brought in at night. Every recess was occupied by beds. Diphtheria broke out. There was patient abuse. When one patient died there, his widow ordered that an autopsy be done, and it was revealed that he had suffered a broken jaw, which had abscessed. Despite the abscess, the hospital claimed the fracture occurred after his death, and the DA dropped the case.[57] There would be no stalwart guardians of patients' rights.

A small furor broke out in Napa's city council in 1936 when councilman S. J. Cinnamond—a man with a mustache alarmingly like Hitler's—objected that certain politicians in Solano County were exerting undo influence on the selection of a Napa County dairy inspector. In an editorial that week, the *Journal*'s Luther Gibson referred to Napa as Vallejo's "sister city" in a way that suggested Napa was Solano County's lesser sibling. Soon afterward, his brother Elmer took over as publisher and general manager (and moved to Napa), and Luther Gibson involved himself more openly in Solano politics.

Fed up with its out-of-town bias, Napans dropped their subscriptions to the *NJ*. "It is no secret," the paper confessed, "that the *Journal* has lost almost all its local advertising support."[58] Elwin Muller and James T. Ritch bought the paper from the Gibson family, but many were now reading the evening newspaper, the *Napa Register*. John Walden's old daily continued to languish under the new regime. George Provine bought it in February of 1937. He came up with a new slogan, which he ran on the paper's masthead: "A Land Without an Apology: The Napa Valley." Readers came back, but they were wary.

---

[57] *NJ*, 4-19-1935.

[58] *NJ*, 7-29-1936.

Chapter Eleven

Land Without an Apology

M ost people driving through the "land without an apology" in the late 1930's approached it from Vallejo on State Route 29. Route 29 ran past Napa State Hospital, 50 years old and even scarier-looking than it had been in its infancy, because parts of it were creepily decrepit. A writer for Roosevelt's Works Progress Administration described NSH as "a jumble of gingerbread gables, turrets and cupolas" that epitomized "the architectural extravagance of its age."[1]

Route 29 then became Soscol Avenue and ushered travelers past an unattractive string of small stores and the shells of former businesses gone belly-up. There was no bridge over the Napa River south of town. Motorists could catch occasional glimpses of the barges and freighters that still carried goods up and down the river, however, because much of Soscol was still undeveloped in the late '30's. Just past the Adobe Inn (old even then), there was a Y in the road. The east branch was called Bell Avenue, named for the politician-hero who by the end of the 1930's was all but forgotten. Napans pressed to have it considered part of the Silverado Trail and renamed accordingly, a wish that was granted. A few miles north, this branch connected with the road that went to Monticello and the

---

[1] Federal Writers' Project of the Works Progress Administration, *California: A Guide to the Golden State*, Hastings House, NY, 1939, p. 413.

largely undeveloped Berryessa Valley. It was possible by 1938 to take the Silverado Trail all the way to Calistoga.[2] The going was rough, though, because it wasn't all paved, and neither was Monticello Road.

Most drivers veered west at the Y and continued along Soscol Avenue past the electric train station and the Depot Hotel, where Theresa Tamburelli, a widow now, still cooked up malfattis every afternoon and made loans to East Napans. She had money hidden all over her house.

George Blaufuss converted his brewery back to the "Western Cider Works." It burned to the ground in 1938 in a spectacular fire that drew hundreds of spectators who blocked the way out of town for an hour.[3] He rebuilt it right away.

The largest active operation on Soscol was Rothman's Rough Riders on the west side of the street, abutting the Napa River. Living up to its founder's predictions, it was a major Napa employer.

Soscol ended at Third Street, with the Palace Hotel standing as a sentinel at the traditional entrance to town. Like many Napa businesses, unfortunately, the Palace had become a dilapidated casualty. Ownership had changed several times, and its most recent past owner, Esther Ahearn, had been dinged by the police for operating slot machines there. The new owners promised to turn the dive into a splash hit.[4] This would require a lot of money. The lobby was shabby, the guest rooms did not have private baths, the banquet room was too small to host club luncheons, and the elevator was frightening.[5]

---

[2] The completion of the Trail had been the pet project of County Supervisor Charles Tamagni, a Swiss immigrant.

[3] *NJ,* 10-16-1937.

[4] After she sold the Palace, Mrs. Ahearn started something called "Mom's Log Cabin," a bar and grill in East Napa. One summer day while drying her hair on the roof of the bar next door, she accidentally fell through the skylight and was killed.

[5] *NJ,* 3-21-1939.

The Francis Bridge spanned the river at Third and Soscol, its concrete still white with youth. There were a few businesses north of the bridge, along the banks of the Napa River, including the Cavagnaro family's sprawling liquor distributing company. Dave's commanding public relations skills and Ray's beer coup had translated into significant economic success by the late 1930's.

The city began in earnest on the river's west side. The Napa Hotel, a landmark on the corner of First and Main for as long as anyone could remember, burned in 1937, but not to the ground. It was rebuilt. Route 29 went through the business section, where each little enterprise seemed to sport a neon sign. Once stables and blacksmiths had lent their aromas to the heart of the little city. Their places were taken by gas stations and car dealerships, like Hugo Zeller's at Third near Soscol and Gasser Motors on Third near Randolph.

The square at the Courthouse was an attractive oasis of greenery in the center of a small, struggling county seat longing to be modern. It, too, had been threatened by a recent fire that had started around the desk of the often less-than-sober Judge Percy King and nearly destroyed the upper floor, but the damage was restored quickly.

Napa could also be approached from the west. The old road to Sonoma—a poorly paved, pot-holed adventure ride—intersected with Jefferson Street near the County Infirmary. The sharp bend at the junction there continued to be the scene of frequent bad accidents and still bore the ominous nick-name "death curve."

The City of Napa had much in common with many other small towns in America: relatively low violent crime rate, relatively clean air, relatively little racial diversity, relatively uninformed populace. A handful of men ran the place. They served on many boards and committees simultaneously, their sons often followed in their footsteps, and their daughters married into other influential families. Charles Otterson was by 1940 the oldest, longest-serving active fire chief in America, which may or may not have had something to do with the fact that Napa suffered more than its share of fires toward the end of the 1930's. Percy King had been the leading judge in the county and Jack Steckter the sheriff since the

231

days of Prohibition. The county's leaders were mutually protecting good-ol'-boys, a condition that prevailed in many small American towns and was not limited to county lines. Thus when the parents of a Madera boy sued Sheriff Steckter for the fatal injuries their son incurred in a "fall" at the Napa County jail, the Madera judge cleared Steckter, despite the questionable nature of the fall and the fact the injured boy did not receive prompt medical attention. "Every sheriff in California would be harassed by similar suits," said Steckter, "should a precedent be set."[6] The California State Sheriff's Association had unanimously voted him President in 1936, and it would have been nearly impossible for any private citizen to loosen Steckter's grip on Napa County.

The Napa Valley's reputation for yokelism became painfully clear in 1940, when RKO decided to use the Nick Fagiani ranch in Oakville as the site of a movie, *They Got What They Wanted*, a comedy starring Carole Lombard, Charles Laughton and Harry Carey. The plot had to do with an aging Italian vintner from the Napa Valley who marries a beautiful young woman from San Francisco. The two do not meet until the night of the wedding, and because the vintner is shy, his courtship consists of letters written by another, younger man—accompanied by the younger man's photo. The screenplay is offensive by today's standards, referring to Italians as "Dagos" and "Wops."

Nick and Anne Fagiani, owners of the Mount Eden winery, tore down their house and built a villa when they learned that RKO had selected their property for the film. RKO erected a house of their own in the Fagianis' vineyard, saying the family's new home was too modern. Impressed by the family's sudden fame, Napans elected young Anita Fagiani Queen of the County Fair, at least partly because the excitement over the movie gave her outstanding name recognition.

The local newspapers enthusiastically followed the progress of the shooting. Fred Abruzzini extended the hospitality of the Beringer winery to the cast, and the Davis family opened up their

---

[6] *NJ*, 1-4-1940.

Cedar Knolls home for an Allied Relief Committee fund-raiser which the movie stars attended, with Judge Percy King serving as master of ceremonies. Some hoped out loud (and in print) that RKO would have opening night in Napa at the commodious Uptown theater, which was built in 1937 and was one of the few up-to-date structures in town.[7]

But shortly after the film was completed, the *New York Herald-Tribune* published a mocking piece about the "natives" of the Napa Valley, who were "dazzled over the flesh and blood appearance of actors and actresses." They were "completely overcome with the 'thrill of their life,' upon the arrival of the company," the article said. But for the movie, "these natives would still be innocent of the mysterious world of the motion picture." When they saw Carole Lombard with her husband, Clark Gable, it concluded, "the inhabitants had all they could do to keep from dropping dead."

Silver Screen, a national magazine, picked up the thread of the *Tribune* article just before the film debuted. Carole Lombard had to sleep at the Fagianis' ranch, it reported, because there were no hotels in Napa. (An untruth, although the Napa hotels were hardly first-rate.) The daughters of the local elite fought with each other over who could serve her soup, it said; even the local bank president's daughter signed on as a maid, just to catch sight of a real, live movie star. Napans were outraged at the media's trivializing characterization of them. When the film made its rounds to the Uptown, the local newspapers barely made mention of it.

The charge of Napa Valley yokelism was not without merit. After the RKO fiasco had boiled down a bit, Calistoga editor Charles Carroll addressed the issue. The Women's Improvement Club had just hosted a formal dance for young people at Grace Church's Bourn Hall in St. Helena. It was an important event for the youths who attended, he said.

> They are too apt to leave their homes in small communities like this, almost uninformed concerning the

---

[7] It was heralded as offering "every discovery and device of scientific research."

accepted manner of doing things. Unconsciously, they realize their inadequacy for certain situations, and   one of two things results—they either shrink from social contacts, or they throw themselves the easily recognized screen of "defense," which inevitably makes them seem stupid or foolish to others.[8]

Drivers heading for the Up-Valley usually left the county seat via Jefferson Street/State Route 29. There was a large curve in the road just after Napa High School and another just beyond that. Route 29 then became a modest, two-lane country road that slipped past an occasional home and orchards of prune, plum, cherry, apricot, pear, peach, walnut and apple. The fruit trees were interspersed with a few vineyards, which became more numerous the farther north one traveled. In the spring the prune trees flowered with a gorgeous profusion of white petals.

Three miles south of Yountville there was a junction with a dirt lane that crossed the Valley and eventually led to the State Game Farm, manned by patients from the State Hospital. Fifteen-thousand pheasants hatched there annually, along with a number of other game animals, all of which were released each year.[9] The Game Farm required a lot of water, and this was a problem, because Napans were unhappy about sharing the heavenly liquid with facilities run by the state. The Civil Works Army readied to build a dam at Rector Canyon east of the Game Farm in 1935 to service the H2O needs of the big state facilities in Napa County, but the project never got beyond the initial surveys and the building of some service roads.

After passing a stand of eucalyptus trees, the curving country road went through the small, unkempt town of Yountville, population about 360, well-known to people of the '30's for its bootleggers, bandits and bordellos. Several outlaw saloons served the needs of the nearly 2,000 patients at the nearby Veterans' Home, another state-owned institution that used water. Alcohol was still illegal within a quarter-mile radius of the Home, a fact that did

---

[8] *WC*, 1-3-1941.

[9] Federal Writers' Project, Op. Cit., p. 412.

not deter proprietors from selling it. The incorrigible Andy Zandro was arrested again in the summer of 1936 for 17 counts of bootlegging, operating a slot machine, tax evasion and theft at his "infamous Yountville Veterans' Club."[10]

Past Yountville the vineyards gradually became more numerous. The vines were not necessarily planted in neat rows, and vineyards usually featured several varieties mixed in together. Very few vineyards enjoyed the advantage of a rigorous weed abatement program. In the fall the grape leaves turned a rich, dark red, the result of a virus. There were many groves of olive, walnut, fig and the ubiquitous prune.

The road passed through microscopic Oakville, population 219. The enormous tree for which the hamlet was named had engaged in many battles with automobiles. Rather than reroute the road to save the tree (and the drivers who ran into it), the county chose to fell the oak. Julius Caiocca and Louis Tonella operated a little grocery store in Oakville. Big, old wooden To-Kalon Winery burned completely to the gound in June, 1939, in a blaze so enormous it could be seen in Lake County. It took some adjoining buildings along with it and started a grass fire. Dorothy Churchill Hess, the owner, had removed all the wine from the place before the fire began; its 500,000 gallon storage vats were completely dry. The family was never prosecuted for arson.[11]

Martin Stelling, a real estate developer from San Francisco, now owned the Benson/Doak mansion. The San Francisco *Chronicle* described his wife as "one of the 10 most beautiful women in San Francisco."[12] The stately, blonde Caroline Stelling happened to be the granddaughter of Len Owens, owner-manager of Aetna Springs in Pope Valley.[13] As part of his contribution to the local economy,

---

[10] *NJ*, 7-18-1936.

[11] A few years later, when the high-ranking Nazi Rudolph Hess parachuted into England, a rumor began that he had been her husband. He wasn't.

[12] *NJ*, 1-4-1939.

[13] Owens' daughter, Frances Marion, was a famous screenplay writer in her day.

Stelling bought an old building on the southeast corner of Coombs and First Streets in Napa, tore it down and built a new one.

Oakville melted into Rutherford, which was nearly the size of Yountville but more respectable. Beaulieu and Inglenook were the biggest wineries there, and both had undergone recent changes. On his last trip to France, Beaulieu's impeccable gentleman vintner Georges de Latour had met a young Russian aristocrat name Andre Tchelistcheff, who was working at the viticultural experimental station in Paris. He invited Andre to emigrate to California and become his winemaker. After much consideration and discussion with his wife, Tchelistcheff agreed. The California Wine Institute and UC Davis helped Tschelistcheff acquire a visa, and the family arrived in the Napa Valley in 1938. Tchelistcheff found the methods and machinery at Beaulieu to be pathetically provincial and introduced the locals to winemaking as the French were now practicing it. People clung his every word.

Carl Bundschu left Inglenook at about the same time and was replaced by a new manager, Niebaum family member John Daniels. Daniels' genius was in sales and marketing. He had his work cut out for him: 1938 was a very bad year for the industry. A bumper crop glutted the market, and grapes were selling at 14¢ a ton. A small group of vintners were able to persuade Congress to subsidize the conversion of a portion of their grapes to brandy, which eased the problem somewhat. The terms of this "prorate" bailed out both growers and vintners. Andre Tchelistcheff used the opportunity to turn some of Beaulieu's poorer quality, less stable wines into brandy at the government's expense.

Wineries became more common as the road went on, but there were few places to eat. It would be decades before restaurateurs would seize upon the idea that high-class eateries could make money in the wine country. California in the later 1930's was gourmand and not gourmet.

All along the way, the highway paralleled the tracks of the electric railroad, a struggling concern that had spent most of the 1930's in the red. It was Route 29 itself and the vehicles that drove on it that brought the line to extinction. The venerable old

Monticello Steamship Company went out of business first,[14]
followed by the interurban, which carried its last commercial
passengers on February 13, 1938.[15] In September of 1937 it
substituted motorbus and truck transport for its trains, and the
February 13 trip was merely ceremonial.

As Route 29 curved gracefully up the Valley, time seemed to
fall away. Millions of gallons of wine slept in their barrels, and the
pace of life itself slowed to a crawl. St. Helena, home to 16
wineries and about 1,600 people in the late 1930's,[16] was pretty
much the way it had been in 1917. Battered by the Germanophobia
of the Great War, the influenza virus, Prohibition and the Great
Depression, St. Helena needed a rest. The most important
innovation in town was the inauguration of parallel parking. Folks
clamored for a new post office, too, a landmark event that would
indeed occur in 1940.

In the tranquil setting of the quiet village, author Jessamyn West
sat in her study—a converted water tower that once belonged to the
Fuller family—and wrote books and short stories about life among
the Quakers during the Civil War, including *Friendly Persuasion*,
which became a movie. She only needed to stroll downtown to get
a feel for sheltered living in a troubled time. Her husband, Harry
McPherson, was the principal and superintendent of the high school
from 1936 to 1940. The family then moved to Napa, and
McPherson continued there as an educator.

St. Helena was saddened by the recent loss of its newspaper
editor, Frank Bennett MacKinder, who died at 12:15 on a Friday
afternoon in February, 1937, just as he was settling in to inspect the
newest release of the *Star*. He was "a man without an enemy," the

---

[14] George Harlan, *San Francisco Bay Ferry Boats,* Howell-North Books,
Berkeley, 1967. The Golden Gate Ferry Company bought the Monticello
Steamship Company in 1927. The steamer *Napa Valley* ended up in
Bremerton, Washington, where it was re-christened the *Malahat*. It burned
down to the water line in March, 1943.

[15] *NJ*, 2-6-1938.

[16] *NJ*, 8-30-1935.

obituary said, "in spite of the rugged honesty of his character."[17] His stepson, Starr Baldwin, took over.[18] Baldwin was a photography buff and a good writer, and the paper soon took on a new look. Like his predecessor, he did not print much world or national news, and he barely touched on happenings outside the Up-Valley, but he continued close coverage of the wine industry.

Baldwin was bursting with civic pride for St. Helena. He wrote an editorial early in his career that may have made some in the Valley squirm:

> We wonder how many people realize the great
> change that is going on around us. New people
> coming into the valley, people with money, people
> who are coming here to make their homes for
> the rest of their lives. It is a significant influx,
> and one that bodes much for St. Helena in the
> way of a fine place to live.

> These people are the very antithesis of the dust
> bowl refugees, with all respect to the innate worth
> of the latter. The St. Helena emigres are not broke,
> they do not need jobs, they will never become a
> problem. They are, in fact, with their resources
> and their culture, a great contribution.[19]

Brag as he might about St. Helena's attraction for the upper crust, most St. Helenans were actually down-home, regular people. Many still harbored deep resentment against the government and the lost decade of the 1920's. Some still tried to manufacture their own illegal liquor and provided work for the State Board of Equalization, successor to the state Prohibition unit. Others gathered at the bar on the corner of Railroad Avenue and Hunt Streets, drank beer, aimed juice from their chewing tobacco at the

---

[17] *SHS*, 2-26-1937.

[18] Mackinder had married Baldwin's mother three years earlier. Lola Baldwin Mackinder was the daughter of St. Helena pioneer John Mixon.

[19] *SHS*, 5-12-1939.

still extant cuspidors and jawed with proprietor Felix "Gee Gee" Freilone about the old days.

The St. Gothard Inn was a favorite gathering place for the new St. Helena aristocrats. It sat on a hill above Route 29 just past the town. Built by John Money for vintner Seneca Ewer,[20] it was a grand place with 21 bedrooms. Each room had a large bath and opened onto a wide verandah on the building's second floor. The servants' quarters were above, under the roof. The lower floor had a cocktail bar, a lounge and a big formal dining room that could seat 100. There were tennis courts and a croquet lawn, as well, with adjoining patios for spectators. There was nothing else like it in the Valley, and St. Helena vintners could entertain important visitors there quite fashionably.

The Beringer winery and its imposing Rhine House were just beyond the St. Gothard. It was selling about 15,000 cases of wine nationally, mainly to buyers in New York, Chicago and New Orleans—the traditional markets for fine wine beyond the state of California. Its distillery operated 24 hours a day and employed 35 workers. Beringer's made a sea of high-alcohol brandy and also a large amount of apple jack—hard cider distilled from apples from the orchards of Sebastopol in Sonoma County.

The Forni family sold their Lombarda Winery in 1939 to a partnership that proved far more worthy than the Cantina group who had tried to operate it back in 1934. Albert "Abbey" Ahern, a businessman from southern California, was the leader of a threesome that also included Charles Freeman and Mark Foster. Combining their names, they called themselves "Freemark Abbey."

Pacific Union College, the bastion of temperance in the hills to the northeast, seemed to live in an even older time zone than St. Helena. Still true to the visions of its Christian mystic founder, Ellen G. White, PUC matriculated some 500 students a year to

---

[20] _SHS_, 5-27-1938. After Ewer died it was home to the Vance family (pre-Prohibition vineyardists) and the Schultz family, a convalescent hospital and then an Inn. It has had a number of other incarnations, including its present life as "Grandview."

become the doctors, nurses and teachers who were the pillars of the denomination and a source of healing for the community at large. The village of Angwin was up there, and beyond that Pope Valley. The roads were unpaved. Many people carried guns for protection against rattlers and rustlers.

Sheep and cattle fed in the meadows and on the hillsides past St. Helena along Route 29. The old Bale Mill, its huge waterwheel immobilized by tangles of thick-growing vines, was a silent relic of an even older period, the days of the first pioneers. Beyond that was Paradise Park, which claimed to have California's longest bar. The place was owned and operated by the Bothe Brothers, Ren and Al. The family of Lillie Hitchcock Coit had once owned the thickly forested park. In 1938 the old Hitchcock mansion, "Lonely," burned down, with Ren and Al's mother, Carolyn, age 76, inside. The exit was blocked by fire and smoke, so she jumped from a second floor window. She broke a leg but managed to drag herself to safety.

Calistoga, population almost an even 1,000, held its breath and wondered how long it could support itself. It was a dusty, sleepy little country town, proud of its pioneer past. Charles Carroll of the *Calistogian* was probably the best-known man there. He was very active in Rotary and Vice President of the reorganized Bank of Calistoga. The Bank of America, still hungry for purchases, swallowed up the Bank of Calistoga just as 1936 was coming to an end. No community was too remote for the B of A's appetite. Some in Calistoga may have taken comfort from the thought that it saw a future for their little town.

Wisely, perhaps, Calistoga diverted some of its attention from the wine business and concentrated on walnuts, a crop that was just coming into its own.[21] Walnut production in Napa County rose 400% in just 13 years. By 1940, 1,374 acres were in production,[22]

---

[21] Napa Valley farmers had been growing walnuts since the 1850's when William Nash planted them near what is now Bothe State Park. Napan John Hartley developed the extra-large Hartley English walnut at his orchard on Big Ranch Road before 1910.

[22] *NJ*, 8-1-1941.

and there were vast walnut orchards in Lake County, as well. J.H. Wheeler, the former St. Helena vineyardist, had replanted most of his Zinfandel Lane ranch with them. Before the '30's were over, Calistoga would build an immense walnut processing plant on the railroad just south of the business section. Considered by many to be the finest in the state, it housed $40,000 worth of machinery. John Ghisolfo, newly elected Mayor, gave his first important speech at the plant's opening. His remarks were followed by a grand march to a large cake and a mound of prune ice cream. The evening ended with a dance to music from a phonograph.

Motorists traveling east at the Y in Soscol south of Napa would eventually find themselves in Berryessa Valley, 10 miles long, a quarter mile wide, home to more cattle than people and more rattlesnakes than cattle. Wild and innocent, it bore little resemblance to the County's prune-, wine- and walnut-producing communities.

Berryessa had long been a frustration to the scores of investors who had hoped to find oil and gas there. The most persistent of the "wildcatters" was Walter B. Griffiths, a Napa realtor, state assemblyman (1909-1913) and self-styled petroleum expert.[23] Like the prospectors who preceeded him around the turn of the 20th Century, he had struck modest, short-lived pockets of oil and gas several times in the early 1920's. Also like those before him, he had turned for assistance to Theodore Bell. Bell had helped him establish the Griffiths Oil Company in 1921 and had raised $25,000 for the enterprise. Griffiths' strike and Bell's involvement inspired others to speculate. When someone claimed to have found oil and coal on the McCormick ranch on Spring Mountain in St. Helena,[24] a rush of speculation started, and a hatch of new companies appeared, among them the Sugarloaf Oil Company of Los Angeles, the Wreden Oil Company of Los Angeles, the Cappell Corporation, the Napetro Oil Company and a few others. A moderate-sized

---

[23] See Edith R. Griffiths, *Exploring for Oil in the Berryessa Valley*, Napa County Historical Society Gleanings, I, May, 1970, #1.

[24] *NJ*, 1-26-1923.

company, Associated Oil, sublet Griffiths' land and produced about 10 barrels of oil a day, "very high grade and clear as crystal," according to Griffiths.[25] But it wasn't enough, and Associated ordered the hole closed and the riggings removed.[26]

After Bell's death, Rodney McCormick, the local Democratic Party chairman, took over Griffiths' real estate business so that the latter could devote himself full-time to his Berryessa project. Griffiths convinced some Hollywood stars[27] to invest. He persuaded California's Secretary of State, Frank C. Jordan, to buy shares in his company, and Jordan recruited a few others. Local Napa businessmen also bought into Griffiths' dream. But when a geologist from Los Angeles came to inspect the site, the expert advised folks to pull out. All the other little oil companies that had popped up in Berryessa soon reeled in their cables, too, and disappeared.

Convinced that Berryessa would yield oil, the driven Griffiths sank what was at the time the deepest hole ever drilled in Northern California. At 3,710', his 25'-long, heavy steel drilling cable snapped off. The line he used to rescue the cable also broke, and he had to seal the hole with cement. He tried again with another well nearby, but this time it was he who busted. He found a Los Angeles firm that was willing to finish the job on contract, but then the stock market crashed and no one had the cash to sink into questionable oil well investments. As before, the only people to profit from Berryessa's gas and oil reserves were the lawyers who drew up the contracts.

The people of Monticello may have viewed the two oil rushes with mixed emotions. They loved their quiet little valley and their miniscule town, which consisted of a general store/ post office/ telephone exchange/ notary public/ bank/ insurance office/ dilapidated jail/ gas station, all under more or less the same roof and all run by the McKenzie family. There was a school to the

---

[25] *NJ*, 9-14-1922.

[26] Griffiths, pp. 1-6.

[27] an actor named Bert Lytell and his wife, Evelyn Vaughn

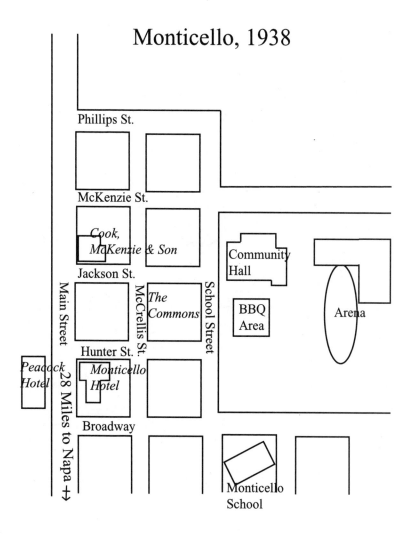

Monticello, 1938

Phillips St.

McKenzie St.

Cook,
McKenzie & Son

Jackson St.

Main Street

28 Miles to Napa →

McCrellis St.

The
Commons

School Street

Community
Hall

BBQ
Area

Arena

Hunter St.

Peacock
Hotel

Monticello
Hotel

Broadway

Monticello
School

Horsemanship was extremely popular in Napa County, and riders like the Avists, above, spared no expense.

southeast of town, and there were two hotels, the Monticello and the Peacock, the latter having been built in the 1860's. There was also a cemetery. Across a tree-lined street from the village proper were the rodeo grounds and a huge barbeque pit. The corrals, arena and grandstands were a symbol of the respect the townsfolk held for cowpunching. The cattle themselves munched, regurgitated and munched again in the broad meadows just past town.

Monticellans hauled down grain each summer to the warehouse at the Napa Milling Company on Main and Fourth Street in Napa. But the warehouse, which shared the lot with the Hatt Building, burned down near the end of 1935, taking bins and sacks of wheat, oats and barley with it and thus a portion of the farmers' very modest income. Hundreds of excited onlookers came to watch the Berryessa grain growers' harvest go up in smoke. A few ranchers were ruined and sold out that year.

Monticello's main claim to fame in the 1930's was not its illusory oil fields nor its good, honest grain, but its annual rodeo and barbeque. It had been attracting thousands since 1926.[28] An outgrowth of the little valley's annual springtime cattle round-up, it was one of the first in California to feature professional contestants.[29] The Monticello Community Club hosted the event on the first Sunday of May for 15 years, and the program was always the same. The night before the event, the barbecue committee built a bonfire of oak wood in a big pit next to the Monticello community hall. When the timbers became white-hot coals, the men and women of the committee sprinkled on a thin layer of loamy dirt and then dropped in some prime hindquarters of local-grown beef, which had been wrapped in many layers of cheesecloth. They covered the meat with more loam and then built a new fire over it all, which glowed all night. Meanwhile, they cooked up several huge kettles of pinto beans.

---

[28] See Robert McKenzie, "The Monticello Rodeo and Barbecue," *Gleanings*, Vol. I, #4, Napa County Historical Society, May, 1975.

[29] Inspired by what he saw there, Stan Gomez of nearby Capell Valley went on to become one of the premier ropers in US Rodeo.

Late the next morning, the smell of roasting beef greeted the jam of cars that pulled into town from just about everywhere. Those who arrived early could play in a pick-up baseball game on the diamond next to the barbecue pit or just sit around and enjoy John Philip Sousa music provided by a live band, which performed all day. Early in the afternoon the barbecuers lifted the roasted beef from the pit with big hooks. An endless supply of beer was available, both during and after Prohibition, as was an endless supply of cake.

Then the rodeo began. There were saddle- and bare-back bronco riding, bull riding, calf roping and wild cow milking. There were races. There were clowns. There were courtships. Between the Blue Ridge hills to the east and the chapparal of Cedar Roughs to the west, under the hazy May sky in a gentle, grassy valley, there was a sweet, simple, down-home joy.

Napans had always admired good horsemanship. The Monticello rodeo helped to reinspire community interest in riding. The annual Fourth of July festival in Calistoga in 1940 was re-named the "Silverado Fair and Horse Show." It featured more than 150 rodeo entries, and Napa Roping Club members won praise for "sticking to the brones and tossing a mean loop."[30] Thousands attended that event, too. With more than 200 horsemen, the opening parade went on for hours.[31] In August, down at the County Fair in Napa, all the men who came had to wear beards and 10-gallon hats like in the "good old days." (Ten gallon hats, of course, were a Hollywood invention. In the good old days of the 1880's, Napans wore top hats and bowlers, not cowboy hats, and at least half spoke with foreign accents.) So well-financed and well-attended were the Silverado Festival and the Napa County Fair that St. Helena stopped holding its Vintage Festival. Horses, not grapes, were now the great attraction.

---

[30] *NJ*, 7-3-1940.

[31] The 1941 parade broke the records for spectators, with an estimated 10,000 driving to the little city for the festivites.

Napa, Solano and Yolo Counties met near a gorge dubbed "Devil's Gate, " through which ran Putah Creek. George Washington Goethals, the engineer who had built the Panama Canal, had inspected Devil's Gate back in 1907, when he was on the US Army's General Staff.[32] Goethals and other experts agreed that Devil's Gate would be an ideal place to build a dam.[33] Impounding the water of Putah Creek, however, would mean flooding the little town of Monticello and drowning the cowboy haven of Berryessa Valley. To many, and especially to those in Napa County, that seemed like too great a price to pay for water.

Others, however, believed that Northern California didn't really *need* Berryessa Valley; Putah Creek, however, could be very useful. The Gibson family floated a brief story in the *Journal* about a proposed dam on Putah Creek early in 1936. It was the first many people in Napa County had heard about such an idea. "Construction of Putah Creek dam is temporarily held up," the article said, "by the refusal of one party to sign an easement allowing his property to be flooded. The expenditure of $15,000 is being jeopardized by this refusal."[34] The story named neither the refusing party nor the source of the $15,000. Meanwhile, the *Journal* gave florid praise to the newly completed reservoir system on Spring Mountain Road in St. Helena.

By 1940, Solano County's large urban centers (Vallejo, Fairfield and Vacaville) were experiencing much more robust population growth than the cities of Napa County. Solano's parched, flat terrain knew little moisture in the hot months, and civic leaders there worried about where the water to support their people and enterprises would come from. Neighboring Yolo County also suffered from arid conditions. The soil would yield generous harvests if it could be irrigated. Yolo and Solano farmers saw that the introduction of water to the San Joaquin Valley had

---

[32] With him on that assignment was William Mulholland, who later led the drive to divert water from Owens Valley to irrigate Los Angeles.

[33] Harold Rubin, *The Solano Water Story*, Solano Irrigation District, Vacaville, 1988, p. 5.

[34] *NJ*, 3-27-1936.

enabled orchardists there to grow plumper, juicier (if less sweet) fruit. Northern California fruit growers were losing market share.

Launcelot Gamble, heir to a soap fortune, was aware of Yolo/Solano's greedy gaze on Berryessa as a receptacle for water storage. He bought up as much land as he could and held on tight. Basalt President Al Streblow did the same.

Napans, too, needed water. They were making do with an antiquated system that also had to supply the needs of the Game Farm and the State Hospital. Back in 1883 the Napa City Water Company, a privately owned organization,[35] had hired local stone mason J.B. Newman to dam Milliken Creek about a half-mile north of Trancas Street, thus creating a small lake. Newman fit together a number of large squares of stone to create the dam. Pipes brought the water to an old locomotive boiler filled with sand, where it was purified (after a fashion) and collected in a cistern.[36] The water was then pumped to the hill above the cistern. The original system had a capacity of 3,000,000 gallons; Napa doubled it during the building boom that followed the '06 earthquake and built a separate 100,000-gallon reserve above the general reservoir for use in case of fire.[37]

A pipeline from the reservoir followed the Silverado Trail to a point near its intersection with East Avenue. It passed under the Napa River and delivered water to six wells in various locations around town and then finally to the main city water tower, which was located on Pine Street near the end of Seminary.[38] By 1922 the system was already obsolete, and the city had to build another dam, this one at Milliken canyon above what is now the Silverado Country Club. The project was finished in 1924. Despite Napa's

---

[35] created by George Goodman, Samuel Holden, E.W. Churchill and George Cornwell

[36] which was located where Hagen Road intersects the Silverado Trail.

[37] See Mario J. Tortorolo, "History of the City of Napa Water Supply," in *Gleanings*, Napa County Historical Society, Vol. 2, #2, May, 1978.

[38] close to today's Shearer Elementary School.

slow growth, the Milliken Canyon reservoir proved insufficient, especially since the State facilities used the water, too.

Experts had been surveying Rector Canyon (east of Oakville off the Silverado Trail, near the Game Farm) for years as a possible site to impound water. Through various measures, more than $600,000 had already been appropriated toward a dam's construction at Rector, but other than some primitive access roads in the chapparal, no building had yet begun. The Army Corps of Engineers, meanwhile, had conducted a survey of its own of another, much larger potential dam site: Conn Valley, northeast of Rutherford, which was fed by Sage, Chiles, Moore and Conn Creeks. Conn Valley, the Army's report said, was the only location the Federal Government would consider as a dam site; the cost of any other location would exceed the value.[39]

Back in 1927, an Oakland-based company called Utility & Service had bought land in Conn Valley for $28,310 from Nathan F. Coombs with the purpose of building a dam there.[40] The water would go to Vallejo. Napa Valley people vigorously protested what they felt was the absconding of their water by their "sister city," and bad feelings developed. Angry locals met at the Rutherford Grange to "protect what is by heritage the property of the people of Napa County."[41] County Supervisors declared they would not allow a right of way for Utility & Service to lay pipelines. The issue went fallow, with Utility & Service holding land they could not develop and Napa and Solano Counties still thirsty for water.

In March of 1941 State Senator Frank L. Gordon introduced a bill requesting funds to construct a dam at Conn for use by the state

---

[39] Conn Valley had enjoyed a rich history of human habitation long before the American poineers came there to settle. When word leaked out that this and not Rector might be the site for a new dam, the WPA sponsored an archeological survey of the area. It was the first of its kind in California.

[40] Presumably Coombs' involvement had been as an agent for the County of Napa.

[41] *NJ*, 1-19-1928.

facilities. The bill included measures for flood control. Gordon assured his fellow politicians that the water would not be used to supply the cities of Napa County. Those who looked at it closely, however, saw that it provided for "the beneficial utilization of any surplus of waters" by Napa Valley municipalities. The bill authorized the Department of Finance to acquire land for the dam, build it and cooperate with the federal government in its management and development.

Some of the most powerful men in the county drove to Sacramento to testify, lobby and cheer for the bill's passage, among them Calistoga Mayor John Ghisolfo and Councilmen E. J. Stevens and Howard Butler; St. Helena City Councilman Dr. H. L. Byrd; Veterans' Home Commandant Col. Nelson Holderman; labor leader George Bobst; Stanly Jones of the Napa Valley Water Conservation League; Ed Hennessey of the Napa City Council and Thomas Maxwell, chairman of the County Board of Supervisors. They were surprised, perhaps, to find that another Napa Valley group was arguing the other side. Dean A. Calkins of Pacific Union College sent a panicky telegram protesting against the Conn Valley site. A dam there, they claimed, would cost the college between $100,000 and $250,000, because they would have to install a new sewage system. This huge expense would be a disaster for the privately run institution, something California's 30,000 Seventh-Day Adventist constituents would resent deeply and remember at the polls. Mary Grigsby, owner of a gravel pit on Conn Creek, also spoke out against the project, saying a dam would destroy her business and that she would expect compensation for this.

The bill went to the Department of Finance for study at the end of April. In a hearing before the Finance Committee, Utility and Service claimed that they would not consider selling the site to the State for anything less than $260,000. Assemblywoman Jeannette E. Daley observed that the state should pay no more than $125,000 for the site, three times its assessed value.

The Ways and Means Committee voted to approve Rector, not Conn, as the site for the dam. The Conn site, they said, would "put the state in the water business," and they did not want to be responsible for refurbishing the sewage system of Pacific Union

College or losing the SDA's vote statewide. They allotted $757,000 more for the project, resulting in a total of $1,377,000 to be set aside for a dam in Rector Canyon.

Two weeks after its detailed coverage of the Conn Valley issue, the *Napa Journal* lost its designation as the "official newspaper of Napa County." On June 29, 1941, publisher George Provine announced that henceforth, the paper would only come out once a week, leaving the *Register* as the only daily in the Valley. He cited a lack of manpower as the reason. While a thin staff may or may not have been the direct cause of the *Journal's* sudden failure to thrive, the manpower problem was very real. Just a few years ago there were masses of unemployed workers begging for jobs. What happened?

Provine's personnel problem had roots far from Napa County. In March, 1938 Adolph Hitler seized Austria, which offered no resistance. The following summer Nazi armies invaded Poland and began a brutal program of "ethnic cleansing" there. Britain declared war on Germany in September, 1939, followed immediately by France and Canada. The American stock market awoke from its decade-long slumber, with spectacular buying of steel, copper, aviation, chemical and truck shares. Airplane companies cried for more workers, and so did shipyards. Although the American public was strongly isolationist, Roosevelt and Congress would not be caught napping. They foresaw a war on the Atlantic and were pumping out air and sea power as fast as they could.

In January of 1940, Mare Island employed 6,700 workers and was expanding quickly through a string of major appropriations. They built submarines and sub tenders. By August, France and the Netherlands had fallen, and the Nazis had grabbed Spain. Germany was pounding England with a torrent of deadly bombs, and as flames engulfed London, Congress authorized more and more dollars for Mare Island and the nation's other defense facilities.[42] The Navy built an $8,000,000 radio station on Skaggs Island. It was a three-way relay that could both receive and transmit. By

[42] MI was the nation's fourth largest.

September 1, 1940 the workers at Mare Island and related facilities numbered 10,460, and their daily wage was much better than most local employers could afford to pay. Thousands of local workers dropped what they were doing and signed on with the defense industry. Now it wasn't only George Provine who had a labor problem. Hardly anyone was around to harvest the crops. The schools opened late so that students could pick prunes, grapes and walnuts.

The Basalt Corporation was involved with the American defense build-up, too, first with a contract to supply rip-rap to the air base at Alameda in the East Bay and then with much larger orders to build steel cargo-hold barges, freighter lighters and tugboats. Al Streblow's quickly growing Basalt company bought land along the Napa River to manufacture and launch the vessels.

The biggest nearby operation was not in Napa County, however, but in Richmond. The Kaiser shipyard employed tens of thousand of workers, most of them former dust bowl refugees. They worked at assembly lines and mass-produced Liberty Ships, slow-moving cargo vessels that supplied the materiel needed to wage war on foregin shores. Some of these workers moved to Napa County, too, partcularly to Napa and Napa Junction, which were within comfortable commuting distance.

Roosevelt ordered the nation's first peacetime draft. On October 16, 1940, Napa's eligible draftees stood in line, signed in and got a number.[43] More than 1600 Napa County aliens were also required to make their presence known, most of them employees at the State Hospital. As was the case just before World War I, many men did not wait to be called up; they enlisted. Georges de Latour's son-in-law, the Marquis Henri Galcerand de Pins, left the Valley to enter the service in France against Hitler. Wally Everett joined the Napa Home Defense Guard and became its Captain. Frank Dunlap left the law offices of Nathan F. Coombs in April of 1941 and took a commission in the Navy. Ensign Dunlap sailed to Midway, which for a while may have seemed calmer than his law firm.

---

[43] Twenty-four year-old Elmo Doughty was the Napan whose number, 158, was drawn first.

As the nation tooled up for war, the quicksilver/mercury industry enjoyed a rebirth because of the toxic mineral's use in marine paints and explosives. The biggest mine in Napa County was the Oat Hill, north of Calistoga, where an old-fashioned armed robbery just before dawn one summer morning diverted the Valley's imagination from the horrors in Europe. Two bandits wearing black hoods overpowered H. Carr, the only man on duty, dragged him over a slag pile and tied him to a tree with leather thongs. They took $3,000 from the safe and 14 flasks of quicksilver. Carr wriggled loose and telephoned his brother, Floyd, in another part of the mine. The thieves heard the phone ring and took off with their loot in a large sedan. Calistoga Police Chief Ed Light and Undersheriff John Claussen sped to the scene of the crime and found, in the slag, a heel plate dropped by one of the thieves. When two "strangers" showed up in a large sedan in Healdsburg a few days later, Light produced the heel plate and induced a confession.

The ghost town of Knoxville rose briefly from the dead when George Gamble bought it and tried to get it up and running, but its reincarnation proved brief: The ore had run out. Despite the loss of this one-time big producer, Napa County could boast of 20 operating mines, making it the third largest supplier in the state.

Other minerals were also drawn from the ground to help in the defense effort. The owners of the Palisades silver mine north of Calistoga reported striking a new, rich ledge of ore. Twenty-one men worked the mill there 10 hours a day to extract it from its matrix. In Berryessa near Steele Canyon, other, less lucky men labored in an asbestos mine, inhaling the fine filaments that fluttered in the air about them. It was one of only three such operations in the country. Miners were considered vital, so a federal law was passed "freezing" them to their jobs; they were not allowed to seek employment elsewhere.[44]

Mare Island and Basalt attracted men and women to Napa and Vallejo like magnets and worked them in rotations 24 hours a day,

---

[44] *NJ*, 9-18-1942.

seven days a week, starting in May of 1941. The tenders *Fulton, Nereus, Sperry, Neptune* and *Bushnell*, and the submarines *Wahoo, Whale, Sunfish, Tinosa, Tullibee, Tunny, Tuna, Silverside* and *Gudgeon* were all born at MI, which by the summer of '41 had also gone into the mass production of submarine torpedo tubes and guns for cruisers and destroyers.

In October of 1941, the old landing strip that had been installed in the 1920's—grown over and forgotten about by most—saw a second life, but very soon saw death, as well. Within two weeks of its revival, a bomber crashed into the hillside 10 miles east of Napa, killing all three crewmen.[45] It was clear that the landing strip was inadequate for government needs, so county leaders searched for a more suitable location that they could sell to the Defense Department. When the war ended it would convert to civilian use.[46] They chose 800 acres south of Napa, farming land in the possession of six families.[47] All but one of the families eventually consented to selling their land. The holdout, John Almada, took the county to court but lost. He appealed, and the Appellate Court ruled that the county "exceeded its jurisdiction" in snatching Almada's land from him. Later on he lost it anyway.

By mid-November MI employed 22,444 people. Napa was declared a "defense housing area," which meant people could buy homes with 0 to 5% downpayment. A mill in Napa Junction went into the production of material for prefabricated houses, most of which went up in Vallejo. Napa became home to fleets of trailer homes and to as many new cottages as there were lots on which to build them. Most of the little defense houses had two bedrooms, a bath, a big living room with a fireplace, a dinette, a kitchen, a laundry cove and a garage. Napa Councilmen voted several times to incorporate new developments within the city limits, thus the county seat expanded both in population and in area. Each man, woman and child who came to live in the area needed water,

---

[45] *Napa Shopping News,* 10-31-1941.

[46] NJ, 11-13-1942

[47] the Kelly estate, the Dutton estate, Manuel Almada, John Almada, Harlow Greenwood and Victor Leveroni

turning the water shortage problem into a crisis. A companion crisis also intensified: where to dispose of waste. The Federal Housing Administration was unhappy with sewage conditions in Napa, but people kept on coming, and builders kept on building.

Chapter Twelve

Heroes

itler's assault on the Old World seemed unstoppable. Swastikas flew on the Crimean peninsula; Rommel's tanks ground their way through North Africa, and parts of the Mediterranean seemed like a Nazi lake. Doris Pellet, the St. Helena emigree, left her beloved Mallorca again. "The danger of a concentration camp was growing so imminent," she wrote, "that it was madness to stay on."[1]

Roosevelt declared an "Unlimited Emergency." The military would be brought to a basis of readiness to repel an invasion; the raw materials usually intended for domestic and municipal use would be diverted to make this possible. As if the imminent shortages would have no effect on the Napa Valley, the City of Napa decided to buy the Conn Valley dam site from Utility and Service for the $260,000 that U&S demanded, with payments to be made over time after an initial $30,000 down. On Friday, December 5, 1941, the city placed Nathan F. Coombs in charge of negotiating with U&S and rendering an opinion on all legal matters connected with it. Crews immediately dug "borrow pits" from which they could take dirt to build the dam.

Elsewhere in America, all eyes were focused on Hitler and Europe. There was mounting tension, too, however, on the other side of the globe, where Japan continued to plunder China and was making incursions into Southeast Asia. The United States and

---

[1] *SHS*, 1-2-1942.

Britain trickled occasional aid to Chinese leader Chiang Kai-shek and worked together to embargo scrap iron, steel and aviation fuel. Japan still relied on the US for 80% of its oil.[2] America's always tenuous relationship with Japan frayed further after Hitler invaded Russia in June of 1941. The US sent oil and other supplies to the invaded country, which had long been Japan's enemy. Japan protested the shipments and the moderate embargo it was enduring, but the freeze deepened, and by the end of summer the US had stopped shipping anything at all to Japan, leaving the Imperial Navy with about 18 months of oil. To replenish their tanks, Japan would either have to pull out of China or conquer the oil-rich Dutch East Indies.

Special Japanese envoys met repeatedly with Cordell Hull to get the United States to at least lift the embargo.

> Were the situation not so grim [wrote Provine of the *NJ*], loud laughter would greet the solemn assertions from Tokio that Japan is being driven to take drastic action by the "insufferable hostility" of Britain and the United States...[T]he current limited boycotts...can better be described as moderate restraints aimed at preventing Japan, for her own good, from participating in a conflict which would mean national suicide for her.[3]

But Japan would not cede what it had taken from China, and the United States would not ship them any more oil. While Nathan Coombs was plotting how to finagle with Utility and Service, an armada of battleships, cruisers, destroyers and subs carved through the Pacific Ocean, and in the center of this formation steamed six aircraft carriers, fully laden. On the morning of December 7, 1941, 350 planes burst forth from their decks like ripe seeds and headed toward Oahu. Napan Harry Gruver was aboard the supply ship *Wright* when the raiders came, and his gun crews fired on them,[4] but the war for which Mare Island, Basalt and the nation had been preparing was suddenly a reality. Another Napa Valley man, a

---

[2] Kennedy, p. 505.

[3] *NJ*, 11-21-1941

[4] *NJ*, 9-14-1945.

shipfitter on the *Oklahoma* named Algeo Malfante, died in the bombing. He was the first of what for the Napa Valley would be way too many.

The same day the Japanese attack force headed for Hawaii, a second flotilla embarked for the Philippines and the string of islands leading to the Dutch East Indies. Within days of the attack on Pearl Harbor, Hong Kong, Guam, Wake Island, Indochina, Thailand and British Malaya fell to Japan. Several men and one woman from the Napa Valley were killed or taken prisoner.[5] Among them was a WWI veteran, St. Helenan Hjalmar Erickson, a senior medical officer on Cavite. The Japanese hauled him and other prisoners to Manila, where he was thrown into a dank, ancient Spanish prison. He witnessed the torture and execution of fellow prisoners. A devout Seventh-Day Adventist, Commander Erickson drew upon his deep faith to survive the ordeal.[6]

Now the Valley's proximity to the big defense plants became a liability. Sheriff Steckter took charge of the county's defense preparations and instructed the citizens on what to do in the event of air raids. Complete blackouts were mandated. Citizens were to drape heavy blankets over their windows when the siren went off: one blast of one minute long followed three seconds later by a blast three seconds long, repeated at one-minute intervals. The "all clear" was a minute-long blast. Citizens were to stay indoors, and motorists were to pull to the curb immediately, turn off their lights and stay still until it was over. Civilians were not to use the telephone, and the phone company offices painted their exterior windows black so they could operate in an emergency.

Marjorie Hetland Wright found herself in an emergency during the first Napa blackout. Nine months pregnant, she went into labor in the darkness and soon delivered Edgar Wright III. Her husband, Edgar Wright, Jr. was far away on the jungley island of Corregidor, expecting the Japanese.

---

[5] The woman was Elizabeth Donnelly, a bacteriologist working in Manila, who was captured by the Japanese.

[6] *NJ*, 7-27-1945.

Neighbors were encouraged to police each other for blackout violations. An old Italian named Augustino Arbaco, who had lived for years on the corner of Fulton and Railroad Avenues in St. Helena, not only refused to turn off his porch light during a blackout, but insisted on turning it on again after a ranger at the fire suppression camp across the street extinguished it for him. He also refused to turn off his radio, with which he had plagued the neighborhood for many years by playing at full strength. He was fined $15 for the light and had his radio (which contained short-wave radio equipment) confiscated.[7] Far less fortunate was Juzo Hamamoto, 43, a Japanese rancher who had lived in the Valley for 13 years. He was arrested and jailed as a spy.

Undersheriff Claussen gave a class on what to do if incendiary bombs fell, and it was suggested that residents roof their houses with asphalt shingles, which withstood fire better than shake. Northern California received the unsettling news that the months of June, July and August would be the most likely for an attack, because the Pacific fog bank allowed aircraft carriers to come relatively close to shore. The defense committee found locations outside of the Napa city limits which would serve as shelters if the dread possibility of an air raid occurred.

The State Guard and all other military units prepared for full mobilization. A guard was posted at Milliken dam to prevent sabotage, and when Johan Carl Nisson, a German alien, mentioned to some fellow Napans that he wished he could help Japan, he was arrested and held for investigation.

As has been seen, the war paranoia of 1917 led to the persecution of the Germans and Austrians in the Napa Valley and other places in America. Many remembered the hysteria of those times and vowed not to repeat it. Nevertheless, as a matter of national security, citizens of countries with whom America was now at war were required to register at their local post office. In Calistoga, postmaster Owen Kenny registered 24 "enemy aliens." Joe Galewsky signed up 89 in St. Helena, and there were 165 in Napa. As has also been seen, however, persons of Asian ancestry

---

[7] *SHS*, 1-9-1942.

had never enjoyed the embrace of full acceptance by their Caucasian neighbors. Thus, when Roosevelt signed Executive Order 9066 declaring that all persons of Japanese ancestry must leave the "Western Defense Command" of Washington, Oregon and California, few voices protested.

"Zone A-1" of the Western Command—the area considered the most sensitive for national security—carved Napa into two sections. Everything west of Jefferson and South of Third Street fell within it. No Japanese, whether citizen or not, was allowed to be there, nor could other "enemy aliens," i.e. Germans or Italians. Everything east and north of this was a "restricted" area. "Enemy aliens" could remain in the restricted area for the time being, but they couldn't move about and had to obey a curfew, which was enforced. When Angelo Casagga of Calistoga was discovered away from his home at 9PM, for example, he was arrested and sent to a facility in San Francisco.[8]

The "restricted" zone included the heavily Italian East Napa. About 10% of the Italians in the United States were not US citizens, and there was some public outcry about labeling these people—often elderly and non-English speaking—as risks to national security.[9] On Columbus Day, 1942, Roosevelt had the "enemy alien" label lifted from the Italians, but not from the Japanese or Germans.

Fifty-four Japanese people were ordered to leave Napa County at once, all but 10 of them *Issei*: first-generation immigrants who had been denied citizenship by the Immigration Restriction Act of 1924. Three of them were farmers,[10] and only one owned the farm he operated. Some, like Joe Fullert, were only partly Japanese. Joe's brother Richard managed to escape to Switzerland, but his mother and other siblings were shunted to a relocation camp, where Joe died.[11] Those lucky enough to be in Zone B remained until May of 1942, when the increasingly paranoid Lt. Gen. John L. Dewitt of

---

[8] *WC*, 7-24-1942.

[9] Kennedy, *Op. Cit.*, p. 750.

[10] *NJ*, 11-10-1944.

[11] *NJ*, 6-23-1944

the Western Defense Command ordered all Japanese out of Napa, Marin and Sonoma Counties and into internment camps. As soon as they were gone, "qualified farmers" wishing to take their land were invited to register for it at a given location.

Public outcry was minimal. Starr Baldwin revealed the depth of his racial prejudice when he wrote that since Japan was America's enemy, all Japanese should be interned, because, he claimed, there was no way of telling which were loyal and which were not.[12] "And there is nothing in the Japanese character, as exposed to us over almost a century of relations, that can permit us to ever trust that race again,"[13] he said.

While California's Japanese lost virtually everything, the rest of the population had to make do with shortages of certain supplies. The first thing to be rationed was tires. The Napa Horsemen's Association immediately put together a committee to install hitching posts in the county's towns so that residents could ride their horses to work and shop, as they had within the memory of many. The Horsemen's Association was such an effective lobby that the Army allowed the Association's Second Annual Spring Horse Show to go ahead as planned at the fairgrounds. It was one of very few such public gatherings permitted in 1942. Nearly 130 horses were entered in it, and people used precious tire tread to journey to the fairgrounds to watch and compete.[14]

July's Silverado Horse Show and Fair in Calistoga, however, was cancelled, as was the Napa County Fair in August, due to the rubber shortage.[15] Folks living in outlying areas like Pope, Chiles and Berryessa Valleys were more or less marooned there, only daring to come to the larger towns every few weeks to gather supplies. Shopkeepers in Napa enjoyed business as usual because

---

[12] *SHS*, 4-24-1942.

[13] *SHS*, 6-4-1943. In another editorial he wrote that "Japan is in like situation with the South, save that she has no moral ground on which to stand."

[14] Because they were still potentially useful in warfare, horses and mules between the ages of 3 and 10 had to be registered.

[15] Calistogans made do with a festive gymkhana.

of the great influx of Mare Island workers, but merchants in Calistoga and St. Helena suffered.

People were urged to recover all the scrap rubber they could find and donate it to the war effort. The response was satisfying. Not everyone, however, was patriotic-minded. Rings of young bandits stole tires from cars, and at least one local man was arrested for "bootlegging" them.

Sugar rationing began in March, bringing new life to the bee-keeping industry. Gas rationing began in November. Nearly 15,000 drivers came to 21 schoolhouses around the Valley to pick up mileage ration books. Defense workers were entitled to more miles and different ration books, a situation that was immediately confusing to everyone, including, perhaps, the staff working under local ration chief Marcus Stanton, who had to spend so much time explaining the procedure to people that lines grew long and tempers grew short.[16] The inundation of red tape resulted in a shortage of paper.

Metal of all kind was rationed. The state department of transportation switched from steel to wooden road signs. Bottle caps for beer were in short supply, so people were urged to buy their brew in quart sizes or larger, an ironic twist to the situation faced by thirsty citizens during the previous war. Cloth was also in limited supply (although not rationed), which had a shortening effect on women's hemlines and led to the introduction of the two-piece bathing suit.

Cork was no longer available for the county's 45 wineries, and much was made of a grove of 60 cork oak trees in Oakville. Hans Hansen helped to plant them from acorns in 1878, when he was five years old and his father was superintendent at the old *Far Niente* winery. The land had changed owners a few times, but the trees were still there, and Hans was still tending them. He watched with great satisfaction when the first corks were taken from them in 1940, but early in 1942 he fell from a ladder while tending his stately old charges and died.

---

[16] *NJ*, 12-4-1942.

The wine industry contributed to the war effort in several ways. Wine itself rolled out of the Napa Valley Co-Op Winery in unprecedented amounts, some of it destined to be consumed by armed forces officers in points around the globe. Beringer wine was included for a time as part of the ration packet for French soldiers in the Far East. Wine by-products had numerous uses. American wineries became the world's only source of tartrates, which were used in the manufacture of medicines and rayon and in photography. Tung oil, an ingredient in aircraft paint, was an export from China and no longer available; grape seeds yielded a substitute for it. Tannic acid from skins and stems could be used in the treatment of burns.

Hedgeside Distillery announced it would manufacture 190-proof alcohol for war purposes. Hedgeside may have produced a lot of whiskey from time to time, but it apparently had trouble selling it. Owner De La Montanya tripled its payroll in 1937 and introduced a line of rum made from prune mash. The Distillery went idle in 1938. Later, when the inventory of brandy it had stored on Brown Street appeared to have shrunk, the IRS may have suspected that Montanya was actually one of the last of the bootleggers. By 1939 Hedgeside was barely able to pay its taxes. The Schenley Corporation bought it in 1941, with a portion of the inventory going to something called World Wide Industries.

Japan breezed across the Pacific throughout the early months of 1942. The British possession of Singapore surrendered on February 15, and the Japanese launched a major naval invasion of the Dutch East Indies, winning the Battle of Java Sea on February 17. The Indies fell by mid-March. On April 9 Bataan surrendered, followed by Corregidor, and the Imperial Army dealt sadistically with the American and Philippino prisoners it captured. One who managed to slip away was Edgar Wright, whose son had been born in Napa during the blackout. He ducked into the jungle, where he would spend the next two-and-a-half years years on the run as a guerilla.

News of these Allied losses was withheld from the American public, but sailors home on leave told their personal stories to breathless audiences. One who had a tale to tell was Armand

Holderman, son of the Commandant of the Veterans' Home. The younger Holderman was an Ensign on the *USS Lexington*, in command of the port bow gun battery. The first torpedo to hit the huge aircraft carrier landed just below him, but was a dud.

"What's that?" asked one of his sailors. "A torpedo?"

"Nah," said another, "we just hit a reef." An explosion then rocked another part of the ship, and the sailor added, "Damned shallow water around here, isn't it?" The *Lexington* shot down 40 Japanese planes in 45 minutes, Holderman said.[17] He was one of the last to leave as the big ship disappeared beneath the rolling swells of the deepest part of the Pacific. After recuperating with his parents at the Veterans' Home, he went back to train as a pilot.

President Roosevelt made a secret, surprise visit to Mare Island in September, and one of the items he came to inspect was a two-man submarine taken from the Japanese, nick-named the "Tojo Cigar." Like the "Trophy Train" that came to Napa during the First World War, the "Tojo Cigar" became a great propaganda tool. For the price of a war bond, spectators could view the little vessel and even poke their heads inside. Calistoga led the entire state in response to the sub. Its 1,124 citizens spent an average of $22.88 each to see and touch an actual Japanese submarine.

Each week more young men and women left the Valley to don uniforms and serve their country. Defense workers continued to move in, however, so despite the drain of Napa Valley natives, the population of the city of Napa grew steadily. In September, 1942, it was the seventh-fastest growing city in the west. In October it was the third.[18] Mare Island and the other building sites demanded workers, and with so many men gone to war, women took their places on the assembly lines.

The rapid change in demographics was not without consequence. On the plus side, the increase of recently arrived, two-income families enabled Napa merchants to enjoy the most lucrative Christmas ever in 1942. But the recipients of these gifts became a source of aggravation for the police department, as the

---

[17] *WC*, 6-12-1942.

[18] The population of Vallejo tripled between 1940 and the end of 1942.

incidence of juvenile delinquency spiked. A curfew of 10PM was instituted in Napa after some 15 young people staged a two-day drunken orgy in a private home on River Street.[19] Children habitually skipped school, often with the knowledge and blessing of newcomer parents who themselves had not received much education.

For many of the recent arrivals, Napa was just another place on the map. Breaking into the tightly knit, xenophobic community was not easy, and civic pride was slow to develop. No one did much about it when the junk yard at Randolph and Second Streets mounted into a disgusting trash heap. The high-maintenance Napa River banks became gorged with garbage; people simply held their noses and continued on their way. Some said it was the filthiest river site in Northern California. A great, hideous dying of fish near Trancas Street seemed to confirm this.

Napa's civic apathy spilled over to other things, as well. When the Office of Civil Defense tried to muster up 1,000 volunteers for the municipality's Home Guard, only 115 people signed up. "This week has clearly demonstrated," sighed the *Journal*, "that the majority of us do not care what happens to us."[20] And despite the fact that the population was three times what it had been in 1940, there were actually 1,263 fewer registered voters on the books when it came time for the town to elect new leaders. The only important measure to be voted in was a bond issue for the creation of a local community college, which 90% of the voters approved. The guiding force behind it was Harry McPherson, husband of author Jessamyn West and superintendent of the Napa schools.

The situation in Calistoga could not have been more different. Its population boasted neither swarms of newly arrived, poorly educated defense workers nor paragons from the San Francisco society page. In every drive for war-related funds it oversubscribed, including the Red Cross's pledge program in the first part of 1945,

---

[19] *NJ*, 12-11-1942.
[20] *NJ*, 11-6-1942.

where it was the first town in America to meet its quota.[21] Each Christmas Calistogans assembled gift packs for their men and women in the service that included gum, cigarettes, games and a special edition of the *Weekly Calistogian* entitled "Greetings from Your Calistoga." The Rotary Club extended an open invitation to any service person passing through town to attend a meeting, and it pledged to find a job for any returning local veteran. Calistoga's experience of World War II was a therapeutic reversal of the deep discomfort it had experienced in the prior war.

New leadership in the county seat was critically necessary. Not only was Napa very poorly run, but certain members of the good-ol' boy system had gone on to other things and other places. After 14 years on the City Council, Napa Mayor Oliver Hoffman died unexpectedly in December, 1942, and long-time Councilman S.J. Cinnamond assumed his unexpired term. Because of new federally mandated term limit legislation, Rodney McCormick had to relinquish his postmaster position, handing the reigns over to George Provine, whose family continued to publish the *Journal*. In St. Helena, Joe Galewsky retired after decades as postmaster there for the same reason.

There were other changes. Congressman Frank Buck, very popular with Solano County voters but perhaps somewhat less so in Napa County, dropped dead of an apoplectic stroke in Washington, DC, just before the big 1942 elections. Governor Olson lost his bid for re-election to an upstart Republican lawyer named Earl Warren, whose terms of office would have enormous consequences for some in the Napa Valley.

Of most immediate import for the Valley, though, was the death of Percy Simpson King, the hard-drinking Superior Court judge who had reigned over Napa's judiciary since 1927. He died of a heart attack, and with him went the heart and soul of the good ol' boy system. Melvin Lernhart, an honest lawyer who had served briefly as District Attorney, replaced him.

---

[21] *NJ*, 2-16-1945.

After King died, Charlie Otterson finally stepped down from his post as fire chief. He insisted on assuming a less demanding role in the department, a favor that could not be granted for long, because his health was failing. The big, mustachioed Swede had basked in Napa's limelight since 1905, coming to town along with the electric railroad. He had survived earthquakes, train wrecks, car wrecks, fires, stab wounds, stray bullets and, until the death of Judge King, small town politics. He died within a year of his retirement at the age of 75. Members of the department he had loved and dominated for so long carried him to his mausoleum at Tulocay.

Napans had the opportunity to elect new leadership in May of 1943. Long-time Council member S.J. Cinnamond ran against a rookie to city politics, Charles Moffitt, who owned a car dealership. Moffitt won and brought in with him another first-timer, Charles Hare. District Attorney Wally Everett went to Europe with the Army, and Daniel K. York became the new DA.

With Judge King gone, the new guard grabbed the old system by the collar and shook it hard, and out fell a pair of good ol' rascals. Lernhardt and York hired an outside auditor to review in depth Napa County's finances, ostensibly for just the past two years, but in fact the probe went far deeper. The first rat they nabbed was the sheriff, Jack Steckter. Working in concert with the Grand Jury, the auditor was able to determine that Steckter had been illegally pocketing other peoples' money since 1927. Part of his job was to transport prisoners and psychiatrically disturbed patients to various venues in the area, and his office was reimbursed for this. The money was supposed to go back into the county coffers, because the transportation of prisoners was part of his job, but the bucks stopped in Steckter's personal bank account, instead. Meanwhile, when his deputies transported prisoners, they had to use their own cars and were not reimbursed. Other monies that found their way to his bank included bail bonds, litigants' deposits, food allowances for certain prisoners, trust funds and the personal effects of some of the people he arrested. In its report, the Grand Jury also stated that

> excess amounts were collected from citizens for services
> rendered in civil matters, and refunds had not been made

> to them; the proper fee only and not the full fee collected
> being deposited with the County Treasurer.[22]

Steckter resigned after 24 years in office. The Grand Jury did not investigate his activities on behalf of well-placed bootleggers, if indeed there were any. Undersheriff Claussen was not implicated in the Steckter scandal, and he stayed on, but two of Steckter's closest associates in the Sheriff's Department, Deputies Gaffney and Graham, left with him, although they were not involved in Steckter's malfeasance, either. Joe Moore of Berryessa accepted the invitation to become Napa's new sheriff.

The second rat they trapped was the County Coroner/Public Administrator, Theodore Treadway, who was also one of Napa's morticians. Like his dishonored predecessor, William Blake, Treadway had never bothered to keep files on the activities of his office, and each year when the Grand Jury came by to review his department, he took charge of the audit himself. The outside auditor had to do a great deal of detective work to untangle the rodent's nest Treadway had created. He found 49 estates with "irregularities" and another 18 with "unsatisfactory verification of financial transactions." The irregularities and lack of verification inevitably resulted in a profit for Treadway; indeed, "the principal assets of the Estates were transferred to the Treadway Funeral Chapel" in many cases.[23]

> [C]ash and various kinds of personal property have been
> held by the Public Administrator without any official
> record thereof having been made…[P]ersonal property
> has been received, sold and the funds derived therefrom
> disbursed before there has been any official record of the
> property being owned by the Estate.[24]

---

[22] Napa County Grand Jury Report, 1943, A.J. Frommelt, Chairman.

[23] "Audit Report of Theodore J. Treadway, Public Administrator, June 30, 1943," p. 14.

[24] Ibid, pp. 6-7.

The Grand Jury report cited case after case of Treadway's apparent, sometimes ludicrously macabre malfeasance, including one instance where there was no record of the body even being buried.

Treadway tacked random, unjustifiable fees onto the deceased's estates, almost all of them illegal, which often drained the estates of all of their assets. The estate of George W. Quick was an example:

```
County Clerk fee.............................7.00
Napa Journal advertising.....................9.00
County Treasurer's fee.......................1.22
Theodore J. Treadway, administrator's fee....8.56
King & King, Attorney's fees.................8.56
Webber Funeral Parlors......................87.89
```

The only fee in Quick's case that was legal was the last one listed.[25] "Such payments would appear to have the sole effect of increasing the compensation of the Public Administrator or his attorney," said the audit report.

Upon taking office, Treadway swore to a notary public (Percy King, Jr.) that he himself was not "interested" in (i.e., would not profit from in any way) his role as County Coroner, a misstatement that brought up serious questions of perjury. The truth was that the deceased very often managed to find their way into Treadway's own funeral parlor. From June of 1927 through July, 1943, Treadway's business received a total of $17,002.71 as a direct result of his work as Public Administrator.[26] The Grand Jury urged that future Coroner/Public Administrators not also be morticians.

As the "Official Newspaper of Napa County," the *Journal* received $9.00 for each death notice it ran for the Public Administrator, drawn from the decedent's estate, an unlawful practice in which had also engaged in Walden's time. Perhaps because it, too, had profited along with Treadway, the *Journal* did not expend much ink reporting the details of Treadway's legal problem.

The Treadway case went through several levels of litigation. Percy King, Jr. defended him. At one point, Percy Jr. argued that

---

[25] Samuel J. Webber was Treadway's competitor.

[26] "Exhibit E, Audit Report of Theodore J. Treadway."

the presence of an out-of-county judge, Matthew J. Brady, intimidated the jurors at the presentation of evidence, thus the verdict should be thrown out.[27] It was still not completely resolved in the spring of 1945, when the defendant dropped dead during a fishing trip on the Eel River in Garberville. In its eulogy, the *Journal* did not mention the scandal that accompanied his final term of office, but it did note that he wasn't a politician "in the narrow sense" of the term. He "played politics all year round," it said.[28]

The Steckter/Treadway scandal may have drawn California's new Governor to investigate Napa County more closely. Earl Warren made Napa State Hospital one of the first focal points of his new administration. Arriving at Imola in the beginning of October, 1943, he was "greatly distressed" by what he saw. "We must act immediately," he declared, and he ordered the fourth floor of the main building to be evacuated at once. His concern was fire. Three hundred patients were crammed into a stuffy upper story with no fire exits, wooden walls, narrow halls and rickety, claustrophobic stairways. It was a miracle that a tragedy hadn't already occurred. The experience at Imola, coupled with the Steckter/Treadway revelations, may have negatively conditioned the Governor's opinion of the Napa Valley.

Another important figure in Napa's Old Guard also left a post of responsibility in 1943. After 25 years of faithful service, Mrs. Franklin W. Bush resigned as chair of the Napa County Chapter of the American Red Cross, leaving the vital volunteer organization in the hands of younger women. The war effort placed a huge burden on the Red Cross. Especially in the Up-Valley, where fewer wives worked, women gathered to knit and prepare relief supplies for soldiers in battle. They sold war bonds, hosted rallies, even put on a parade in St. Helena that featured a motorcade of some of the town's leading ladies. Driving down Main Street on the topside of cars like candidates for homecoming queen were its organizers,

---

[27] NJ, 7-7-1944.

[28] *NJ*, 3-24-1945.

Mrs. Harold Smith and Mrs. John Daniels. The parade helped bring in more than $16,000 in donations.[29]

Numerous organizations awoke, almost simultaneously, to the fact that women constituted a viable, hitherto untapped resource. Representatives of the WACS, WAVES and SPARS rolled into the Valley seeking to enlist the wives and girlfriends of the guys in uniform.[30] Mare Island and the other defense plants continued to broadcast urgent pleas for more women to apply for work there.

Women were also actively recruited to stand watch during daytime hours in the airplane observation posts constructed in Calistoga, St. Helena, Pope Valley and other places throughout Napa County. (Men took the watch at night.) The lookout towers were part of a network that spanned the entire West Coast into Canada. Volunteers learned to identify the shapes of all known kinds of airplanes. If they spotted anything unusual, they were to call the Fourth Fighter Command in San Francisco on a high-priority phone line. There were two observers to a watch, and watches lasted four hours. Occasionally the women in the watchtowers would be scared out of their wits when pairs of Air Force planes suddenly dropped down from the clouds and flew low with their engines roaring to practice strafing. One such plane actually crashed into a field just north of St. Helena, barely missing the town. The pilot parachuted to safety.

Wartime responsibilities were time-consuming enough, but there was another problem that insinuated itself even more directly into the everyday lives of women in the Napa Valley and most other places in the Northern Hemisphere: the rationing of food and other essential items, which began in earnest in 1943. Bottles, jars and cans of commercially packed fruits, vegetables, juices and soups and extras like chili sauce and ketchup were all rationed, as was coffee, but not milk, wine, beer or booze. All meats, canned or

---

[29] *SHS*, 4-2-1943.

[30] St. Helena's Helen Ballentine joined the St. Helena Rifles, a California State Militia cell. She was thought to be the first woman inducted into the CSM. She became the assistant company clerk. Napa's Virginia E. Weimers was among the first American women to join the Marines.

fresh, and most cheeses made the ration list, along with shortenings (salad oil, butter and margarine). Other everyday items also fell within the Ration Board's purview: shoes, for example (three pairs per person per year), and pressure cookers, of which Napa County was allotted 75.

Shoppers received books of ration stamps that could be traded for these various commodities. The procedure for buying dried beans, peas and lentils was more complicated. The consumer had to go to the Ration Board and fill out a special form stating the purpose for which the seed would be used and the amount desired. The board issued a certificate that the shopper presented to the merchant at the time of purchase. The few restaurants in the Valley had to submit their menus to the Board to prove that they stayed within the prescribed limits. Governor Warren appointed a Napa Valley woman who had worked hard for the American Legion, Mrs. A.R. Jewell, to chair the Women's Civil Service Corps in helping the War Council on matters regarding food and nutrition in this time of induced scarcity.

With so much being parceled out by the Ration Board, householders resorted to growing and making whatever they could on their own. "Victory Gardens" sprang up in practically everyone's backyard, and the art of home canning was revived. Gone were the afternoon whist parties with little tea cakes and sandwiches that had been the fare of genteel ladies in the gentle days before Pearl Harbor. A new diversion became popular, however—the cocktail party,[31] a social mingling fueled by alcohol and the smoking of cigarettes, which dampened appetites. Upper middle-class women drank and smoked and spoke of war with other women in the afternoon and in mixed groups in the evening, but editorials in the newspapers urged them not to reveal details regarding the names of the ships or units where their loved ones served, nor the locations. Western Defense Commander Dewitt saw fifth columnists[32] in the woodwork and was broadly quoted as uttering one of the more paranoid comments of the entire war:

---

[31] Helen Moodey Clark, Op. Cit., introduction.

[32] spies

The fact that enemy raids have not taken place is…an indication that the danger is very real, and all agencies of civilian defense are urged to be constantly on the alert.[33]

One difficulty with the wartime social institution of cocktail parties was that good alcohol was hard to find. Distillers' product was diverted to the war effort. Some alcohol producers tried manufacturing booze out of fruit juices—Hedgeside, for example, made their aforementioned concoction from prune mash—but cocktail partiers sought "the good stuff," especially bourbon, Scotch, gin and vodka, the latter three typically coming from countries immersed in war. (A couple of years after Schenley bought Hedgeside's inventory, it acquired Greystone and made the huge stone winery part of Cresta Blanca, its wine-producing subsidiary.[34] Small, independent vintners felt uncomfortable about the presence of a corporate giant among them.)

Dave Cavagnaro had always been able to find beverages for his clientele, even when others could not. He was thinking about retiring now, and his son Ray was taking over the reins. If they failed to find a source of liquor, however, there would be no reins to take over, especially if someone else located a supplier before they did. Stymied, Ray consulted with a fellow *paisano* who still had connections back East, Louis Stralla. Stralla told Ray to stuff a suitcase full of money and present it to whoever answered the door at a certain address in New York City. Good things would come from this, said Stralla.

Ray gathered all the cash he could find and flew to New York with airline tickets that Stralla procured for him. He located the address and delivered the suitcase. He flew home and waited anxiously, suddenly impoverished.

---

[33] *SHS*, 3-5-1943.

[34] Cresta Blanca/Schenley bought Colonial, the Fruit Industries winery, in 1942.

The young men and some of the women were gone to war; their parents were watching airplanes, canning their own food, sewing their own clothes and trying somehow to hold together a system that was groaning under the strain. To the crops growing in the fields, however, it was life as usual, and when it came time to pick them there was hardly anyone around to work the harvest. Workers were imported from Mexico and housed in a unit constructed at the State Farm, which ceased to function as a hatchery for game. There were too few workers to handle the load, and worse, for perishable crops like pears, there was no room available for storage or transport—everything was being used by the military. The federal government, moreover, ruled that operators of fruit dehydrators must dry fruit at the same price they charged in 1941, despite the fact that the cost of living had increased. Jealously guarding their own profits, Napa Valley growers who had their own dehydrators refused to dry the fruit of their neighbors. Much of the pear crop rotted; the rest went to brandy distillers in Madera and Sausalito.

For many months the news media did not inform Americans about the events in the Pacific Theater, because Roosevelt and his War Department knew that in so doing, they would be informing Japan, as well. Long distances and an immense ocean were making it difficult for the Japanese to keep tabs on American strength and numbers. And for the first several months, such knowledge would have given much aid and comfort to the enemy, for the battle did not go well for the Stars and Stripes. The first US success did not occur until June, 1942, near Midway Island, when the Navy sank three Japanese carriers. The War in the Pacific continued to go in Japan's favor until early 1943, when the Imperial Navy was forced by disease, poor judgment and starvation to pull out from their southernmost stronghold, Guadalcanal in the Solomon Islands. Slowly, the tide began to recede for the victors of Pearl Harbor. An attack on the American mainland seemed less and less likely, and by October of 1943 the aircraft observation outposts in Napa County and elsewhere no longer seemed necessary.

Had any of the observers been inclined to celebrate this initial victory over Japan, they could have done so with a cocktail party, and they wouldn't have needed to drink prune mash. Ray

Cavagnaro was flabbergasted one afternoon to learn that an entire train car full of premium booze had arrived with his name on it, sent without comment by the recipients of the suitcase full of money. The Cavagnaro family's wholesale liquor distributorship would live on, thanks to the help of Lou Stralla and his connections.

Some other friends of Lou's also made an important move around the same time. Lou had leased the old Charles Krug winery for a few years before buying the Covich winery in Oakville. He lacked the cash to buy Krug outright, although he would have liked to. The Mondavis, however, had done quite well with Sunny St. Helena, and son Robert wanted to parlay this modest success into a bigger one. Vintner John Ballentine was the first to suggest that the Mondavis should consider reviving Charles Krug's pioneer stone winery. He took Bob through the place one day in 1943 and confided to him: "This," he said, "should belong in your family."[35] A month later, Paul Alexander (manager of the Bank of America in St. Helena) reiterated the idea that buying Krug would be a good move. Better act quickly, though, he added, because owner James Moffitt was about to sell it to someone else. It would not be the last time Giannini's bank would play a key role in advancing the wine industry.

Robert drove to Lodi and broached the subject with his father, but Cesare was cool to it. Later that night he asked his mother, and to his surprise, at breakfast the next morning Cesare suggested a trip to St. Helena. Paul Alexander arranged an interview with Moffitt and the Mondavis to discuss the potential for a sale. Shortly after the meeting began, Moffitt's phone rang. "I'm sorry," he said to the caller, "I just sold the property to Cesare Mondavi."[36] Robert and Peter sat wide-eyed while the older men spoke of interest rates, and when they walked out of the room they were the new owners of 147 acres, an old stone building and a familiar brand name. The total cost was $75,000. It would be a business the whole family could run together and pass on to their heirs, they hoped, just like

---

[35] Robert Mondavi, *Interviews and Reminiscences, III*, p. 199.
[36] Ibid, p. 201.

in the old country. The Mondavis kept Sunny St. Helena going while they planned the resuscitation of Krug.

Three Bay Area couples who traveled in more or less the same circle also found the Valley in 1943. Jerome and Virginia Draper purchased acreage on Spring Mountain that had belonged to wine merchant C. Schilling back in the days of the California Wine Association.[37] They brought the vineyards back into production and found that they grew superlative wine grapes.

Bay Area businessman J. Leland Stewart and his wife knew the Drapers. They also knew a bargain. They purchased the defunct Rossini place on Howell Mountain and began to transform its neglected vineyards and old stone facility into a fully operational winery. Stewart was perhaps the first non-vintner in the post-Prohibition era to set his comfortable life aside and try his hand at winecraft. He needed—and received—plenty of help from his new Up-Valley friends, among them the Drapers, Andre Tchelistcheff, Dr. Maynard Amerine (an enologist at UC Davis who lived in St. Helena) and local printer and label-maker Jim Beard. At Beard's suggestion, the Stewarts called their winery "Souverain."

Fred and Eleanor McCrae, also friends of the Drapers, bought 160 acres on Spring Mountain for $7,500. The land had never been planted in grapes; it was the family ranch of the pioneering Griffith family, at least one of whom fought in the Bear Flag Revolt of 1846. It would take several years, but the vines that they planted for their "Stony Hill" would also produce extraordinary wine.

Meanwhile, there was a war going on. Napa Valley men participated in the military action on both sides of the globe, often with great distinction. Sergeant Robert Braswell bagged a Messerschmidt over Augsburg; Sergeant Ernie Guiducci did the same over Central Italy.[38] Harold Christiansen was cited for "exceptional gallanty" when he and the rest of his bomber crew flew a series of low altitude reconnaissance flights over enemy territory. A St. Helenan, First Lieutenant Oliver Eisan, navigated

---

[37] And before that, to Rudolph Lemme.

[38] *NJ*, 4-31-1944,

the first B-29 super-fortress to land in India. He flew most of the way at night to avoid detection.[39] First Lieutenant Richard Simpson, also a St. Helenan, was among the first men to pilot a precision bombing P-38. Zooming down to tree-level, he demolished seven German locomotives, seven river barges, an oil tank car and two box cars. His prowess at the controls won him a Distinguished Flying Cross. Lieutenant Clinton Covery flew seven night missions against Japanese shipping in Dutch New Guinea. Despite heavy anti-aircraft his crew and he sunk seven small ships and eight barges. He also flew 10 air-sea rescue missions and won a "Distinguished Flying Cross."

On the ground, Pfc Wayne Johnson saw heavy fighting in Italy. The Nazis cut in half his 88th Infantry division platoon, but he managed to take eight German prisoners and capture an arsenal. Corporal John Montelli won a Bronze Star for the pinpoint accuracy of his rifle fire at Kwajalein, a battle site that claimed the lives of several Napa Valley men. Edward Jones was another Napa Valley soldier who received the Bronze Star. Leading his platoon across a German mine field under severe small-arms and machine gun fire, he secured a position from which his men could successfully engage the enemy. His five-day demonstration of "outstanding leadership and combat skill" earned him a battlefield commission.

Future St. Helenan Carl Wehr was at sea almost constantly after Pearl Harbor, on the lookout for Japanese ships:

> On one of these patrols we made contact and attacked one of the Japanese Fleet submarines—an "I" boat—which we destroyed. It was the first submarine kill of the Pacific War. Our depth charge barrage brought her to the surface and, as she rose about 2,000 yards on our port beam, she gradually assumed a vertical position. With nearly half the vessel out of the water, she slowly began to descend. It was an awesome sight and left one with a feeling of extreme sadness.[40]

---

[39] *NJ*, 7-14-1944. Eisan was later killed in action.

[40] Carl Wehr, "Up Through the Hawse Pipe," St. Helena, undated, unpublished manuscript, p. 30.

Among the most fortunate Napa County men to serve in Europe was the former DA, Wally Everett, whose absence (along with Judge King's death) enabled Dan York to nab Treadway and Steckter. Perhaps because of his connection with the wine industry, Major Everett served on the staff of General Dwight Eisenhower in Great Britain. Close to the brains of the entire European operation, Everett said that he found his assignment "extremely interesting,"[41] although fraught with peril. Everett had a close brush with death as machine guns strafed his motorcade in France.

Another lucky man was 28-year-old Russell Henry Porterfield, a sailor in the merchant marine, whose ship was torpedoed and sank in the dark ocean. Porterfield grabbed his life jacket and sea-bag and raced for the deck, where he made it into a lifeboat with 19 other men as the ship was going down. "We kidded each other most of the time," said Porterfield. "When anyone looked like he was going to crack, we kidded him out of it."[42]

Sgt. Lawrence Horgan of Napa was touched by a friendly fate. He was hunkered down in his foxhole when the nose of a 9-inch, 85-pound mortar shell burrowed in alongside him.

> I felt something pushing underneath my back, and after hearing an explosion near me I was too excited and shaken up from the impact to think about it. It felt more like a gopher pushing itself into the dirt, but much heavier.[43]

Murray Longhurst was doing aerial reconnaisance over Germany when his plane was hit by flak. His engine caught fire, and because he was flying too low to parachute, he maneuvered the craft into a grove of trees and managed to worm his way out before it exploded. Running by night and hiding by day, he schemed his way into France, where he was taken to a hospital and treated for exposure. He was able to relay much information about the

---

[41] *Napa Shopping News*, 7-5-1944.

[42] *NJ*, 4-24-1942.

[43] *NJ*, 1-5-1945.

enemy's strength and position in the area through which he had just traversed.[44]

But many were not so lucky. Napa Valley men died in North Africa, Italy, Holland, France, Asia and in the skies over Germany. Among the most inspirational stories was that of Pierre Ferran, who fought with the Marines in the Philippines. After his platoon leader was wounded and evacuated, he crawled across an open field in full view of the enemy and assumed control of the men. He was severely wounded in the process, but nevertheless urged his platoon on until they held their gains. He died on the battlefield. Ferran was awarded the Silver Star posthumously.

Allied victory in Europe was by no means a foregone conclusion. By the spring of 1944 England was down to its last gasp. Operation Overlord—the code name for a massive invasion of the French coast that would bring the US Army into the war at full strength—had been pushed back so many times that Stalin was losing patience, especially since his country was up to its neck in Nazis. Finally, on June 6, under the direction of Wally Everett's boss, General Dwight Eisenhower, fluffy parachutes started dropping out of the moonless night sky onto Normandy, bearing the US 82nd and 101st Airborne Divisions and a similar British group. Nearly 6,500 Allied vessels and a cloud of aircraft surged across the Channel just behind them, and when dawn broke the endgame was at hand, although it would be another year before the whole thing was finished.

Napa Valley soldiers participated in D-Day. Technical Sergeant Karol Southard of Napa was with the first flight of paratroopers who billowed into France. Later he jumped into Holland and Alsace. "Rusty" Quirici and Kenneth Hull, both paratroopers, were among the wounded. Quirici lost a leg; Hull recovered, only to die in Holland. "Punch" Cavagnaro's son Bill and Private First Class

---

[44] *NJ*, 2-23-1945.

Laurence Larson survived D-Day but were killed in the drive toward Paris.[45]

Those who could, marched on.

Napa Valley civilians got a taste of war's horror at exactly 10:17 PM July 17, 1944, when two immense explosions, five seconds apart, blew up Port Chicago, a weapons-loading facility not far from Mare Island. The first came as a loud, distinct BOOM and produced an ascending, billowing, mushrooming column of orange and red gas punctuated with firework-like sprays of independent explosions. The second blast, by far the greater, began as a brilliant white flash that went from yellow to orange and was accompanied by a deep, muffled roar. It started on the pier and spread in all directions including up, the ensuing cloud reaching an altitude of more than 12,000 feet. It dug a 27-foot crater in the bottom of the Bay and created a small tidal wave.

So profound was the concussion from the combined blast that in Calistoga, Charles Carroll's old, deaf bulldog ran under the couch to hide. Horses in a corral south of St. Helena ran madly in circles. It blew out windows in Napa, Vallejo, Benicia, Martinez, Pittsburg, Crockett, Concord, San Francisco and Vacaville, and the Navy base of Port Chicago—now the Concord Naval Weapons Station—was flattened. At ground zero, the Liberty Ship *E.A. Bryan* was vaporized. Her companion, the 7,000-ton *Quinault Victory*, blew into bits. The *Quinault's* bow rocketed into the night sky, and her propeller catapulted across Suisun Bay.[46] A locomotive went airborne, too, splashing down some distance from the pier on which it had been standing; eight freight cars and several small boats became smithereens and matchsticks. Shockwaves blew in the doors and blasted off the top of a 200-foot Union Oil tanker cruising a few thousand yards away. It sank, riddled with shrapnel from the *Quinault Victory*. Dismembered body parts of a Port Chicago work battalion were hurled starward

---

[45] *NJ*, 8-11-1944.

[46] David Caul and Susan Todd, "Port Chicago—50 Years," *Napa Sentinel*, January, 1990.

and rained on nearby Roe Island, and other Navy, Coast Guard and civilian personnel met instant death.[47] Clean-up crews found only 80 bodies, and only 30 of those could be identified.[48]

The sky lit up. "Plainly visible here," wrote the *Journal*, "was the towering pillar of flame that flared into the southern sky. The hills of the Napa Valley were momentarily illuminated by sunshine." Tom Sweet happened to be standing on his patio on Spring Mountain and saw "a sudden mushroom of white light, followed an instant later by another, then a few moments later [there was] the intense roar and the concussion of the blast."[49]

Ensign Newton York, a Napan, was in the base recreation hall. He was lifted from his feet and hurled across the room. Napan Tom Shaw, a construction worker, was in a building one mile away. He, too, was pitched across the room.

The telephone operator on duty at the base's central office was likewise sent airborne, and most of the phone lines at Port Chicago were destroyed. With the information hub of the complex thus compromised it took hours for the general public to ascertain what had happened. Napa Valley folks immediately assumed the worst, and the worst varied from person to person. Some were sure that the long-dreaded Japanese aerial attack had finally commenced. An Atlas Peak resident telephoned Sheriff Claussen and "breathlessly reported" that three Japanese planes had passed overhead moments before the explosion.[50] Many believed that the arsenal in Benicia had blown up, taking with it their loved ones. Most, though, feared a calamity had occurred at Mare Island, and scores of panicked citizens converged on the police station, demanding information. As soon as the details began to emerge, Napa County Red Cross Chairwoman Mrs. Bert Hennessey gathered some friends and drove

---

[47] Strangely, a Navy photographer poised a safe distance away took pictures of the entire debacle.

[48] Carl Wehr, *Op. Cit.*, p. 33.

[49] SHS, 7-21-1944.

[50] Paul Donovan, "Highlights," *NJ*, 7-28-1944. (There were no Japanese planes.)

to Port Chicago to aid the survivors. They were turned away from the scene by security-anxious personnel.

The US Navy sent Carl Wehr, now on land and a Lieutenant Junior Grade, to inspect. All he could see of the ships was a single propeller protruding from the water. He could not determine the exact cause of the disaster, because all the eye-witnesses had perished. He learned that the *E.A. Bryan* was loaded with high explosives: It was, in effect, a seaborne bomb. The pier between her and the *Quinault Victory* had borne an additional trainload of ordnance, including torpex bombs, highly destructive devices that "had a propensity on rare occasions to detonate with rough handling."[51] Something probably caused the explosives on the pier to ignite, thought Wehr, and their ignition exploded the *E.A. Bryan*.

Three hundred twenty-two men lost their lives, more than two-thirds of them black.[52] When their compatriots were ordered to return to work immediately after the catastrophe and told to load the same kind of munitions that the dead crew had handled, many refused. They were charged with mutiny, a ruling that was later softened when a lawyer with a future—Thurgood Marshall—advocated for them.

Violence begat violence. On Halloween night, 1944, 500 kids felt entitled to roam the streets of the Napa County seat armed with tomatoes and rotten eggs, with which they pelted buildings, police officers and the firemen who tried to quell their riot by shooting water at them from high-powered hoses. The downstairs corridor of the court house was transformed into a temporary juvenile detention center, but many of the apprehended youths went upstairs, opened the windows and climbed down the drain pipes to riot some more.[53] There was no such hooliganism in the county's other towns. Vallejo, on the other hand, had to hire 75 more

---

[51] Wehr, Op. Cit., p. 34.

[52] Still ignorant of concepts regarding civil rights, the US relegated black soldiers to menial, often back-breaking tasks, like loading high explosives, for which they were given little training.

[53] *NJ*, 11-3-1944.

policemen to deal with the unprecedented wave of crime there. Rape and attempted rape there reached an all-time high.

Napa had achieved the population growth for which it had longed half a century, but it lacked the infrastructure to cope with its success. A few short years before, Napa and its "sister city" Vallejo were just small saloon towns. They were ill-prepared to absorb the tsunami of newcomers that washed in with the war. Mayor Charles Moffitt attempted to introduce a "city manager" plan of municipal government, but it did not take hold. Neither he nor Charles Hare chose to run again in 1945, and S.J. Cinnamond was elected Mayor, collecting three times more votes than his opponent, H.W. Sawyer.

Franklin Roosevelt, whom American voters had chosen four times, did not live to see the end of World War II. He died on April 12, 1945 of a cerebral hemorrhage. "From prince to pauper," said the *Journal*, "expressions of condolence and intense grief snowed the White House from every nook and cranny of the world."[54] His replacement was a hard-headed politician named Harry Truman who had on May 8 the honor of proclaiming the war in Europe to be over. Now only Japan remained.

Peace after four years of conflict would mean a re-ordering of things. Persons of vision moved to position themselves for the new era. The Spreckels ranch went up for sale. Its 334 acres were planted in wheat and housed a small dairy; the new owner would turn the stables into housing units and subdivide the rest. The Stanly family sold their ranch, too. It had belonged to them since the end of the Civil War. Len Owens sold Aetna Springs to George Heibel. Owens' son-in-law, Martin Stelling, handled the deal. Stelling himself had recently acquired vast acreage in Oakville and Rutherford as well as in the city of Napa and was now a major player in the wine grape business. Among his purchases was the Churchill family's To-Kalon vineyards, the winery itself having perished in the suspicious fire before the war; and the Benson/Doak ranch adjacent to it. Charles Forni made major purchases of

---

[54] *NJ*, 4-13-1945.

vineyard land north and south of St. Helena. A San Francisco restaurateur, George Mardikian, bought the old Snowball ranch in St. Helena and brought to the Valley his impressive collection of rare books, including cookbooks. His Omar Khayyam restaurant, however, remained in San Francisco.

Seven winery executives established the Napa Valley Vintner's Association to promote the wine industry for their mutual benefit. The founders were:

Louis M. Martini........................Louis Martini Winery
Mrs. Georges De Latour...............Beaulieu Vineyard
John Daniel, Jr..........................Inglenook
Elmer J. Salmina........................Larkmead Vineyards, Inc.
Robert Mondavi.........................C. Mondavi & Sons
Charles Forni............................Napa Valley Cooperative
Louis Stralla............................Napa Wine Company

There was work for them to do right away, because the ante-Prohibition feud of wine growers vs. raisin growers looked to be heating up again. Within months of the NVVA's inception, the Office of Price Administration stepped in to reduce by more than half the price of wine grapes, from $108 a ton to $52. Furious, Napa County growers charged the OPA and the War Food Administration of deliberately doing injustice to wine growers in order to benefit raisin growers.

Inch by inch, island by island, Japan was losing its ill-gotten gains in Asia and the South Pacific. On Corregidor, Napan Edgar Wright, Jr. finally emerged from the jungle lean and hard after fighting nearly three years with a group of American guerillas. He ate second helpings of everything the cook at the US command post set in front of him and saw for the first time a picture of his three-year-old son.

Once intoxicated with victory, Japanese pilots now grew crazed with despair. Many turned their planes into bombs, crashing into American vessels hoping to sink them, a strategy that sometimes worked. *Lexington* survivor Armand Holderman was now attached to the aircraft carrier *Wasp* in the South Pacific as a Navy pilot. He was patrolling the skies above his ship when he saw a would-be *kamikaze* drop down from the clouds. He got on its tail and gunned off its left wing. It fell into the sea just short of the *Wasp*, and the other men got to calling him "Holy Joe Holderman." The Navy called him a hero and awarded him a Gold Star and the Distinguished Flying Cross.[55]

When the US recaptured the Marianas, those islands became the final staging area for the powerful new B-29 "Superfortress" bombers, which could carry a serious payload a long distance.

Late one night Carl Wehr received a telephone call from a lieutenant at the Oakland Naval Supply Depot. Two express cars had just arrived, the caller said, with a load of classified material code-named "Bowery." They were under marine guard, and the lieutanant didn't know what to do with them. The next morning Wehr asked his commanding officer for instructions regarding "Bowery."

> He leaped to his feet and shouted, "Where the hell did you learn about 'Bowery'? Only the Admiral, the Chief of Staff and myself know of this!"[56]

"Bowery," Wehr later discovered, was the first atomic bomb. It made its way onto the cruiser *Indianapolis* and then to Guam, from whence it sailed to Manila and then Tinian in the Marianas, where it was loaded onto the Superfortress *Enola Gay*.

On August 10, 1945, the Japanese city of Hiroshima ceased to exist, blown away by a detonation that made Port Chicago seem tame. A week later a second atomic bomb obliterated Nagasaki. A terrified Japan surrendered to General Douglas MacArthur on the *Missouri*.

The jubilant people of the Napa Valley truly danced for joy. Napans celebrated with noise, paper streamers, an impromptu Drum and Bugle Corps parade and the breaking of some downtown windows. St. Helenans, in contrast, prepared all week for the

---

[55] *NJ*, 9-20-1946.

[56] Wehr, Op. Cit., p. 36.

inevitable and were primed for what Starr Baldwin called a "bang-up" party. It began with Methodist minister A.A. Chapman ringing the church bell. The firebell and siren quickly joined in, along with Harley Morrison's ambulance. Dogs howled, and folks poured onto Main Street for a parade, their vehicles already spiffy for the occasion. Malcom Paulson and Kenneth Rahn mounted a make-believe cannon on the roof of a car, through which issued a flapping of doves. A formal program followed the next day at Lyman Park, with Mayor Metzner as the emcee and President Klooster of Pacific Union College the main speaker. It was wonderful, and no one had to wear gauze masks.

Sheriff Jack Steckter (left, from a campaign ad in the Napa Journal) and Theodore Treadway (right, courtesy of the Napa County Historical Society).

Superor Court Judge Melvin Lerhnart, DA Dan York, and Sheriff John Claussen (left, center, right) opposed the "good-ole-boy" system that had long dominated Napa County politics. Their terms of office brought reform.

Napa Residents Must Help Man These Battle Stations!

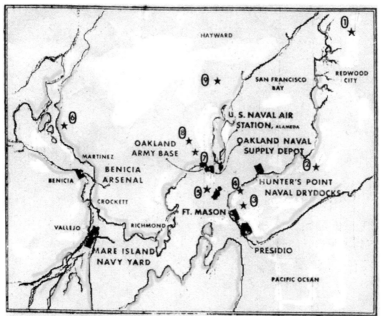

KEY TO ARMY-NAVY INSTALLATIONS--1.Dibble General Hospital, Menlo Park. 2. U.S. Naval Advance Base Personnel Depot, San Bruno. 3. 12th Naval District Labor Board. 4. U.S. Marine Corps Quartermaster Depot. 5. U.S. Naval Training and Distribution Center, Treasure Island. 6. California Quartermaster Depot. 7. Oakland Army Base. 8. Pacific Overseas Air Technical Service Command. 9. Ordnance Service Command Shop, San Leandro

A cry for help that ran in several newspapers, including the Napa Journal. *The Quartermaster Depot (6) was soon expanded to become Port Chicago.*

Napa Valley civilians had a taste of the horror of war when Port Chicago, above, was flattened by two immense explosions. The Navy's Carl Wehr was sent to investigate the next day and found nothing but rubble.

Former prisoner of war Paul Cerbe sent this letter to the Julius Jaeger family of Rutherford, on whose farm he was interned as a prisoner of war. He wrote from the Magdeburg region, soon to be part of East Germany. "You shall be astonished to get a letter of Germany. Before two years I was still with the men grape cut by you. You will remember the Prisoners of War, who were in the camp in front of your farm. There I had a good time. For we had enough to eat and the treatment was good. From California I came to England. There I was still August 1947. After four years prisoner time I came to Germany. I found my mother and my brothers still healthy. But our farm, where we lived, musted my mother and my brothers leave. They musted the farm leave, without any things. All horses, cows and machines musted remain..."

Photo courtesy of Yountville Veterans' Home

Armand Holderman, son of WWI hero Nelson Holderman,
served with distinction both at sea and in the air during WWII.
Known as "Buddy" by his friends at Napa High, he was
called "Holy Joe Holderman" by his shipmates on the carrier
Wasp, which he protected during a kamikaze raid near the war's end.

Chapter Thirteen

Water and Wine

The much-maligned local rationing office closed its doors for good the last week of 1945, leaving sugar as the only commodity still portioned out. As building materials necessary to the war effort became available again, progress could be made on the county's big projects, the dams at Conn and Rector.

Watching the erection of Conn Dam was a popular pastime for most of 1945, with cars full of onlookers parked for hours along the side of the road. Bulldozers bulldozed, dump trucks dumped, and engineer August Kempkey engineered the completion of the 180-foot-high, 1,000-foot-long earthen barrier. When the winter rains finally came, it began to fill with water. Dirt roads that had only days before been crowded with looky-loo's slowly submerged. War shortages precluded the installation of pipes from the reservoir to the city of Napa—they would be installed later—so once the dam was full, some water had to be released. A steady stream thus flowed from Conn throughout 1946, monitored closely by Ed Hennessey, the long-time Napa councilman who was in charge of the city's water department.

Mayor Walter Metzner urged St. Helena's city council to purchase some of Napa's new water resource for its own use. The council agreed. For the first time since anyone could remember, running out of water was not going to be a fear.

285

Neither was running out of fish. Anglers rejoiced over the fact that 35,000 fingerling rainbow trout had been planted at Conn, although they were forbidden to cast for them until the fish had matured a little. An additional 100,000 fingerlings wriggled into the murky depths a few months later, and more went in after that.

Work began on Rector Dam in March of 1946. Workers drilled a 600' tunnel into hard rock, through which would extend the main outlet pipe, once pipes were available. Governor Earl Warren came to speak at the Rector Dam site. He was feted afterward with a luncheon at the labor camp site just off the Silverado Trail. Unbeknownst to many, the camp site had recently been housing not Mexican laborers, but 250 German and Italian prisoners of war. Orchardists and grape growers utilized this source of free labor to work the 1945 harvest. They were sent from camp in groups of 20 under the watchful eye of an armed guard and labored nine hours a day, six days a week. It was a cushy placement, as POW camps went. One of the prisoners escaped but posed no threat to the populace, wishing only to blend in and become Americanized. He probably succeeded, for no mention was ever made of his capture.

County residents were also scrutinizing the progress of another dam. In September of 1945, two Napans[1] attended a meeting of the Central Valley Water Project, the huge irrigation and riparian management program that sought to control the state's liquid wealth. They raced back to the County Board of Supervisors with word that 26 California counties had passed a resolution favoring the construction of a dam at Devil's Gate. Official bodies in Solano County, they said, would make a "concerted effort" to have work proceed. The Napans vigorously opposed it, and the resolution was sent to the Project's executive committee without action.[2]

Surveys of the area continued nevertheless. An idea for the proposed dam that stirred up additional controversy was to drill a tunnel from Clear Lake to Putah Creek so that floodwaters from Clear Lake could be collected in the dam, thus removing a winter

---

[1] George Soloman and August Brucker

[2] *SHS*, 9-14-1945.

weather problem that had troubled owners of Lake County resorts. Already unhappy that Lake County had sucked tourist dollars from the Napa Valley, local leaders were disgusted that beautiful Berryessa might be utilized as a holding tank for someone else's floodwater. The Clear Lake water proved to be too full of boron and other chemicals unfriendly to plant-life, however, and the idea went away.

While the forces in favor of the dam were formidable, there were a few agencies outside of Napa County that withdrew their support once they understood the Berryessa residents' position. The California State Chamber of Commerce, for example, recanted an earlier stance and came out against to the project. Every piece of good news was music to the ears of Monticello's worried grain farmers and cattle ranchers, whose labors produced a sixth of the county's agricultural wealth.[3]

The Bureau of Reclamation presented a bill to Congress in the summer of 1946 urging early approval of the Devil's Gate dam. Nathan S. Coombs[4] drew up a resolution seeking a delay while other places further up Putah Creek could be investigated as alternative sites. Berryessans donated $4,000 for the problem to be professionally studied and sought matching funds.

The Board of Supervisors hired hydraulic engineer August Kempkey to concoct the stratagem that could save Berryessa, and by March of 1947 he was ready to report. His proposal required the active cooperation of Napa's "sister city." It had three key components:

- Vallejo should relinquish its reservoir in Gordon Valley to other Solano County users, namely Suisun, Fairfield and the Benicia Arsenal;
- Conn dam should be heightened and its capacity increased so that the City of Vallejo could receive all its water from Conn;

---

[3] *SHS*, 2-15-1946.

[4] There were at this time three Nathan Coombses in Napa: Nathan F. (the former DA), Nathan S. and Nathan H.

- Putah creek should be dammed in uninhabited Coyote Valley, and the water impounded there should be added to the Conn supply. Other small dams should also be built in remote locations.

Some in Vallejo liked Kempkey's plan, but there had been friction between the two cities recently, and the political atmosphere did not favor cooperation. Just prior to the Kempkey proposal, for example, there had been an unfortunate *contretemps* involving Napa's invitation to Vallejo to use its existing Conn Valley supply. For months Napa had been asking Vallejo to commit one way or another to buying Conn water, but Vallejo had refused to answer. Delay meant postponing the installation of water pipes. Finally, after Vallejo ignored Napa's final ultimatum for an answer, the Napa City Council voted not to sell any water outside the county. The next week, Vallejo said it might like to buy some water. Napa refused. Vallejo then asked Napa County to help fund a full-time lobbyist in Washington who could represent the area's needs. Napa politicans questioned why they should pay someone "to slit our throats." The "sister cities" now loathed each other.

The Kempkey plan had some flaws. Karl Kadie, district manager of the US Bureau of Reclamation, put it bluntly. The value of the water in the dam, he said, was greater than the value of the land beneath it. The Devil's Gate plan was relatively cheap; building a series of smaller dams would be too costly.

Saving Berryessa was not consistent with newly emerging thought regarding resource management. The state of California now viewed itself as a huge thirsty organism, a gigantic system of mutually interdependent needs and resources. Water from the proposed Monticello Dam, for example, would not only irrigate Yolo and Solano farmland, but some of it would be sent to the San Joaquin Valley to supplement their water supply, which came from the dam at Shasta. This would leave more water at Shasta for use in generating power. Capturing and taming Putah Creek would, moreover, abate some of the winter flood problems experienced by the Sacramento River. Seen from this perspective, little valleys like

Berryessa, and even large ones, like Owens in the south, could be sacrificed if necessary for the good of the whole.

Governor Earl Warren was mainly interested in the big picture. He assured a delegation of Vallejo businessmen and Mare Island representatives that he would do everything in his power to insure them a water supply as expeditiously as possible, as soon as the Bureau of Reclamation and the State Division of Water ironed out the details.[5] When Vallejo selected vociferously pro-Dam publisher Luther Gibson as "Man of the Year," Warren spoke at the dinner given in his honor, while Al Streblow, Whit Griffiths, George Provine and other anti-Dam Napans listened quietly, sadly sipping their soup.

Napa and Solano drew up competing plans to form "irrigation districts" that would use Putah Creek water, a formality that preceded any final decision regarding a dam site. In the Napa plan, a "Berryessa Irrigation District" would use water from Coyote Valley and other uninhabited locations. In contrast, 757 Solano County residents petitioned for a "Solano County Irrigation District" that would drown Berryessa.[6] Chief among the dam's promoters was the Chairman of the Solano County Board of Supervisors, Frank O. Bell, a nephew of the late Napa County politician. Twisting and omitting key facts regarding the Conn Valley pipeline controversy, Bell accused Napa County at a public forum of hypocritically withdrawing its offer to share Conn water with its sister city and selfishly voting to retain all its water for its own uses. Solanan W.E. Andrews then bitterly assailed Napa for "misrepresenting the facts" regarding the dam. The meeting erupted in a furor of outraged Napans.

County Supervisor Lowell Edington flew to Washington to garner whatever help he could in fighting off the dam. He also tried to find money to improve the Napa River, a perennial problem that never seemed to get resolved. What he found was that, despite the big muscles behind the Monticello Dam movement, Congress itself was preoccupied with something having nothing to do with water

---

[5] *NJ*, 2-28-1947.
[6] *NJ*, 10-10-1947.

management. Both houses were crammed with bills to fight Communism. The House Committee on Un-American Activities was identifying certain members of the entertainment industry as disloyal, and a Congressional sub-committee was reading through junior high school textbooks seeking pro-Red propaganda. A Southern California politician named Richard M. Nixon was riding to power on the crest of anti-Communist paranoia, together with a frightening hate-monger named Joseph McCarthy.

The fear was not limited to Communists within. The Soviet Union had been rattling swords of war in eastern Europe. China, too, had fallen under Communist rule, and when Japan withdrew from Korea in 1945, Chinese soldiers took over the northern part with suppport from the Russians. Due to the urgency of these matters, Congress sidelined the issue of building a dam at Devil's Gate. Thanks to the federal obsession with Red and Pink, ranchers could watch a few more seasons play out in the green and gold little valley of Berryessa.

Economically, Napa County was in good shape when the war ended, and many locals participated in America's unprecedented post-war prosperity. Individual income in Napa County had more than doubled during the war. The population reached 42,700, up 50% from 1940. Families were reproducing like rabbits. Some weeks County Clerk Ralph Dollarhide recorded the birth of more than 20 new babies.

People could afford to buy houses[7] and relax a little. A huge new roller-skating ring/entertainment hall, the Glidrome, opened its doors in East Napa, occupying a block bounded by Clay, Juarez, First Street and the Silverado Trail. Cowboy groups gave concerts there.

Supervisor Lowell Edington was secretary-manager of the 1946 Napa Fair, the first to be held since the outbreak of war. It was a sparkling success, with some 20,500 people paying to get in. Dave Cavagnaro organized the pre-fair parade, said by many to be the best ever. Twelve thousand people witnessed it. Five hundred of

---

[7] A builder named P. Devita built many of them in Napa.

them also saw a Napa fire engine accidentally run over and kill Dave's brother, "Punch," who still worked for the police department as he had since the days before Prohibition. It was a bizarre tragedy, and the courtroom drama that followed was also odd, with lawyers for the police department accusing lawyers for the fire department of whitewashing the fireman's negligence.

Jack Steckter ran for Sheriff again in 1946, and Theodore Treadway's mortuary partner, Henry Wigger, ran for Public Administrator/Coroner. Both men lost, which was sign that the good-ol'-boy system was beginning to wear down. Nathan F. Coombs, son of Frank, ran unopposed for the state senate the next year.

Up in St. Helena, Harley Morrison bought and paid for some first-class playground equipment so that the town's growing juvenile population could swing at Lyman Park. It was a public-spirited act of generosity that endeared him to the community, and he wasn't even running for office.

Grown-ups had a new place for their toys in Calistoga. A runway and "air park" were installed across the road from Paradise Park, whose "longest bar in the West" was a potentially lethal temptation for amateur pilots.

A well-known St. Helenan fell prey to lethal temptations and provided a macabre diversion for gossip-mongers. One evening retired bootlegger Lloyd Crellin, Wally Everett's party-loving uncle, told his wife and visiting brother-in-law that he had taken poison. They called Dr. George Wood, to whom Crellin had in the past confided suidical feelings. Crellin died some seven hours after he said he injested strychnine, and a subsequent autopsy revealed that he had actually succumbed to a heart atttack associated with the poison. He had also been severely intoxicated. He was buried. A San Francisco toxicologist, however, read about the case and decided that the Napa Valley medical personnel who dealt wirh Crellin's case had mishandled it and that Crellin had actually been murdered, because Crellin could not have survived seven hours with all that rat poison in his system. Suspicion was cast on his wife.

Furious that an outside "expert" was attempting to make Napa County professionals look like a pack of rubes, DA Dan York resisted the toxicologist's efforts to have the body exhumed. Exhumed it was, however, and a new autopsy was performed. The jury determined that Crellin, had, indeed, died of a heart attack brought on by the poison and that the reason he lived seven hours was because all the alcohol he had drunk slowed down his digestive process. The jury ruled his death a suicide.

The Crellin case helped county personnel regain some esteem. Clearly, DA Dan York and Superior Court Judge Mervin Lernhart were not the small-town tyrants many of their predecessors had been. This fact became abundantly clear to the "dapper, debonnaire Nemesis"[8] of the Napa County Traffic Court, Justice of the Peace David Wright. Not unlike Steckter, Wright kept for himself a portion of the fines paid by six motorists charged with moving violations. He falsified public records and made fraudulent entries regarding them, and he was caught. At first he pled innocent, citing clerical errors, but when York threatened to reveal a host of other defalcations beyond the original six, Wright conceded. He was sentenced to a term at San Quentin.

Other things were changing, some for the good, others not. Calistoga mourned the passing of the man who had, more than any other, held the little city together. After 53 years at the editor's desk of the *Calistogian*, Calistoga's beloved Charles Carroll died on December 9, 1946.[9] He was in San Francisco attending a meeting of the California Newspaper Publishers' Association and had addressed the group only two nights earlier. In frail health, the event may have taxed him beyond his resources. He was 73.

Governor Earl Warren's trip to Napa State Hospital back in 1943 had raised his awareness regarding the plight of the mentally ill. With the input and backing of reformers like Portia Bell Hume, he supported a new outlook in the area of mental health, and Napa State Hospital benefited. By 1948 the institution was reshaping its

---

[8] *NJ*, 10-3-1947.

[9] He had turned the paper's editorial duties over to Roger Winston the prior summer.

image. No longer content to be a prison for the hapless, it promoted itself as a "stopping-off place for those too troubled to continue."[10] It would be a rehabilitation center. Patients were encouraged to find themselves through the medium of earnest physical labor, which was available through a number of venues. The hospital's farm allowed patients to tend fruit trees, irrigate pastures and feed poultry. In addition, the hospital opened a shoe factory, a cannery, a machine shop, a laundry, a wood shop, a beauty parlor and a barber shop. The vocational experience it provided helped patients get jobs outside its walls—a new and far-reaching concept in psychiatric care. Emotionally damaged men and women could gain a sense of identity by doing work of which they were proud, and, through the experience being valued, they began to heal.

Another of Warren's innovations was the creation of a State Department of Public Health, with local offices in each county. The county public health division would address the control of communicable diseases and environmental sanitation, health education and maternal and child care. It would maintain records that could be used as a database, and it would operate an outpatient clinic. Napa County's new health department opened in September, 1948, under the direction of Dr. Kenneth Haworth.[11] It was housed where the old county infirmary had been, on the road to Sonoma just past "death curve."

Modern times were moving into the Valley. Resistance was futile. Those who could not rise with the tide would drown in it. The local wine industry was one institution whose survival in the second half of the 20th Century was in question. True, there were a few important names, like Beringer, Beaulieu, Inglenook and Martini. But none was large enough to compete successfully for long with the giant firms of the Central Valley. Nor did any of

---

[10] *NJ*, 12-17-1948.

[11] Warren's reform-minded thinking impressed his Republican peers. In 1948 presidential candidate Thomas Dewey chose him as his running mate. They lost, but Warren was appointed to the Supreme Court. He became Chief Justice in 1954.

these wineries have significant market share outside of California. Wine-drinkers in New York and other centers of sophistication almost always chose European brands, expecting California wines to lack distinction. Robert Mondavi wanted to change all that. The family sold Sunny St. Helena to Martin Stelling and focused exclusively on Krug.

The name "Napa Valley" meant little to most people beyond the borders of Northern California, although those who remembered the Pan-American Exhibition and *They Got What They Wanted* may have recalled images of ethnic, barefoot people stomping grapes and partying. A few probably still identified the Valley as a source of supplies for activities proscribed by the 18th Amendment. But as a name associated with items of great value, the Napa Valley was largely unknown.

Bob Mondavi knew something of marketing from his college days at Stanford. He understood, for example, that it would be counter-productive to send premium wines to the eastern market; they would be snubbed. So he divided Charles Krug winery into two parts. The Mondavis' "CK" brand consisted of gallons and half-gallons of run-of-the-mill wine which they directed toward the eastern market for many years. The better stuff they labeled as "Charles Krug Fine Wine," and they sold it exclusively in California in fifths and tenths. It was important to them that the two lines never mingle, at least not until Charles Krug was identified as a quality wine.

The Mondavis believed that premium wines would only be given the credit they were due when the Napa Valley itself was recognized as a unique region within California. Toward that end, the family hired a well-connected, well-traveled *bon vivant* from New York, Francis "Paco" Gould, to handle Krug's PR. Besides running their innovative public tasting room, hosting parties and serving as general hospitality manager, Gould wrote a quarterly publication called *Bottles and Bins*. Knowledgeable visitors had come to the Valley and written about it; Gould was the first insider to send regular word to the world outside. His unusual mailer—"uncorked and poured from time to time by Charles Krug

Winery"—was part news and part hype that touted not just the winery, but the Valley and wine itself:

> *Bottles and Bins*, should you be favorably disposed, will come to you, from time to time to remind you that Napa Valley wines are worthy of pride and praise and that the wines made by Cesare Mondavi and his sons at Charles Krug Winery, St. Helena, are worth even more—a place in your wine bin.[12]

For the next 30 years, Gould delivered his humorous and entertaining monograph with the help of Jim Beard. If someone with the background and erudition of a Paco Gould found merit in Krug and the Valley, others like him should, too, hoped the Mondavis.

Paco Gould and Andre Tchelistcheff were cut from the same cloth. Both men had exquisitely developed sensory faculties that brought them great pleasure. Both loved to linger over elegant meals featuring an endless flow of wine and wit, followed by brandy or armagnac and cigars. Both wanted to share their love of sense with the world. "Establish the primitive tastes first," Tchelistcheff advised.

> Then bring all your sensory perceptions to bear: your eyes as well as your palate. Look for clarity, brilliance and color reflection in the wine. If it is sherry, look for the brownish orange tinge. For testing and tasting take a quarter of a wine glass only. Don't swallow the wine intended for testing until you are out of the amateur class in wine appreciation, or the after-taste will serve to confuse you. The after-taste itself is a final part of wine testing when you have graduated to the finer and more delicate wines.[13]

While Gould and Tchelistcheff were waxing eloquent about wines, the vineyards of the Drapers, McCraes and Stewarts were

---

[12] Francis Gould, *Bottles and Bins*, Vol. I, No. 1, July, 1949, St. Helena, CA.

[13] *NJ*, 3-12-1948.

coming into their own. The Stewarts' Souverain won the first of many gold medals at the California State fair in 1947. His specialty was white wines, especially White Reisling and Green Hungarian.[14] The McCraes also made outstanding white wines. Jack and Mary Taylor's Mayacamas Vineyards in west Napa, once the property of the bootlegger Brandlin, was beginning to bear, and it joined Souverain and Stony Hill as part of the new generation of smaller post-Prohibition wine-making concerns. None of the new winery owners had a background in wine-making or viticulture; all were persons of culture and taste. They turned to the experts for advice not on how to brew up quantities of grape soup to be sold in tankers to the markets back east, but on how to craft fine wines. This was exactly what Robert Mondavi had in mind.

Martin Stelling did not seem to share this view. His empire of prime vineyard land in the heart of the Valley was an investment whose fruit he sold mainly to blenders in the Central Valley. One summer night in 1950, while on his way home from a business meeting in San Francisco, the 55 year-old financier lost control of his Cadillac and crashed into a power pole in front of the cemetery in Yountville. He died a few hours later. Over the next decades viticulturalists who knew the true potential of his properties bought up Stelling's vineyards and from them began to produce legendary wines.

The success of these newcomers would be inspirational to dozens and eventually hundreds of other entrepreneurial adventurers. A more refined Napa Valley was about to bud forth, grafted on to rootstock that had resisted the ravages of plague and pestilence, corruption and chicanery, flood, fire and war. From this grafting would emerge the new Napa Valley.

---

[14] See Charles Sullivan, *Napa Wine: A History*, Wine Appreciation Guild, San Francisco, 1994, p. 243.

Calistoga's Mayor John Ghisolfo served his
community for many years.

Bon Vivant Paco Gould introduced Charles Krug wines and the Napa Valley to the wine-loving world through his word and example.

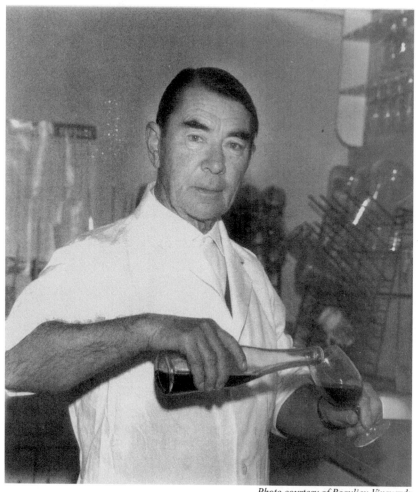

Beaulieu's Andre Tchelistcheff brought European expertise to a struggling industry.

Napa Vallley wine industry leaders meet at the Bourn estate in St. Helena, 1949. Left to right: Brother Tim, Christian Brothers; Charles Forni, Co-op Winery; Walter Sullivan, Beaulieu; Aldo Fabrino, Beaulieu; Michael Ahern, Freemark Abbey; Peter Mondavi, Charles Krug; Robert Mondavi, Charles Krug; John Daniel, Jr., Inglenook; Louis M. Martini, Martini Winery; Charlie Beringer, Beringer Brothers; Martin Stelling, vineyardist; Fred Abruzzini, Beringer Brothers.

BIBLIOGRAPHY

<u>Newspapers:</u>
The Napa Daily Journal
The Napa Journal
The Napa Register
The Napa Sentinel
The Napa Shopping News
The New York Times
The Placer County Republican
The San Francisco Call
The San Francisco Chronicle
The San Francisco Examiner
The St. Helena Star
The Weekly Calistogian

<u>Periodicals:</u>
Gould, Francis. *Bottles and Bins*, Vol. I, No. 1. St. Helena: July, 1949.
Griffiths, Edith R. "Exploring for Oil in the Berryessa Valley." *Gleanings*,
    Vol I, No. 1, Napa County Historical Society. May, 1970.
Hutchinson, W.H. "Prologue to Reform: The California Anti- Railroad
    Republicans, 1899-1905," in *Southern California Quarterly*,
    Historical Society of Southern California, September, 1962.
McKenzie, Robert. "The Monticello Rodeo and Barbecue," *Gleanings*,
    Vol. I, #4, Napa County Historical Society, May, 1975.
Meers, John R. "The California Wine and Grape Industry and Prohibtion."
    The California Historical Society Quarterly, Vol. XLVI, No. 1.
    California Historical S ciety. March, 1967.
Posner, Russell. "The Bank of Italy and the 1926 Campaign in
    California." *The California Historical Society Quarterly*. Vol. 37,
    No. 3. California Historical Society. September, 1958.

Prchal, Dolly. "Mr. Calistoga: The Life and Accomplishments of John B. Ghisolfo." *Gleanings,* Vol. III, No. 3. The Napa County Historical Society. December, 1985.

Tortorolo, Mario J. "History of the City of Napa Water Supply," in *Gleanings,* Napa County Historical Society, Vol. 2, #2, May, 1978.

Wheaton, Donald W. *Quarterly of the California Historial Society,* V, No. 3, September, 1926.

Wichels, John "John Lawley: Pioneer Entrepreneur." *Gleanings,* Vol. 3, Number 1. Napa County Historical Society, February, 1982.

Unpublished Manuscripts:

Bordwell, Rita Harren. "History of the Napa Fire Department from 1859 to 1962." Napa: n.d.

Clark, Helen Moody. "Profile of a Varied and Busy Life." St. Helena, n.d.

Crawford, James. "The Democratic Party of California and Political Reform, 1902-1910." Berkeley: University of California. Unpublished Masters thesis, 1959.

McCormick, Rodney. "Recollections of Rodney McCormick of Grandfather York, Vol. 2." St. Helena: unpublished manuscript, 1938.

Quinn,Tony. "A History of the Salmina Family of Corcapolo and St. Helena." self-published, np, September, 1994.

Wehr, Carl. "Twenty Years at the Helm: A Story of Greystone." St. Helena, n.d.

Wehr, Carl. "Up Through the Hawse Pipe." St. Helena: undated, unpublished manuscript.

Other Publications:

Napa County Grand Jury Reports 1900-1950

The People of the State of California vs. Charles Forni. Napa, 1933.

_____ *Oil and Gas Prospect Wells Drilled in California Through 1980.* Sacramento: California Division of Oil and Gas, 1982.

_____ *History of Napa Valley: Interviews and Reminiscences of Long-Time Residents,* Vols. I-4. St. Helena: Napa Valley Wine Library.

_____ _Yearbook of the United States Department of Agriculture,_ Government Printing Office, Washington, 1903.

Books:

Allen, Frederick Lewis. _The Big Change: America Transforms Itself, 1900-1950._ New York and Evanston: Harper & Row, 1952.

Behr, Edward. _Thirteen Years That Changed America._ New York: Arcade Publishing, 1996.

Birmingham, Stephen. _California Rich._ New York: Simon & Schuster, 1980.

Black, Joyce M. and Esther Matassarin-Jacobs. _Medical-Surgical Nursing._ Chicago: Harcourt Brace & Company, 1997.

Botting, Douglas. _The U-Boats._ Alexandria, Virginia: Time-Life Books, 1979.

Cashman, Sean Dennis. _Prohibition: The Lie of the Land._ New York: The Free Press, 1981.

Chang, Iris. _The Rape of Nanking._ New York: Basic Books, 1997.

Cleland, Robert Glass. _California in Our Time._ New York: Alfred A. Knopf, 1947.

Curti, Merle. _The Growth of American Thought._ New York: Harper & Row, 1964.

Dana, Julian. _A.P. Giannini: Giant in the West._ New York: Prentice Hall, 1947.

Davis, Daniel. _Behind Barbed Wire._ New York: E.P. Dutton, 1982.

Delaplane, Kristin. _Solano's Gold: The People and Their Orchards._ Vacaville: Vacaville Museum, 1999.

Deverell, William. _Railroad Crossing._ Berkeley and Los Angeles: University of California Press, 1994.

Eby, Gordon. _Napa Valley,_ Napa Valley: Eby Press, 1972.

Federal Writers' Project of the Works Progress Administration. _California: A Guide to the Golden State._ NY: Hastings House, 1939.

Feldman, Herman. _Prohibition: Its Economic and Industrial Aspects._ New York: D. Appleton and Company, 1927.

Fellmeth, Robert C. *Politics of Land*. New York: Grossman Publishing, 1973.

Ferrell, Robert H. *Woodrow Wilson and World War I*. New York: Harper & Row, 1985.

Galbraith, John Kenneth. *The Great Crash: 1929*. New York: Houghton Mifflin Company, 1997.

Gentry, Curt F. *The Madams of San Francisco*. New York: Doubleday & Company, 1964.

Gilbert, Martin. *The First World War: A Complete History*. New York: Henry Holt and Company, 1994.

Gould, Francis Lewis. *My Life with Wine*. St. Helena: self-published, 1972.

Gould, Romilda Peri. *Con Brio*. Calistoga: Illuminations Press, 1988.

Gregory, Thomas Jefferson. *History of Solano and Napa Counties*. Los Angeles: Historic Record Company, 1912.

Harlan, George. *San Francisco Bay Ferry Boats*. Berkeley: Howell-North Books, 1967.

Hawkes, Ellen. *Blood and Wine*. New York: Simon & Schuster, 1993.

Hichborn, Franklin K. "The Party, the Machine, and the Vote," in *California Historical Society Quarterly*, XXXIX, No. 1, March, 1960.

Hill, Gladwin. *Dancing Bear: An Insiide Look at California Politics*. Cleveland: The World Publishing Company, 1968.

Hutchinson, Fred. *T.B. Hutchinson of Napa*. Napa: 1950.

Iezzoni, Lynette. *Influenza 1918*. New York: TV Books, 1999.

Innis, Lori Bryant. *Martha Louisa Bryant: Pinoeer Teacher*. Calistoga: self-published, 1995.

Issel, William, and Robert W. Cherny. *San Francisco 1865-1932: Politics, Power and Urban Development*. Berekeley: University of California Press, 1986.

Kennedy, David M. *Freedom from Fear: The American People in Depression and War, 1925-1945*. New York and Oxford: Oxford University Press, 1999.

Kerr, K. Austin. *Organized for Prohibition*. New Haven and London: Yale University Press, 1985.

Klingaman, William A. *1929: The Year of the Great Crash*. New York: Harper & Row, 1989.

Lange, Dorothy and Pirkle Jones. *Death of a Valley*. Aperture, Inc., 1960.

Lewis, Oscar. *The Big Four*. New York: Alfred A. Knopf, 1966.

Manchester, William. *The Glory and the Dream: A Narrative History of America.,1932-1972*, I. Boston: Little, Brown & Company.

Mini, Carolyn and Martin C. *Two Families: Cavagnaro and Guisto*. Napa: self-published, 1998.

Mowry, George E. *The California Progressives*. Chicago: Encounter Paperbacks, 1951; and Chicago: Quadrangle Books, 1963.

Pinney, Thomas. *A History of Wine in America*. Berkeley and London: University of California Press, 1989.

Pringle, Henry F. *Theodore Roosevelt*. Orlando, FL: Harcourt & Brace Company 1931 and 1984.

Roberts, J.M. *The History of the World, 1901 to 2000*. New York: Viking, 1999.

Roosevelt, Theodore. *America and the World War*. London: John Murray, 1915.

Rubin, Harold. *The Solano Water Story*. Vacaville: Solano Irrigation District, 1988.

Scharlach, Bernice. *Big Alma*. San Francisco: Scottwall Associates, 1990.

Schlesinger, Arthur M., Jr. *The Coming of the New Deal*. Boston: Houghton-Mifflin, 1958.

Schlesinger, Arthur M., Jr. *The Crisis of the Old Order, 1919-1933*. Boston: Houghton Mifflin Company, 1956.

Sorensen, Lorin. *Beringer: A Napa Valley Legend*. St. Helena: Silverado Publishing Company, 1989.

Stanton, Ken. *Mount St. Helena & R.L. Stevenson State Park:*. Calistoga: Illuminations Press, 1993.

Sullivan, Charles. *Napa Wine: A History*. San Francisco: Wine Appreciation Guild, 1994.

Swett, Ira L. and Harry C. Aiken, Jr.. *Napa Valley Route: Electric Trains and Steamers*. Glendale, CA: Interurbans, 1975.

301

Terkle, Studs. *Hard Times: An Oral History of the Great Depression.* New York: Pantheon Books, 1970.

Thomas, Gordon, and Max Morgan-Witts. *The Day the Bubble Burst: The Social History of the Wall Street Crash of 1929.* Garden City: Doubleday, 1979.

Thomas, Gordon and Max Morgan Witts. *The San Francisco Earthquake.* New York: Dell Publishing Company, 1972.

Trimble, Paul C. *Interurban Railways of the Bay Area* Fresno Valley Publishers, 1977.

Verardo, Denzil and Jennie. *The Bale Grist Mill.* Oakland: California State Parks Foundation, 1984.

Weber, Lin. *Old Napa Valley*, St. Helena: Wine Ventures Publishing, 1998.

Yergin, Daniel. *The Prize.* New York: Simon & Schuster, 1991.

307

Roots of the Present: Napa Valley 1900-1950

309